THE FEDERAL
TRADE COMMISSION

THE FEDERAL
TRADE COMMISSION

A STUDY IN ADMINISTRATIVE
LAW AND PROCEDURE

BY

GERARD C. HENDERSON

NEW YORK
AGATHON PRESS, INC.
1968

Copyright, 1924, by Yale University Press

Reprinted, 1968, by

AGATHON PRESS, INC.
150 Fifth Avenue
New York, N. Y. 10011

Library of Congress Catalog Card Number: 68-16354

Printed in the United States of America

THE FEDERAL
TRADE COMMISSION

THE FEDERAL TRADE COMMISSION

A STUDY IN ADMINISTRATIVE LAW AND PROCEDURE

BY

GERARD C. HENDERSON

NEW HAVEN · YALE UNIVERSITY PRESS

LONDON · HUMPHREY MILFORD · OXFORD UNIVERSITY PRESS

MDCCCCXXIV

INTRODUCTORY NOTE

THE Commonwealth Fund in 1920 set aside certain funds for the encouragement of legal research and appointed a committee to recommend projects and to have executive responsibility for the carrying on of such research as might be adopted. That Legal Research Committee is constituted as follows:

JAMES PARKER HALL, Dean, The University of Chicago Law School, *Chairman*,

CHARLES C. BURLINGHAM, of Burlingham, Veeder, Masten and Fearey, New York,

BENJAMIN N. CARDOZO, Associate Judge of the Court of Appeals in the State of New York,

MAX FARRAND, Adviser in Educational Research, The Commonwealth Fund, *Secretary*,

JOHN G. MILBURN, of Carter, Ledyard and Milburn, New York,

ROSCOE POUND, Dean, Law School of Harvard University,

BARRY C. SMITH, General Director, The Commonwealth Fund,

HARLAN F. STONE, Dean, Columbia University School of Law.

The vast changes wrought in the social and economic aspects of society during the nineteenth century, due to the introduction of new mechanical forces, the penetrating influence of science, large scale industry and progressive urbanization have reflected themselves in a steady extension of legal control of social and economic interests. State intervention at first expressed itself largely through specific legislative directions depending, in most instances, for enforcement upon the rigid, cumbersome and inevitably ineffective machinery of the criminal law. More recently, legislative regulation of economic and social interests has resorted to administrative instruments in the enforcement of legislative policy. Inevitably, this has greatly widened the field of discretion. It has created, in a sharp form, new aspects of the familiar conflict in the law between rule and discretion.

This great extension of legal control by a vast congeries of administrative agencies has directed the attention of the legal profession to the legal issues involved in their powers, and the relation of their powers to the traditional system of Anglo-American law. To this body of legal problems the term "Administrative Law" is now generally applied. The pervasive influence of this branch of legal control, the comparative suddenness of its impact, the rampant empiricism with which it is allowed to develop, convinced the Legal Research Committee that administrative law presented a need of, and offered an excellent opportunity for, research.

A special committee on Administrative Law and Practice was therefore appointed to investigate this subject, consisting of:

ERNST FREUND, Professor, The University of Chicago Law School, *Chairman*,

WALTER L. FISHER, of Fisher, Boyden, Kales and Bell, Chicago,

FELIX FRANKFURTER, Professor, Law School of Harvard University,

FRANK J. GOODNOW, President, Johns Hopkins University.

The Committee on Administrative Law and Practice recognized at the outset that it must confine the scope of its efforts and proceed piecemeal, without any thought of a comprehensive and exhaustive treatment of the entire field of administrative control. The research thus far undertaken approaches the problem by two different lines of investigation. There is in process a statutory survey of administrative powers which should reveal, so far as the face of legislation can reveal it, the extent to which administrative control has, by modern legislation, been in fact conferred. Secondly, a series of special studies have been projected which should reveal the actual workings of carefully selected administrative organs, in so far as their activities mean law and not mere internal administration. Such intensive studies in administrative law and practice are deemed to be a prerequisite for an appraisal of what administrative law really does, so that we may have an adequate guide for what ought to be done.

The first of these intensive studies, a study of the Federal Trade Commission, is now made public. It is perhaps unnecessary to add that no attempt has been made to influence the character of the investigation or its conclusions, for which the author alone is responsible.

CONTENTS

PREFACE

THE Federal Trade Commission will soon have completed the ninth year of its formal existence. For several years, it is true, its energies were largely absorbed in special work of a transitory character, connected with the prosecution of the war, but even during those years its normal functions were never completely in abeyance, and since the armistice it has had ample opportunity to perfect the organization and develop the procedure appropriate to its main task. The Commission is now a going concern, elaborately organized into departments, divisions, and sections, with a personnel of more than 300 men and women and an annual appropriation of nearly a million dollars. The authority of the Commission and the meaning of the fundamental statutes which it administers have been the subject of numerous court decisions, and the Commission itself has published five volumes of reports embodying its complaints, findings, and orders in administrative proceedings. Not only by court decision, but by force of its own precedents and rules, the Commission's administrative technique and modes of procedure have begun to assume definite form. It is possible now to study the Federal Trade Commission, if not as an organization in its full maturity, at least as a piece of machinery which has been fully designed and assembled, and has been exposed for several years to the test of actual service.

In the early years of growth of a new governmental agency there is necessarily much of trial and error. In its substantive decisions as well as in matters of procedure, it is inevitable that occasional false starts should be made, and that some policies should be pursued which later prove to have been mistaken. Because in the course of this study some practices are referred to which should in my opinion be corrected, and methods criticised which seem to me defective, it should not be assumed that the Commission's work is to be wholly condemned, or that the fundamental policies of the Federal Trade Commission Act are unsound. At the risk of anticipating conclusions, it may not be amiss to record here my belief that the Commission has a valuable and important function to perform, and that the matters criticised in portions of this study are none of them of such a character that they cannot, if the criticisms are valid, be corrected by changes of method and procedure or by minor legislative amendments.

In the course of the investigation, I have been accorded every courtesy and assistance by the members of the Commission and its officers and employees. All proceedings of the Commission, beginning with the issuance of the formal complaint, are matters of public record, and I have spent much time in the Docket Division and the Library of the Commission delving into the material thus available. I have not asked for or obtained access to any records or files not open to public inspection, and I have been careful not to embarrass the employees of the Commission by asking questions concerning matters which could properly be considered confidential.

A word as to the field covered by the investigation. This is a study in administrative law and procedure, and only those activities of the Commission which properly fall within the scope of such a study have been examined or discussed, although they constitute only a part of the Commission's work. Thus the Commission has made, at the request of Congress or of the President, or for the assistance of other government departments, a large number of special investigations and reports, such as its study of grain marketing, of the petroleum and fertilizer industries, of tobacco prices, and of the production and distribution of coal, to mention only a few. During the war, it made extensive investigations into costs of production, to assist other government agencies in arriving at fair prices in the purchase of supplies. It had charge of issuing licenses in the United States for the use of inventions, trade marks, or copyrighted matter patented or registered in enemy countries. It is engaged in administering certain provisions of the Webb-Pomerene Export Trade Act of 1918. For the most part these activities are beyond the scope of this study. Investigations and reports, except in so far as they involve the compulsory production of documentary evidence or compulsory testimony, raise no questions properly within the field of administrative law. The activities immediately connected with the war have no permanent significance, important as they were at the time. The work of the Commission under the export trade law has not involved any formal administrative proceedings. The study has, therefore, been limited to the normal and permanent duties of the Commission in administering Section 5 of the Federal Trade Commission Act, and Sections 2, 3, 7, and 8 of the Clayton Act, in the belief that an intensive study of these peculiarly administrative functions would be more helpful than a discursive treatment of its many other activities.

CHAPTER I

POLITICAL AND LEGISLATIVE HISTORY

THE student of legislation in the United States, especially if he happens to have had some practical experience in legislative matters, cannot but be impressed by the extraordinary difficulties which must have confronted the draftsmen of our anti-trust laws. The statutes concerned problems of trade competition and monopoly, and therefore dealt with some of the most complex features of the intricate mechanism of modern economic life. A complicated situation generally calls for a complicated legal document, as any draftsman of a corporate indenture can testify. To express fully and clearly the intention of the parties it may be necessary to introduce endless details and qualifications, so that nothing is left to implication, and every contingency is anticipated. From the lawyer who drafts such a document for a business client, certainty and completeness are expected above everything else. A statute, however, is a political as well as a legal document. It must stand the test of Congressional debate, and it must be defended on the public platform. The phrases which it embodies must be studied, not only for their legal import, but for their political and ethical quality as well. The enactment and public discussion of an important law is a part of the process of political education, and a statute fails in this respect if it is couched in language which is not comprehensible to the average citizen, or which conveys to the lay mind an imperfect picture of the objects and policies which it embodies.

The difficulty is greatly enhanced where the subject

matter is one upon which popular feeling has run high and formulas and phrases have acquired a political significance. There is in all political discussion a strong tendency to over-simplify the issues. An ethical sense is perhaps a more general attribute of mankind than is the capacity for practical judgment on matters of economic or business expediency, and there is a natural impulse to formulate complicated problems of conduct in simple terms of right and wrong. It has been almost a political necessity to divest the trust problem of its complicated reality, and to clothe it in the simpler raiment of personal ethics. With the best of intentions on the part of the draftsman, the inaccurate phrases and over-simplified concepts of popular discussion tend to force their way into the text of the statute, and necessary details and qualification are rejected because they seem to weaken the legislation from the political and rhetorical viewpoint.

The current vocabulary available to the draftsman of the Sherman Anti-Trust Law was peculiarly lacking in legal precision. The very word "trust" meant one thing to the layman and another to the lawyer, and the word "monopoly" was equally ambiguous. To a lawyer who had some regard for historical accuracy, a monopoly was a grant from the King of or for the sole buying, selling, making, working, or using of anything.[1] The word had acquired a broader meaning only because it was often used in a figurative sense, and because of its convenience as an epithet. Technically speaking, a man who bought up all the grain within carting distance and then raised the price, was an ingrosser,[2] but colloquially he was a monopolist, for his conduct was quite as objectionable

[1] Coke, 3 Inst. 181; Hawk., P.C. book 1, c. 79.

[2] "Monopoly differs from ingrossing only in this, that monopoly is by patent from the King, and ingrossing by the act of the subject between party and party." 1 Hawk., P.C. 624.

as if it had been sanctioned by grant of the King.[3] The words "restraint of trade" also had a dual meaning. When an aging cobbler sold his business to a younger man, and agreed not to practice in competition, the contract was technically in restraint of trade. Whether or not it was enforceable, might depend upon a number of considerations: the territorial extent of the restraint, the character, and at one time the adequacy of the consideration, the need for the restraint as a protection to the purchaser, and other factors. Popularly, however, a restraint of trade was an interference with the liberty of the subject, as objectionable as a monopoly. Indeed to presume to exercise a monopoly was to commit an offense against trade or commerce.[4] A monopoly was, in Blackstone's words, a grant from the King whereby the citizen was restrained in his liberty to trade.[5] In Mitchell v. Reynolds[6] the court spoke of "the great abuses these voluntary restraints are liable to; as, for instance, from corporations who are perpetually laboring for exclusive advantages in trade and to reduce it into as few hands as possible." Again without any attempt at legal precision, without any definition of terms, the words "restraint of trade" came to serve much the same use as the word "monopoly." If all the grain merchants in the vicinity agreed not to sell below a fixed price, they were making a contract in restraint of trade, and attempting to create a monopoly. If a society of tailors attempted to prevent outsiders from getting any business, they were monopolists who were trying to place unlawful restraints on the trade of their competitors.

To endeavor to secure, by research in the common law

[3] *Cf.* The King v. Waddington, 1 East 143, 156 (1800), where Lord Kenyon used the word in its popular sense.

[4] Blackstone, Bk. IV, Ch. 12, Sec. 9.

[5] *Ibid.*

[6] 1 P. Wms. 181 (1711).

books, any comprehensive definition or delimitation of either of these terms is obviously useless, for they were not used where accuracy of expression was needed. Nobody would have thought that the Statute of Monopolies applied to persons who were not exercising or claiming to exercise exclusive rights under royal grant. When it became necessary to define and punish the type of offenses against which the Sherman Law was directed, the more technical words "forestalling, regrating, and engrossing" were used. In the Statute against Forestallers, Regrators, and Ingrossers,[7] these offenses are defined with a precision and detail that are quite astonishing. Indeed this Act, passed in the year 1552, is, from the juristic viewpoint, a much more highly developed product than the Sherman Act of 1890. In its technical aspects it would do credit to any modern legislative drafting service.

Instead of following this excellent model, and describing in simple and yet precise terms the conduct which they wished to forbid, the draftsmen of the Sherman Law chose instead to couch their prohibitions in terms of monopoly and restraint of trade. The words served to indicate strong moral reprobation, but were not helpful in identifying the subject matter to which the statute was applicable. The Standard Oil and Tobacco decisions in 1911[8] revealed clearly the faulty draftsmanship of the law. "Every contract, combination in the form of trust, or otherwise, or conspiracy, in restraint of trade or commerce among the several states" was denounced as criminal. A contract in restraint of trade, the precedents showed, was a contract limiting the right to exercise a trade. The context clearly showed that a broader meaning was intended, and it was fair inference that the law was aimed at agreements, combinations, or conspiracies which

[7] 5th and 6th Edw. VI, Ch. 14.

[8] Standard Oil Co. *v.* United States, 221 U.S. 1 (1911). American Tobacco Co. *v.* United States, 221 U.S. 106 (1911).

had the effect of eliminating or limiting competition between the participants. But the Act said that every such contract, combination, or conspiracy was illegal. If anything was clear from the precedents, it was that a contract might be technically in restraint of trade and yet entirely innocuous and undoubtedly valid and enforceable at common law. Did not Congress mean "every contract or combination or conspiracy in unreasonable restraint of trade"? Or did it mean to send to jail a grocer, living near the state line and delivering groceries in an adjoining state, who retired from business and sold his stock in trade with a covenant not to engage in a similar business in the locality? Did it mean that every regulation of a chamber of commerce or trade association, no matter how reasonable, which limited the manner in which an interstate trade could be transacted by its members, and any trade union rule which affected interstate commerce, had suddenly become an indictable conspiracy? Yet if Congress meant to prohibit only unreasonable restraints, why in the name of good sense did they not say so? Surely the eminent lawyers in the Senate were familiar with the common law distinctions as to restraint of trade.

The explanation, of course, lay in the fact which I have already adverted to, that legislative draftsmen cannot always confine their attention exclusively to legal considerations. Congress was using words to which the precedents ascribed a fairly precise though somewhat irrelevant meaning, but it was using them in a sense which was to be popularly taken to refer to the great trusts and combinations from which the people were understood to be suffering. Was Congress to admit that a trust or monopoly could ever be reasonable? Such a thing was politically impossible. It violated the axiom that all trusts and monopolies were reprehensible. Any qualification or definition or exception tended to weaken the apparently

sweeping and inclusive range of the statute, and hence its
rhetorical value.

In the Standard Oil and Tobacco cases the Supreme
Court took an important although a limited step toward
supplying the legal deficiencies of the text of the Sherman
Act. The court announced that certain common law analogies should guide the judiciary in determining whether
or not a particular contract or combination was in restraint of trade or was an attempt at monopolization, in
the sense in which those words were used in the statute.
The test was that applied by the common law to contracts
restraining the exercise of a profession or trade, namely,
the reasonableness of the scope and terms of the restraint
from the point of view of the parties and of the public. It
may be conceded that the test is not of itself susceptible
of precise and definite application. A court may have good
reasons for concluding that it is not proper for a physician to covenant not to practice his profession within 100
miles of the city of York, but they are not very helpful in
determining whether or not a consolidation of 40 per
cent of the steel industry in the United States is reasonable. The common law analogies do not go far in indicating the principles to be applied in the solution of the
modern trust problem. At most they suggest the frame
of mind into which the judges should put themselves in
arriving at a decision.

The promulgation of the "rule of reason" did, however, bring to the forefront a fundamental question of
legislative policy. The Supreme Court had announced,
what was doubtless fully appreciated by the legislators
of 1890, that the text of the Sherman Act contained no
definite rule of decision, but contemplated that the courts
themselves, with the aid of common law analogies, should
evolve their own rules and precedents as the cases came
before them for decision. Was it in the public interest
that such a sweeping power, in matters of such vital con-

cern, should be entrusted to a judiciary appointed for life and carefully shielded from the influence of public opinion? To put the matter differently, was it possible to develop, out of the storehouse of the common law, a set of legal principles capable of precise application, by which judges could solve all problems of restraint of trade and monopoly by logic and precedent? Or must the decision depend in each case upon the judge's personal notions of expediency and economic policy? At bottom, this was the issue between those who retained their faith in the Sherman Law as interpreted by the Supreme Court, and those who thought that the law should be amended or supplemented by new legislation.

We are fortunate in having, from the pen of the present Chief Justice of the United States, a contemporary defense of the Sherman Law which reveals clearly the issue which the legislators of 1914 were facing. Mr. Taft's book, *The Anti-Trust Act and the Supreme Court,* was published in 1914, and was doubtless suggested by the prospect of new anti-trust legislation at the current session of Congress. The main thesis of the book was that the Sherman Law, read in the light of common law analogies, contained principles capable of logical formulation and precise application, and afforded a certain guide to the judges charged with administering the law, so that supplementary legislation was unnecessary and might even be harmful. As the argument goes to the root of the justification for the new legislation, it is worth examining with some care.

At common law, Mr. Taft pointed out, a contract entered into with the sole object of restraining the exercise of a trade or profession was void. If a tailor should persuade an obnoxious competitor, in a moment of weakness, to sign a bond to cease exercising his trade, the courts would refuse to enforce the bond, for it is against public policy that a citizen should be deprived of his

means of livelihood, or that the public should be deprived
of the advantages of competition. But if a tailor, in-
tending to retire, sells his business, with an undertaking
not to exercise his trade in competition with the buyer,
the agreement is lawful. There is a restraint, but it is
merely incidental. The main purpose of the contract is to
secure a fair price for the business sold, and the restraint
is only to prevent the vendor by subsequent competition
from derogating from the value of his grant. If, however,
the restraint is broader than is reasonably necessary for
the purpose, it is void, for it then becomes apparent that
the purpose of the buyer in exacting the restraint was
not merely to protect the property purchased, but to exclude the seller from a legitimate occupation or to deprive
the public of his services.

By the mere application of the accepted judicial technique of analogical reasoning this common law distinction could, in Mr. Taft's view, be applied to the decision
of the problems of combination and monopoly encountered in the administration of the Sherman Law. Any
agreement between two or more competing business concerns, of which the sole purpose is to restrict competition,
say by fixing minimum prices, or apportioning territory,
or restricting output, is unlawful at common law and
indictable under the Sherman Act. It makes no difference
how laudable the motive, or how beneficial the result; if
restraint alone, whether partial or general, is the sole
purpose of the contract, it is void. If, however, the restraint upon competition accompanies a transfer of
property, or other legitimate business transaction, it becomes necessary to consider the scope and purpose of the
restraint. Every combination of competitors restrains,
because it eliminates, the mutual competition of the combining units, but every such combination is not illegal.
If the purpose is to promote economy and efficiency, the
combination is legal; but if the real purpose is to elimi-

nate competition, as a step toward the control of the market, the transaction is illegal. In substance, this was Chief Justice White's view of the rule of reason at common law, which treated as illegal those contracts "which were unreasonably restrictive of competitive conditions, either from the nature or character of the contract or act or where the surrounding circumstances were such as to justify the conclusion that they had not been entered into or performed with the legitimate purpose of reasonably forwarding personal interest and developing trade, but on the contrary were of such a character as to give rise to the inference or presumption that they had been entered into or done with the intent to do wrong to the general public and to limit the right of individuals, thus restraining the free flow of commerce and tending to bring about the evils, such as enhancement of prices, which were considered to be against public policy.'"[9]

The actual decisions of the Supreme Court, in Mr. Taft's view, were in harmony with this principle. In the traffic association cases,[10] the Addyston Pipe case,[11] the Nash case,[12] and the Bathtub case[13] there were agreements between nominally independent competitors, fixing prices, or otherwise restricting the scope of competition. In these cases restraint was the sole purpose, and the agreements or combinations were illegal. In the Northern Securities case,[14] there was a formal transfer of securities to a holding company, but the real purpose was to avoid competition and monopolize transportation. In the Standard Oil and Tobacco cases[15] there were combinations of

[9] Standard Oil Co. v. U.S., 221 U.S. 1, 58.

[10] U.S. v. Trans-Missouri Freight Association, 166 U.S. 290; U.S. v. Joint Traffic Association, 171 U.S. 93.

[11] U.S. v. Addyston Pipe & Steel Co., 175 U.S. 211.

[12] Nash v. U.S., 229 U.S. 373.

[13] Sanitary Manufacturing Co. v. U.S., 226 U.S. 20.

[14] Northern Securities Co. v. U.S., 193 U.S. 197.

[15] *Supra,* p. 4.

competing units, but the conduct of the defendants had
shown that the purpose in each case was not greater productive efficiency, but the exclusion of competitors by
unfair means, and consequent domination of the market.
In the Reading case[16] a number of coal carrying railroads
and coal mining companies combined to buy up, through
a corporation to which each company subscribed capital,
an independent operator who threatened to build a competing railroad line into the anthracite field. The combination was held illegal, because the intent, to be inferred
from the extent of the control which the combination
exercised in the anthracite field, was not efficiency, but a
more complete monopoly. On the other hand, in the Cincinnati Packet case[17] the covenant restraining competition was sustained because merely incidental to the main
purpose of the contract, namely, the sale of property. In
U. S. v. Winslow[18] the purpose of the combination was
merely to secure greater efficiency, and not to eliminate
competition or control the market; hence an indictment
of the man who engineered the combination was dismissed.

Here was a legal principle capable of logical application and development, which judges could employ without
embarking upon the uncharted sea of economic or social expediency. To determine whether or not a given
contract or combination, though in restraint of trade, is
nevertheless so beneficial in its economic effect as to be
worth protecting, is to exercise a legislative power which
should never be entrusted to the courts. To decide whether
or not such a restraint is merely incidental to a legitimate
business transaction, and not the main purpose of the
contract, is not assuming legislative power at all. "It is
only exercising the function that courts have exercised in

[16] U.S. v. Reading Co., 226 U.S. 324.
[17] Cincinnati Packet Co. v. Bay, 200 U.S. 179.
[18] U.S. v. Winslow, 227 U.S. 202.

applying a well-measured and definite yardstick to contracts incidental and ancillary for now more than three
centuries.''[19]

Mr. Taft's book was completed after the anti-trust bills
of 1914 had passed the House, but before they had taken
final form in the Senate,[20] and of course he reserved judgment as to detailed proposals. He attacked, however, what
later became the two principal features of the new legislation. He was opposed to any amendment of the Sherman
Law by enumeration and legislative definition of specific
offenses. Since the courts had already set up a "well-
measured and definite yardstick," a legislative duplica-
tion of the work would only lead to confusion. On the
other hand he opposed vigorously the proposal to authorize either the courts or an executive commission to
define and prohibit "unfair competition." Such legislation would submit questions to the economic and business
judgment of courts, and not to their legal judgment. "If
this means more than what is included in unreasonable
restraints of trade at common law now denounced by the
anti-trust law, it would seem to be conferring legislative
power."[21]

In sharp contrast was the argument of the friends of
supplemental legislation. Lawyers and laymen alike
pointed out that however suggestive and logically relevant the common law analogies might be, they did not in
practice furnish that definite yardstick of legality which
was claimed for them. Some of the most fundamental
questions of business conduct were at that time still in
doubt, and the best that competent attorneys could do
was to give their best guess as to how the Supreme Court
would ultimately decide them. The frequency with which
important Sherman Law cases have been decided by a

[19] Taft, *The Anti-Trust Act and the Supreme Court*, p. 115.
[20] *Ibid.*, p. 131.
[21] *Ibid.*, pp. 116-117.

closely divided court, both before 1914 and after, of itself
suggests that the yardstick is a flexible one, and that
much may depend on the way in which it is applied.

There were moreover serious practical difficulties in
the application of the theory that a combination is lawful
if the purpose is efficiency, but that it is unlawful if the
purpose is the elimination of competition. If two manufacturers combine, it is inconceivable that they should
not have considered every aspect of the situation, its bearing on technical problems of production, on expenses of
overhead and operation, as well as on the general competitive situation. It does not touch the realities of the
situation to inquire whether the purpose was greater
efficiency or the elimination of competition. Such an inquiry assumes a singleness of motive which is rare in any
case, and would be disastrous in a business enterprise.
Even if the dominance of purpose were clear, it would
hardly be a satisfactory test. Assume that the two manufacturers had admitted in the presence of witnesses that
their real object was to put an end to a mutual competition that was getting too keen to be profitable. Would the
combination be dissolved merely because they did not at
the time profess the correct motives? The decision in the
United States Steel Corporation case,[22] rendered, of
course, since Mr. Taft's book was published, seems to indicate that it would not. In that case, it will be recalled,
Judges Buffington and McPherson, in the district court,
thought that the purpose of the consolidation was to secure certain metallurgical gains in production, and the
better handling of export trade.[23] Judges Woolley and
Hunt thought the purpose was to monopolize and restrain trade, but that the purpose had not been achieved.
All four judges agreed that the bill should be dismissed.
A majority of the Supreme Court were inclined to agree

[22] U.S. *v.* U.S. Steel Corporation, 251 U.S. 417.
[23] *Ibid.*, 223 Fed. 55.

with Judges Woolley and Hunt, although the opinion suggests that more weight should perhaps have been given to the need for integration in the industry. These, however, were matters of past history. "It is against monopoly that the statute is directed, not against an expectation of it, but against its realization, and it is certain that it was not realized." "Whatever there was of wrong intent, could not be executed, whatever there was of evil effect, was discontinued before this suit was brought . . ." The case stands for the proposition that if a number of competing manufacturers combine in one corporation, not for the purpose of promoting productive efficiency, but to eliminate competition and control the market, the corporation will not be dissolved if in fact the field remained competitive and the market free.

The theory is even more difficult to apply in the cases which involve the lawfulness of rules or practices of associations, boards of trade, or commodity exchanges. Organizations of this character, which play an increasingly important part in the business life of the community, very generally endeavor to regulate the manner in which members shall carry on their business. A trade association establishes for its members standards of quality, or of measurement, or uniform terms of discount or credit. A livestock exchange establishes a uniform commission to be charged by brokers, and provides that members may not trade with persons not members of the exchange. A grain exchange limits the types of contracts that may be entered into by its members. These and countless other regulations are familiar in every line of business. Obviously they restrain, in the sense that they limit and restrict, commerce among the members or with outsiders. If some of the commerce happens to be between two states, are the restraints illegal? It seems fairly clear that restraint is the direct and primary purpose of the regulation. There is no transfer of property or other business transaction to which it is merely ancillary. Yet it is certain that such regulations, if reasonable, will be sustained.[24] Here also the case which best tests the theory was decided since Mr. Taft's book was written.[25] The Chicago Board of Trade adopted a rule binding upon all members that purchases of grain "to arrive," made between the close of the "Call" in the afternoon and the opening of the session the following morning, could be made only at the closing bid price at the "Call." Here was a clear restraint on competition; indeed for a limited period it was a rigid price fixing rule. Upon the ground that a bare restraint of competition, without more, was always illegal, the lower court excluded all evidence as to the purpose or economic justification of the rule, and granted to the government an injunction against its enforcement. The Supreme Court unanimously reversed the decision on the ground that certain enumerated economic benefits, such as concentration of sales in the public market, and elimination of the risks and uncertainties of private trading, afforded a justification for the restraint. The method of approach in judging of the legality of such a combination was clearly stated by Mr. Justice Brandeis:

> The case [in the court below] was rested upon the bald proposition, that a rule or agreement by which men occupying positions of strength in any branch of trade, fixed prices at which they would buy or sell during an important part of the business day, is an illegal restraint of trade under the Anti-Trust Law. But the legality of an agreement or regulation cannot be determined by so simple a test, as whether it restrains competition. Every agreement concerning trade, every regulation of trade, restrains. To bind, to restrain, is of their very essence. The true test of legality is whether the restraint imposed is such as merely regu-

[24] Anderson v. U.S., 171 U.S. 604 (1898), and Board of Trade v. Christie Grain and Stock Co., 198 U.S. 236 (1905).

[25] Chicago Board of Trade v. U.S., 246 U.S. 231 (1918).

lates and perhaps thereby promotes competition, or whether it is such as may suppress or even destroy competition. To determine that question the court must ordinarily consider the facts peculiar to the business to which the restraint is applied; its condition before and after the restraint was imposed; the nature of the restraint and its effect, actual or probable. The history of the restraint, the evil believed to exist, the reason for adopting the particular remedy, the purpose or end sought to be attained, are all relevant facts. This is not because a good intention will save an otherwise objectionable regulation or the reverse; but because knowledge of intent may help the court to interpret facts and to predict consequences.[26]

Here is a frank rejection of any rigid legal criterion of reasonableness. Purpose is to be considered, but only as an aid to the interpretation of facts. The ultimate test is economic justification. *Prima facie,* it may be, every restraint of competition is unlawful, but if it is shown to be of such economic value that the effect of the restraint is outweighed, it will be sustained.

These later decisions have made it possible to crystallize what was vaguely in the minds of the proponents of the legislation of 1914. It was felt that in substance, however much they might be reinforced by artificial logic, the decisions of the courts in anti-trust cases depended upon the economic views of the judges rather than upon the application of a policy declared by Congress. It was quite natural that the dicta in the Standard Oil and Tobacco cases should be misunderstood. It was easy to give the impression, and no doubt many critics sincerely believed it was so, that the Supreme Court had boldly grasped the power, intentionally withheld by Congress, to declare which trusts and monopolies were reasonable and which were unreasonable, and to confer immunity upon combinations which, while illegal under the law as enacted by Congress, were in the opinion of the court

[26] *Ibid.,* 238.

economically desirable. President Taft himself, in a vigorous message, had declared that such a power "might involve our whole judicial system in disaster."[27] Even the moderate majority of the Senate Committee on Interstate Commerce, of which Senator Cummins was Chairman, had this to say of the "rule of reason":

> The committee has full confidence in the integrity, intelligence, and patriotism of the Supreme Court of the United States, but it is unwilling to repose in that court, or any other court, the vast and undefined power which it must exercise in the administration of the statute under the rule which it has promulgated. It substitutes the court in the place of Congress, for whenever the rule is invoked, the court does not administer the law, but makes the law. If it continues in force, the Federal courts will, so far as restraint of trade is concerned, make a common law for the United States just as the English courts have made a common law for England.
>
> The people of this country will not permit the courts to declare a policy for them with respect to this subject.[28]

In the Presidential campaign of 1912 the three political parties had joined in demanding that the anti-trust laws be made more specific. "We favor," said the Republican Platform of 1912, "the enactment of legislation supplementary to the existing anti-trust act which will define as criminal offences those specific acts that uniformly mark attempts to restrain and monopolize trade, to the end that those who honestly intend to obey the law may have a guide to their action and that those who aim to violate the law may the more surely be punished."[29] The Democratic Platform expressed regret that the Sherman Law had been weakened by judicial construction, and favored "the prevention of holding companies, of inter-

[27] Message, January 7, 1910, Cong. Rec., 61st Cong., 2d Sess., p. 382.
[28] Report of Senate Committee on Interstate Commerce (February 26, 1913), p. xii.
[29] *Republican Campaign Text Book 1912*, p. 272.

locking directors, of stock watering, of discrimination in price, and the control by any one corporation of so large a proportion of any industry as to make it a menace to competitive conditions.''[30] The Progressive Platform took similar ground: ''We favor strengthening the Sherman law by prohibiting agreements to divide territory or limit output; refusing to sell to customers who buy from business rivals; to sell below cost in certain areas while maintaining higher prices in other places; using the power of transportation to aid or injure special business concerns; and other unfair trade practices.''[31]

The demand came, it would seem, from two sources. On the one hand it came from business men, trade associations, and commercial and industrial interests to whom the uncertainty of the law had become exasperating. They took the view, which may appear naïve to the lawyer, but which seemed reasonable enough to them, that after nearly a quarter of a century of experience with the antitrust law, it should be possible for the statesmen in Washington to make up their minds just what conduct they wished to forbid, and to describe it in language which the citizen could understand. On the other hand the demand came from those who thought that the Sherman Law, either because of original defects or on account of the construction given it by the Supreme Court, had proven ineffective, and who objected upon political and constitutional grounds to the delegation of legislative power which the ''rule of reason'' seemed to imply. Their conception of the trust problem was clearly stated by Mr. Brandeis in his testimony before House and Senate Committees, and was embodied in the La Follette-Lenroot bills, in the preparation of which Mr. Brandeis took an active part. Large combinations of capital, Mr. Brandeis main-

[30] *Ibid.,* p. 279.
[31] Roosevelt, *Progressive Principles,* Appendix, p. 319.

tained, are inherently uneconomic and wasteful, and have obtained and retain their power mainly through the use of certain well known trade practices which tend to exclude competitors from the field. Tieing contracts, contracts for exclusive dealing, price discriminations, concerted boycotting of certain classes of customers, operating through subsidiaries which purport to be independent, driving out competitors by selling articles temporarily below cost, commercial bribery or espionage, and similar forms of unfair or oppressive competition, should be defined in apt language and declared to be unlawful and heavily penalized. To this specific enumeration of offenses every business man could turn and by the light of his conscience guide his conduct. "Everybody who has even read the newspapers," Woodrow Wilson had said, "knows the means by which these men built up their power and created these monopolies. Any decently equipped lawyer can suggest to you statutes by which the whole business can be stopped."[32]

In this program for a clearer definition of offenses, there was necessarily the assumption that there was already at hand the juristic material necessary for such a legislative codification of the law of restraints and monopolies. The second part of the program which began to evolve out of the discussion provoked by the "rule of reason" rested upon a more modest view of the juristic capacity of the legislative branch, or perhaps upon a more vivid appreciation of the inherent difficulties of the situation. The forms of unfair and oppressive competition are myriad. By the time Congress has discovered and defined a dozen, a dozen more will be devised and put in operation. A tribunal should be created, with power to mold and adapt the law to each new situation. Since business and economic problems will be encountered, as

---

[32] *The New Freedom*, p. 172.

well as questions of law, the power should be lodged with a commission composed of eminent lawyers, economists, business men, and publicists[33] which would have "precedents and traditions, and a continuous policy."[34] "The organization should be quasi-judicial in character. We want traditions; we want a fixed policy; we want trained experts; we want precedents; we want a body of administrative law built up."[35]

Senator Newlands had been advocating such a commission for many years.[36] The Industrial Commission in its final report of February 10, 1902, had recommended that a permanent bureau be established in the Treasury Department to secure and publish information regarding corporations engaged in interstate or foreign commerce.[37] The following year Attorney General Knox had recommended the creation of a commission with similar powers.[38] On February 14, 1903, the Bureau of Corporations had been established in the Department of Commerce and Labor. The Bureau had no regulatory powers, but it could make investigations of corporations engaged in interstate and foreign commerce, and with the approval of the President, publish the information so acquired.[39] In 1908 President Roosevelt had urged that corporations whose contracts were technically in restraint of trade be permitted to file them for approval with the Commissioner of Corporations. If disapproved, they would be-

[33] Senator Newlands, Cong. Rec., Vol. 51, p. 11083.

[34] *Ibid.*, p. 10376.

[35] *Ibid.*, Senate Hearings, "Control of Corporations," p. 11.

[36] *See* his letter to the Secretary of the Conference on Trusts at Chicago, dated September 20, 1899, cited in report of Commission of Corporations for the fiscal year ended June 30, 1914, p. 3.

[37] *Ibid.*, p. 4.

[38] Letter to the Chairman of the Senate Committee on Judiciary, quoted *ibid.*, p. 4.

[39] Act approved February 14, 1903.

come illegal; otherwise, they should be deemed illegal only if found to be in unreasonable restraint of trade.[40]

On the day on which the Standard Oil decision was rendered, Senator Newlands, using the decision as a text, renewed on the floor of the Senate his demand that an interstate trade commission be established, so that the question of the reasonableness of a restraint of trade should be decided by a single commission as the servant of Congress, rather than "by the varying judgments of different courts upon the facts and the law."[41] Soon thereafter he introduced a bill,[42] providing for a commission of five members, with which all corporations engaged in interstate and foreign commerce should be registered. The Commission was given authority to cancel the registration if the corporation in question had violated any anti-trust decree, or had used "materially unfair or oppressive methods of competition," or had accepted rebates, or refused to allow to the Commission access to its records, or "upon the ground of over-capitalization." Gradually sentiment began to crystallize. The Republican Platform of 1912 declared that in the administration of the anti-trust laws there is "much that may be committed to a federal trade commission, thus placing in the hands of an administrative board many of the functions now necessarily exercised by the courts. This will promote promptness in the administration of the law and avoid delays and technicalities incidental to court procedure."[43] The Progressive Platform contained a similar recommendation.[44]

[40] Message, March 25, 1908; Cong. Rec., 60th Cong., 1st Sess., pp. 3853-3854.

[41] Cong. Rec., 62d Cong., 1st Sess., p. 1225.

[42] Originally introduced July 5, 1911, and again in amended form August 21, 1911.

[43] *Republican Campaign Text Book 1912*, p. 273.

[44] *See* text in Roosevelt, *Progressive Principles,* Appendix, p. 318.

In the hearings conducted before the Senate Committee on Interstate Commerce in 1911,[45] and before the Judiciary Committee of the House in 1912,[46] advocacy of such a commission had been general. The result of a referendum of the National Civic Federation had shown a vote of 614 in favor of an interstate trade commission and only 278 against, and Mr. Seth Low, the Chairman of the Federation, spoke forcefully in its support. Such industrial leaders as E. H. Gary and George W. Perkins were in accord. The report of the Senate Committee on Interstate Commerce of February 26, 1913, already referred to, advocated the formation of a commission, with authority to take over the investigating work of the Bureau of Corporations; to act with greater promptness in passing upon the legality of combinations in restraint of trade; and to assist the courts in disintegrating any combinations found to be unlawful.

This apparently widespread demand for a new administrative agency to carry out the anti-trust laws concealed, however, two radically divergent policies. Especially among the business interests, support of a federal trade commission rested not only upon the expectation that such a commission would administer a policy more tolerant toward large aggregations of capital, but on the belief that it could give to a group of business men, in advance, authoritative advice as to the legality of a contemplated undertaking. Two corporations might desire to combine forces, consolidate their plants and personnel and operate as one. Consolidation would call for financing. If there was a doubt as to the legality of the transaction it would be difficult to market securities. Yet if legality depended upon the view which a court might take

[45] "Control of Corporations," being report of hearings before the Senate Committee on Interstate Commerce.

[46] "Trust Legislation," being report of hearings before the Committee on Judiciary, House of Representatives, 62d Cong., 2d Sess.

as to the reasonableness of the transaction, one could only guess what the result might be. Why could not the parties put the matter frankly and fully before a competent federal tribunal, representing the public interest, and obtain a prompt ruling upon which all parties could rely? A trade association might wish to organize a cost and price information service among its members. Why should it not obtain disinterested and authoritative advice from Washington so that the pitfalls of the Sherman Law could be avoided? Plans presented to the Senate Committee on Interstate Commerce by Mr. E. H. Gary, Mr. Francis Lynde Stetson, Mr. Victor Morawetz, and Mr. George W. Perkins all had in common this theory of "advice in advance"—in the nature of an administrative "declaratory judgment," to obviate uncertainty and litigation.[47] In general these proposals embodied the theory advocated by President Roosevelt, that combinations and consolidations were not of themselves an evil; that there were good as well as bad trusts; and that rather than pursue a policy of indiscriminate warfare against big business, it was the part of wisdom to license big business under competent regulation in the public interest.

Very different were the grounds upon which such men as Senator Newlands, Senator Cummins, and later President Wilson supported a federal trade commission. In their view of the matter such a commission was to be merely a more effective agency for the enforcement of the anti-trust laws. The purpose of the anti-trust laws was to maintain competitive conditions—a field free to all upon equal terms—and this purpose was not to be abandoned. The only object was to eliminate the delays and uncertainties incident to judicial enforcement.

[47] *See* Mr. Gary's plan, Senate Hearings, p. 693; Mr. Stetson's plan, *ibid.*, p. 960; Mr. Morawetz' plan, *ibid.*, p. 1329, and Mr. Perkins' plan, *ibid.*, p. 1089.

It is believed that through the intervention of such a body of men the legislative policy with respect to combinations and monopolies could be vastly more effective than through the courts alone, which in most cases will take no cognizance of violations of the law until months or years after the violation occurs, and when the difficulty of awarding reparation for the violation is almost insurmountable.[48]

"The railroad question," said Senator Newlands, "is practically settled; the settlement of the trust question has hardly been commenced. Had we submitted the administration of the anti-trust act to an impartial quasi-judicial tribunal similar to the Interstate Commerce Commission instead of to the Attorney General's office, with its shifting officials, its varying policies, its lack of tradition, record or precedent, we would by this time have made gratifying progress in the regulation and control of trusts, through the quasi-judicial investigations of a competent commission and through legislation based upon its recommendations."[49]

On January 20, 1914, in an address before both Houses of Congress, President Wilson announced in concrete form the administration program. In part it was no more than an elaboration of the thesis of the Democratic Platform and of *The New Freedom*. President Wilson asked for a "further and more explicit legislative definition of the policy and meaning of the existing anti-trust laws." "Surely," he said, "we are sufficiently familiar with the actual processes and methods of monopoly and of the many hurtful restraints of trade to make definition possible, at any rate up to the limit of what experience has disclosed. These practices, being now abundantly disclosed, can be explicitly and item by item forbidden by statute in such terms as will practically eliminate uncer-

[48] Report of Senate Committee on Interstate Commerce of February 26, 1913, *supra*, p. xv.
[49] Senate Hearings *re* Newlands bill, p. 5.

tainty, the law itself and the penalty being made equally plain.'"[50] As a part of the program, he asked for legislation to prevent interlocking directorates between large corporations and to regulate the issue of securities by railroads.

The second part of the Democratic program, however, went beyond anything that was suggested in the Democratic Platform. A federal trade commission had generally been looked upon as the peculiar political property of the Progressives. Indeed the Rooseveltian conception of an administrative agency to license and supervise the "trusts" had been the target of some of Mr. Wilson's most effective eloquence.[51] In his address of January 20, 1914, however, President Wilson gave his unqualified support to the establishment of an interstate trade commission. "The opinion of the country would instantly approve of such a commission. It would not wish to see it empowered to make terms with monopoly or in any sort to assume control of business, as if the Government made itself responsible. It demands such a commission only as an indispensable instrument of information and publicity, as a clearing house for the facts by which both the public mind and the managers of great business undertakings shall be guided, and as an instrumentality for doing justice to business where the processes of the courts or the natural forces of correction outside the courts are inadequate to adjust the remedy to the wrong in a way that will meet all the equities and circumstances of the case."

The address set the keynote for both Houses, and within a week tentative bills had been drafted by administration leaders. There was a bill amending the Sherman Law by adding sections specifically denouncing discrimination in price with intent to injure a competitor

[50] Cong. Rec., 63d Cong., 2d Sess., p. 1963.
[51] *The New Freedom*, pp. 194-216.

of either the purchaser or the seller, and sales on condition that a purchaser shall not deal in the goods of a competitor of the seller.[52] Another bill[53] declared that the words "restraint of trade" and "monopoly" in the Sherman Law should include any combination or agreement "to create or carry out restrictions in trade" or to acquire "a monopoly" in interstate commerce; to limit or reduce production or increase prices; to prevent competition; or to make any agreement undertaking "to prevent a free and unrestricted competition" among the participants, or any purchasers or consumers. A third bill related to interlocking directorates,[54] and a fourth to intercorporate stockholding.[55] On January 22 Congressman Clayton introduced "A bill to create an Interstate Trade Commission." The bill established a commission of five members, transferred to them the old Bureau of Corporations, and gave them complete access to the books, records, and papers of corporations engaged in interstate and foreign commerce. The Commission was authorized to investigate any corporation believed to be violating the anti-trust laws, and if any violation is found, to report the matter to the Attorney General. Upon request of the Attorney General, or of any corporation subject to the act, the Commission could, after investigation, make formal findings prescribing the readjustments necessary to bring the corporation within the law. These findings could be used by the Attorney General in effecting voluntary reorganization of the law-breakers.[56]

The program encountered difficulties. Members of the committees had strong views, and it developed that the

[52] *See* Committee Print No. 1, Trust Bill, April 15, 1914, p. 23.

[53] *See* Committee Print No. 2, *ibid.*, p. 29.

[54] *See* Committee Print No. 3, *ibid.*, p. 33.

[55] *See* Committee Print No. 4, *ibid.*, p. 37.

[56] *See* H.R. 12120 and S. 4160, on pp. 41 and 51, respectively, of Trust Bills, *supra*.

Attorney General, who had not been previously consulted, objected to some items in the program.[57] In the House a compromise was finally reached. The Trade Commission bill was reintroduced, with changes, by Congressman Covington and reported by the committee on March 16.[58] In addition an omnibus anti-trust law was introduced by Congressman Clayton on April 14.[59] It contained the substance of the bills relating to intercorporate stockholding and interlocking directorates, and of the bill covering price discrimination and exclusive contracts, and in addition elaborate provisions designed to regulate the use of injunctions in labor disputes. The attempted definition of the phrases of the Sherman Law had been abandoned, as had the subject of railroad securities issues. On May 6 the new bill was reported by the committee. On June 5 both the Clayton and Covington bills passed the House with large majorities.

The bills went to the appropriate committees of the Senate. In the meantime, however, there was an important change of Administration policy. The Trade Commission bill, as it passed the House, gave to the Commission no regulatory or quasi-judicial powers. It was to be an investigating and advisory body, and indeed hardly more than an adjunct to the Department of Justice. On the other hand, the Clayton Act was a criminal statute, with which the Trade Commission would have no concern. On June 12, however, it became known that the Administration had approved the substance of a bill previously introduced by Congressman Stevens, of New Hampshire, which had apparently been rejected by the House Committee. This bill authorized the Commission to issue restraining orders against the use of unfair competition in

---

[57] See Young, "The Sherman Act and the New Anti-Trust Legislation," Vol. 23, *Journal of Political Economy*, pp. 305 ff.

[58] H.R. 14749, Trust Bills, p. 479.

[59] H.R. 15657, Trust Bills, p. 3.

interstate and foreign commerce. The Senate Committee accepted the proposal, and on June 13 reported the Trade Commission bill, as amended, to the Senate. With changes in matters of detail, the bill passed the Senate on August 5, and on September 26, after further changes in conference, became law. In the meantime the Clayton Act had been amended in the Senate, by striking out the sections relating to price discrimination and exclusive contracts, upon the theory that these matters would be dealt with by the Trade Commission. In conference, the sections were restored, but the penal provisions eliminated. Instead, the conferees inserted in the bill sections analogous to those contained in the Trade Commission bill, authorizing the Federal Trade Commission to issue restraining orders to prevent the corporation from carrying on the practices described in the restored sections. On October 15, this bill also became law.

The new anti-trust legislation of 1914 was not intended to cover the whole field of monopoly and restraint of trade. The Sherman Law remained intact, nor was any attempt made at a legislative definition or specification of the offenses to which it relates. Emphasis was laid on the fact that the new legislation did not purport to amend the anti-trust act of 1890, but merely to supplement it. To this extent it is apparent at the outset that the movement for clarification and definition, at least in so far as it rested upon the demand of business men that they be apprised what conduct was and what was not lawful, had made but little progress. The Clayton Act described certain practices, and declared them unlawful, but there was no declaration that practices not enumerated or described in the act were to be deemed lawful. The theory of the law was rather that certain practices, whether or not prohibited by the Sherman Law, could be isolated and defined, and guarded against by special prohibitions and methods of enforcement. The new methods of enforcement, however, were not exclusive, for if the practices, either of themselves or in connection with a general course of conduct, were found to be a violation of the Sherman Law, the criminal and equitable remedies of that law were still available.

Before turning to the administrative machinery provided in the new laws, it will be helpful to trace in greater detail the legislative history of the new principles of substantive law which they embodied. Within the field with which we are concerned (disregarding for this purpose sections relating to banks and common carriers, to labor disputes, and other matters beyond the jurisdiction of the Federal Trade Commission) there are five such principles, four contained in the Clayton Act and one in the Federal Trade Commission Act.

Section 2 of the Clayton Act related to price discrimination. In the form in which it appeared in the original Clayton bill as introduced in the House on April 14, 1914, and passed June 5, 1914, it forbade any discrimination in price with the purpose of injuring or destroying the business of a competitor of either the seller or the purchaser. It drew its inspiration from a dual source. It was designed to meet the case of a powerful corporation or combination which, with a view to driving a competitor out of business, starts a temporary and local campaign of price cutting, expecting to return to a profitable price level as soon as the competitor is eliminated or brought to terms. Local price cutting of this sort was clearly an unfair method of competition, and was one of the practices which, in the opinion of the Supreme Court, had given an illegal color to the organization of the Standard Oil and Tobacco Companies. Section 2 seems to have been intended also, however, to cover price discrimination designed to place particular purchasers or groups of purchasers at an unfair advantage as compared with competitors who purchased at a more favorable price. In this respect the policy was that of the Interstate Commerce Act and of the law of public callings. At this stage the bill carried, it will be recalled, a criminal penalty, and it is to be noted that a specific intent to "injure" the business of a competitor of seller or buyer was required to render a price discrimination illegal. A proviso, inserted for greater caution, made the prohibition inapplicable to price discriminations based on differences in grade, quality, or quantity, or in costs of transportation. A second proviso declared that "nothing herein contained shall prevent persons engaged in selling goods, wares, or merchandise in commerce from selecting their own customers."

The Senate Judiciary Committee reported the bill, with amendments to Section 2, designed to perfect the language. The first proviso was changed to permit discriminations based upon selling costs as well as transportation costs; and to permit "discrimination in price in the same or different communities made in good faith to meet competitors and not intended to create monopoly." The right to select customers, in the second proviso, was confined to "bona fide transactions and not in restraint of trade." After the report was filed, however, but before the bill was reached on the calendar, the Trade Commission bill had passed the Senate. Accordingly, on the floor of the Senate, a new amendment was adopted, eliminating the section entirely, on the ground that the practice was already covered by the phrase "unfair methods of competition" in the Trade Commission bill.

It was only after it had been restored to the bill in conference that Section 2 assumed its final form. The criminal penalty was eliminated, and the practice was merely declared to be "unlawful." The operation of the section was confined to commodities sold for use, consumption, or resale within the United States or places subject to its jurisdiction. The provisos were inserted substantially as suggested by the Senate Judiciary Committee, except that the words "and not intended to create monopoly" were omitted from the first proviso. The provision requiring a specific intent to injure the business of a competitor of seller or buyer was, however, eliminated. Instead, a price discrimination was declared to be unlawful only "where the effect of such discrimination may be to substantially lessen competition or tend to create a monopoly in any line of commerce."

Section 3, relating to exclusive or "tieing" contracts, passed through a somewhat similar evolution. In the original Clayton Act,[60] it was made a criminal offense to lease or sell goods, or fix a price, discount, or rebate, on condition that the lessee or purchaser do not use or deal in the goods of a competitor of the seller or lessor. The prohibition was complete and unqualified; an attempt on the floor of the House to amend the section by requiring an intent to establish a monopoly or destroy a competitor's business was defeated by a decisive vote.[61] Substantially without amendment, the section remained in the bill as it passed the House. It is apparent that this section also was designed to cover two types of practices. It was designed to meet the case of a manufacturer of an article, generally a patented machine, who sold or leased it with a stipulation that it could only be used in connection with other machinery or accessories or supplies also made by the seller or lessor, but not covered by patent. Such a "tieing clause," had been sustained by the Supreme Court, in Henry v. A. B. Dick Company,[62] and had been the source of serious complaint in the case of the United Shoe Machinery Corporation.[63] The section was also de-

[60] Section 3 of the bill introduced by Mr. Clayton, and Section 4 of the bill as reported by the House Judiciary Committee.

[61] Cong. Rec., 63d Cong., 2d Sess., pp. 9398-9410.

[62] 224 U.S., 1 (1912).

[63] See testimony of Mr. Brandeis, Trust Legislation, p. 31. In United

signed to cover the case of a manufacturer who required of his wholesale and retail distributors an agreement not to handle the products of the manufacturer's competitors. Such an agreement while probably of itself not a violation of the Sherman Law[64] was looked upon as an instrument by which the normal channels of distribution were closed to competitors.

In reporting the section, the Senate Committee suggested minor amendments,[65] but subsequently, upon the floor of the Senate, this section also was dropped from the bill.[66] Not satisfied, however, that the prohibition of unfair methods of competition would have the result of overruling the Dick case and reaching the tieing clause of the Shoe Machinery Corporation, the Senate adopted instead a section, applicable only to patented articles, prohibiting the use of "tieing clauses" under criminal penalty. In conference, however, the section was restored substantially as reported by the Judiciary Committee, except that the practice was declared to be unlawful only where "the effect of such lease, sale or contract for sale or such condition, agreement or understanding, may be to substantially lessen competition or tend to create a monopoly in any line of commerce."

Section 7 of the original Clayton Act made it a criminal offense for a corporation engaged in interstate or foreign commerce to acquire the whole or any part of the stock of another corporation similarly engaged, "where the

States v. United Shoe Machinery Corporation, 258 U.S. 454 (1922), such tieing contracts were held not to be in violation of the Sherman Law.

[64] See also Whitwell v. Continental Tobacco Co., 125 Fed. 454 (1903).

[65] A "contract of sale" as well as a sale or lease was brought within the section, and it was expressly made applicable to articles "whether patented or unpatented."

[66] Committee amendment striking out the section adopted, Cong. Rec., 63d Cong., 2d Sess., p. 13849; reconsidered p. 14223; and again adopted pp. 14272-14273.

effect of such acquisition is to eliminate or lessen competition between the corporation whose stock is so acquired and the corporation making the acquisition, or to create a monopoly of any line of trade in any section or community.'' A similar prohibition applied to acquisition by a holding company of stock of two or more corporations engaged in interstate or foreign commerce. Stock purchases solely for investment, not used ''to bring about, or in attempting to bring about, the lessening of competition,'' and acquisitions growing out of the formation of subsidiary corporations in order to carry on ''their immediate lawful business, or the natural and legitimate branches thereof,'' were excepted, and rights ''heretofore legally acquired'' were safeguarded. There were no significant amendments either on the floor of the House, or by the Senate Judiciary Committee. The committee substituted ''commerce'' for ''trade'' in the sentence above quoted, and there were changes in the clause preserving vested rights and guarding against legalization of anything forbidden by the Sherman Law. In accordance with the changed program, the criminal penalty was here also eliminated, and the practice merely declared to be ''unlawful.'' On motion of Senator Reed, of Missouri, the word ''is'' became ''may be,'' so that the clause read ''where the effect of such acquisition *may be* to eliminate or lessen competition . . .'' In conference the clause was once more revised. In its final form, intercorporate stockholding was forbidden only ''where the effect of such acquisition may be to substantially lessen competition between the corporation whose stock is so acquired and the corporation making the acquisition, or to restrain such commerce in any section or community, or tend to create a monopoly of any line of commerce.''

Section 8 of the original Clayton Act contained, among other provisions, a paragraph making it unlawful for any person to be a director in any two or more corporations (other than common carriers) engaged in interstate or foreign commerce, "if such corporations are, or shall have been theretofore, by virtue of their business and location of operation, competitors, so that an elimination of competition by agreement between them would constitute a violation of any of the provisions of any of the anti-trust laws." The House Judiciary Committee limited the application of the section to corporations of which at least one had a capital, surplus, and undivided profits of over $1,000,000. The section was adopted by the House without amendment of this paragraph, and the Senate Committee proposed merely verbal changes, aside from the elimination of the criminal clause. Substantially in this form, the paragraph was embodied in Section 8 of the bill as it became law.

The fifth principle of substantive law was in Section 5 of the Federal Trade Commission Act. Neither the original Trade Commission bill nor the revised bill introduced by Mr. Covington contained any substantive principles affecting the law of restraint of trade or monopoly. They were merely procedural statutes. In the Stevens bill, introduced in the House on April 13, the trade commission therein created was authorized to issue restraining orders against "unfair competition," and this bill became the model for the Senate Judiciary Committee. As finally adopted, the phrase became "unfair methods of competition." It was the belief of the committee, as already noted, that the words "unfair competition" would cover the specific practices enumerated in the Clayton Act. "It is believed," said the committee report, "that the term 'unfair competition' has a legal significance which can be enforced by the Commission and the courts, and that it is no more difficult to determine what is unfair competition than it is to determine what is a reasonable rate or what is unjust discrimination. The committee was of the opinion that it would be better to put in a general provision

condemning unfair competition than to attempt to define
the numerous unfair practices, such as local price cutting,
interlocking directorates, and holding companies intended
to restrain substantial competition.'"[67] The contention
was only in part accepted by the Senate, and rejected in
conference. That a campaign of local price cutting is an
unfair method of competition may be admitted. A discrimination in price not aimed against a competitor of
the seller, but forbidden because of the unjust disadvan-
tage to which it puts a purchaser as compared with his
competitors, raises a greater difficulty. It may not be a
method of competition at all. A "tieing" or exclusive
sales contract will generally be a method of competition,
although in view of the decision in the Dick and Shoe
Machinery cases, it might not have been deemed "unfair." As to "interlocking directorates and holding companies" it is difficult to understand upon what ground
the committee considered them to be included in the term
"unfair competition." As was stated by Senator Cummins during the debate, they may furnish a motive for not
competing, but they are not methods of competition (except perhaps in the rare case where a concern has bought
a minority interest in a competitor for the purpose of
harassing its operations).[68] In the debates in the Senate
the meaning of the phrase was much discussed, and there
was no clear agreement. It was admitted that it would
apply to the usual "passing off" cases, or cases involving
misrepresentation, in which no element of restraint or
monopoly existed,[69] although Senator Newlands thought

[67] Senate Report 597, p. 13.

[68] *See* Cong. Rec., 63d Cong., 2d Sess., p. 11103. *Cf.* Senator Newlands' suggestion that an interlocking directorate might constitute
unfair competition if it made the affiliated corporations more powerful
in their competition with outsiders—a somewhat far-fetched theory, it
would seem. *Ibid.,* p. 11106.

[69] *See* colloquy of Senators Sutherland and Cummins, *ibid.,* p. 11105.
Remarks of Senator Newlands and Senator McCumber, *ibid.,* p. 11108.

cases of this sort could often be handled by correspondence or dismissed as "de minimis."[70] An amendment was
offered to substitute for "unfair competition" the words
"competition in commerce the purpose or effect of which
is to cripple or destroy the business of a competitor" but
it was not adopted.[71] The bulk of the discussion, however,
turned about the numerous competitive practices which,
where used by a large corporation or combination in an
attempt to exclude competitors from the field, had been
condemned by the courts as a violation of the Sherman
Act or of similar state laws. Local price cutting was mentioned, and the use of "fighting ships" and "fighting
brands," operation through secret subsidiaries which carried on business in the guise of independents, the use of
"tieing clauses" and contracts for exclusive dealing, and
coercion, intimidation, and similar practices.[72] An article
in the *Political Science Quarterly*, reviewing and listing
a number of unfair competitive practices encountered in
anti-trust suits, figured prominently in the discussion.[73]
Decrees in anti-trust suits in which specific practices, such
as arrangements for exclusive handling of products, the
use of "fighting brands," the granting of discounts based
on quantity, etc., had been forbidden, were referred to.[74]
There were some attempts at generalization. Senator
Cummins believed that conduct, to come within the prohibition, must be "tinctured with unfairness to the public," but Senator McCumber disagreed, taking the view
that unfairness to a competitor would be the gist of the
offense. Senator Newlands thought the phrase covered
"every practice and method between competitors upon

[70] *Ibid.*, p. 11109.
[71] *Ibid.*, p. 11298.
[72] *Ibid.*, p. 11108.
[73] "Unfair Competition," by W. H. S. Stevens, *Pol. Sci. Quart.*,
June, 1914, p. 283. *See* Cong. Rec., p. 11230.
[74] Senator Robinson, *ibid.*, p. 11228.

the part of one against the other that is against public morals, in my judgment, or is an offense for which a remedy lies either at law or in equity."[75] Senator Cummins, on the other hand, asserted that "the only unfair competition that the section will ever touch is that competition which has for its object the destruction of competition. There is no unfair competition that is consistent with the endurance of competition." I mention these expressions of opinion to show the general legislative background. Except in so far as they are persuasive as the well considered views of able and experienced lawyers, they should not greatly influence the detailed construction of the law. Indeed, the debates themselves suggest, what seems obvious from the text of the Act, that it was the Congressional intention to confer on the Commission, subject to court review, the duty of giving a detailed content to the general principle embodied in the phrase, and to employ, in fulfilling this duty, not only the rules and precedents established by the courts at common law and under previous statutes, but the technique of reasoning by analogy and upon principle, with which jurists are familiar.[76]

In a later part of this study, it will be necessary in reviewing the work of the Federal Trade Commission to consider in greater detail the construction and scope of the five rules of law embodied in the new legislation. Some general conclusions apparent from the face of the sections, may be ventured in anticipation.

In Section 5 of the Trade Commission Act, it is obvious that no specific rules of conduct were prescribed. The section stated a general ethical and economic principle, and relied upon the course of administration and judicial decision to give it content. In its scope the principle was in

[75] *Ibid.*, p. 11112.
[76] *See* remarks of Senator Newlands, Cong. Rec., 63d Cong., 2d Sess., pp. 11083, 11084; Senator Hollis, *ibid.*, p. 11178.

some respects broader, in some respects narrower, than the one embodied in the Sherman Law. On the one hand it covered a multitude of deceptive practices which might bear no relation whatever to the problem of monopoly and restraint of trade. Although the popular impression doubtless was that the act was intended to deal primarily with the trust problem, the legislative debates show clearly, as I have indicated, that the use of the broad language was deliberate. On the other hand, it covered only a part of the field to which the law of restraints and monopolies is applicable. It covered only acts of competition, not agreements or combinations limiting or putting an end to competition between the parties. Although the record is not quite so clear, this limitation of the scope of the rule seems also to have been deliberate, on the part of some at least of the legislators. Within the field to which it applied, the phrase was without question a great improvement on the language of the Sherman Law. The Sherman Law used phrases with a common law significance only remotely related to the object which Congress had in mind. The common law precedents to which it pointed confused rather than clarified the issues involved. Indeed in order to give the law the construction which was apparently intended, it was necessary, by a judicial *tour de force,* to divest the words of their technical legal meaning, and attempt to give order and form to the popular beliefs and policies which they were supposed to embody. The task of construing Section 5 of the Federal Trade Commission Act is much simpler. The phrase "unfair methods of competition," both in its technical and its popular meaning, is closely related to the problem at hand; it does not conceal any fundamental ambiguities; and it renders available a store of rules and precedents not only from the common law decisions, but from a section of the law of restraints and monopolies in which the decisions under the Sherman Law had been fairly satisfactory.

In the sections of the Clayton Act which contain substantive rules of law dealing with restraint and monopoly, Congress was, it seems to me, less successful.

In the section dealing with "interlocking directorates," the test of illegality was frankly the test of the Sherman Law. Common directors between corporations engaged in interstate and foreign commerce were prohibited only "if such corporations are or shall have been theretofore, by virtue of their business and location of operation, competitors, so that the elimination of competition by agreement between them would constitute a violation of any of the provisions of any of the anti-trust laws." The difficulty in applying the test lay in the fact that no one could state with assurance under what circumstances the elimination of competition by agreement would constitute a violation of the anti-trust laws. It seemed to have been generally conceded, as we have seen, that if the agreement by which competition was eliminated comprised a transfer of property, and was made with a view to effecting economies, it was legal. There were dicta, on the other hand, that a bare agreement not to compete, without merger or sale, was illegal under any circumstances.[77] Yet under the rule of reason, the test of illegality was the test of unreasonableness at common law, and by the weight of authority an agreement limiting competition between two concerns was not illegal at common law if they controlled between them so small a part of the field that it remained, as a whole, freely competitive.[78] Since

[77] Judge Taft, in U.S. *v.* Addyston Pipe & Steel Co. et al., 85 Fed. 271; Justice Hughes, in Dr. Miles Medical Co. *v.* Park & Sons Co., 220 U.S. 373.

[78] *See* Wickens *v.* Evans, 3 Y. & J. 318 (1829); Collins *v.* Locke, 4 A.C. 674 (1879); Northwestern Salt Co. *v.* Electrolytic Alkali Co., L.R. 1914 A.C. 461; Oakdale Mfg. Co. *v.* Garst, 18 R.I. 484 (1894); Anchor

these agreements did not restrain the promissor entirely from carrying on his business, but merely limited "the mode or manner in which a trade is carried on," they were considered to be merely partial restraints, and to be lawful if reasonable and for good consideration.[79] Yet in view of the dicta in the Addyston Pipe and Dr. Miles Medical Company cases,[80] and of the emphatic opinion of the present Chief Justice,[81] it was not at all clear that this view of the common law would be carried over into the interpretation of the Sherman Law. It is unfortunate, to say the least, that the draftsmen of a statute designed to give clarity and definition to the law of restraints and monopolies, should have permitted the lawfulness of a common directorship to turn upon this highly controversial question.

Section 7, on the other hand, adopts a different and probably more drastic test than the Sherman Act. Intercorporate stockholding is illegal, "where the effect of such acquisition may be to substantially lessen competition between the corporation whose stock is so acquired and the corporation making the acquisition, or to restrain such commerce in any section or community, or tend to create a monopoly of any line of commerce." A mere lessening or prospective lessening of competition between the two corporations is sufficient, regardless of the effect

Electric Co. v. Hawkes, 171 Mass. 101 (1898); Meredith v. New Jersey Zinc & Iron Co., 55 N.J. Eq. 211 (1897); National Benefit Co. v. Union Hospital Co., 45 Minn. 272 (1891). Cases where combinations were held illegal because they included a sufficient number of competitors to give "control of the market," are Morris Run Coal Co. v. Barclay Coal Co., 68 Penn. St. 173 (1871); Central Ohio Salt Co. v. Guthrie, 35 Ohio St., 666 (1880); People v. Sheldon et al., 139 N.Y. 251 (1893); Cummings v. Union Blue Stone Co., 164 N.Y. 401 (1900).

[79] See Lord Bowen, in Nordenfelt v. Maxim Nordenfelt Co. (1894), A.C. 535.

[80] See note 77.

[81] The Anti-Trust Laws and the Supreme Court, p. 11.

upon the market as a whole. Indeed, the careful reservation of "any right heretofore legally acquired" indicates a belief that the section might go beyond the Sherman Law. Yet the result, from the practical viewpoint, can hardly be considered satisfactory. An industrial or commercial corporation does not generally buy a minority interest in a competitor merely in the hope that competition may be somewhat lessened. Unless there was already a community of interest, due for instance to common ownership of a controlling interest in both companies, it is hardly conceivable that less than a controlling amount of the stock would be purchased. A purchase of a controlling interest would of course be illegal under the Clayton Act, yet substantially the same result could be reached, quite lawfully, by a purchase of the assets of the competitor. The practical result of the section is therefore no more than to prevent one particular method of corporate consolidation. Since other methods are available, it seems doubtful whether the section was worth while.

In Sections 2 and 3, the test of legality is embodied in the phrases "substantially lessen competition" and "tend to create a monopoly in any line of commerce." The latter phrase is of course directly referable to Section 2 of the Sherman Act, as interpreted by Chief Justice White in the Standard Oil case. Possibly the use of the words "may be" and "tend" indicates that the section will catch conduct which is somewhat more remote from the prohibited result than would Section 2 of the Sherman Act, but since the meaning of the word "monopoly" as used in both acts is so much enshrouded in doubt, it is perhaps academic to delve too deeply into minor shades of meaning.

The phrase as a whole was said by one of the conferees, on the floor of the House, to have originated in the opinion of the Supreme Court in the Addyston Pipe case, where it was said ". . . that the power of Congress to regulate interstate commerce comprises the right to enact a law prohibiting the citizens from entering into these private contracts which directly and substantially, and not merely indirectly, remotely, incidentally and collaterally regulate to a greater or less degree commerce among the states.'' If this was its origin, it was not a happy one, since the attempt to develop a juristic principle based upon the difference between ''direct'' and ''substantial'' restraints on the one hand and ''indirect'' and ''incidental'' restraints on the other, had not been a success. Moreover, the meaning of the phrase seems to differ with the context. In the Addyston Pipe case the court was discussing the substantial relation of the conduct to interstate commerce. In Section 8 of the Clayton Act, the question is as to the probable substantial lessening of competition between two corporations, as a result of an acquisition of stock. The test appears to be a quantitative one. Competition might be lessened between two corporations, as a result of such an acquisition of stock, in several ways. The acquisition might lead to an agreement that the two concerns would not compete at all in certain territory. Or it might lead to an agreement limiting the scope of competition; for instance, that there should be no competition in price, but only in quality and salesmanship. Or it might result merely in a lessened intensity of competition, a relaxation of effort where the result might be to take business away from the competitor, or an understanding that customers of long standing should be left alone. Probably in any one of these cases competition would be said to have been substantially lessened, although logical difficulties might easily be imagined. Suppose for instance that two newspapers agree not to cut the price of their afternoon editions below three cents, but that, subject only to this elimination of one of the possible factors of competition, the rivalry between them, the attempt to gain advertisers and subscribers at each other's expense, could be shown to have been intensified. Is it possible to balance increased intensity of competition against lessened scope of competition? It is somewhat as if one were asked to determine how many pears make an apple, and suggests that perhaps a purely quantitative test of competition may be illusory. No doubt a practical way will be found of avoiding the difficulty when it is encountered.

In Sections 2 and 3, however, although the language is about the same as in Section 7, the phrase "substantially lessen competition" seems to have a different meaning. Here it is not a question of voluntary diminution of competitive effort, or of a limitation of the field of competition by agreement, but of an act deemed injurious to a competitor or discriminatory as between customers. Such an act can lessen competition only by forcing a competitor out of business or inducing him to compete less vigorously; yet it is difficult to see how the lawfulness of a practice could be made to depend upon the Commission's guess as to its effect upon the number of competitors, or upon its finding that competition will be, say, 10 per cent less intense if the practice is indulged in. A few examples will illustrate the point. A manufacturer puts a new patented article on the market, with a condition that the purchaser use it only in conjunction with a certain unpatented accessory made by the same manufacturer. This seems to be precisely the situation Congress tried to reach in Section 3 of the Clayton Act, yet it is not a case in which competition is *lessened,* since the business is a new one. Indeed competition will be increased, if the patented article and the accessory, combined, compete with other articles designed to serve the same general purpose. It is significant that in the first case of this sort to arise after the Clayton Act took effect, the Supreme Court, rather than face the difficulty involved in construing the qualifying language of Section 3, preferred frankly to overrule its decision in the Dick case, and to hold that such a restriction was not authorized at common law or under the patent act.[82] Suppose again that a manufacturer establishes a discount for all bona fide wholesalers, but refuses to allow the discount to a wholesaler owned and managed on a cooperative basis by a number of retailers. Whether or not such a discrimination in price violates Section 2 of the Clayton Act need not be considered now;[83] to inquire whether or not it diminishes competition seems beside the point. If its object is to eliminate the cooperative wholesaler from the field, and if it is successful, the result might nevertheless be to increase competition, since the constituent retailers, instead of pooling their purchases through one mutual agency, would probably buy their supplies through a number of competing wholesalers. A campaign of local price cutting could perhaps be said to lessen competition if it was successful in driving the local competitor out of business. Giving full effect to the words "may be" in Section 2, such a campaign, even if not ultimately successful, might be brought within the literal language of the section if it had some chance of succeeding. Would the conduct become lawful, if the trier of facts were convinced that the local competitor was too strong or too stubborn to be dislodged? A manufacturer of gasoline secures agreements from all the retailers in a community not to handle the gasoline of a competitor. In self-defense, the competitor installs a filling station of its own, and competition is intensified. Does the result make the exclusive contracts lawful? These illustrations suggest that perhaps, in Sections 2 and 3, the words "substantially lessen competition" have some other than a purely quantitative signifi-

[82] Motion Picture Patents Co. *v.* Universal Film Co. et al., 243 U.S. 502 (1917).

[83] *See* Federal Trade Commission *v.* Mennen Co., 4 F.T.C.D. 258, 288 Fed. 774.

cance. The general purposes of the two sections seem to call for a test dependent upon the quality of the act rather than upon its actual effect on the quantity or scope of competition. Certain types of exclusive sales contracts, or tieing clauses, might be considered wrongful because of their tendency to interpose obstacles to the conduct of business by competitors. A temporary campaign of price cutting with the object of driving a competitor out of business might be considered injurious because the outcome would generally depend upon the relative financial resources of the parties rather than upon their ability to produce cheaply and well. Perhaps Sections 2 and 3 rest upon a dogmatic assumption that such economically wrongful means of competition in the long run impede free and fair competition, and therefore lessen competition and tend toward monopoly.[84] The uncertainty as to the meaning of the phrase of itself indicates that it was not happily chosen.

To the administrative machinery set up for the enforcement of the two statutes the next chapter will be devoted. It may be observed at this point that in the Federal Trade Commission Act, the administrative method is exclusive. No individual can initiate a suit under that act, nor can a court give it any effect in the absence of a prior complaint, finding, and order by the Commission. In the Clayton Act, however, the administrative method is merely supplementary, for in Section 15 the district courts are given primary jurisdiction to restrain violations of the act, upon petition of the United States, and in Section 16 private individuals or corporations are authorized "to

[84] Without anticipating too much the later chapters of this study, it may be said that support for this view may be found in the opinion of the Supreme Court in F.T.C. *v.* Curtis Publishing Co., 260 U.S. 568 (1923), that it is a question of law for the court whether or not an exclusive sales contract may "substantially lessen competition or tend to create a monopoly."

sue for and have injunctive relief" against threatened damage from a violation of the prohibitions of the act. These sections are entirely independent of Section 13, and it is apparently contemplated that both the Attorney General and the Federal Trade Commission could if they were so minded bring simultaneous proceedings against the same party on the same charges.

Aside from its connection with the enforcement of Section 5 of the Federal Trade Commission Act and of Sections 2, 3, 7, and 8 of the Clayton Act, the Commission was given other powers and duties. They fall mainly into two categories: duties of investigation and inquiry, and duties of an advisory character in connection with the administration of the anti-trust laws.

The Commission was authorized to "gather and compile information concerning" corporations engaged in commerce, and their relations to other corporations and to individuals, associations, and partnerships. Upon the direction of the President or of either House of Congress, it was authorized to investigate and report upon any alleged violations of the anti-trust acts by any corporation. And it could investigate, from time to time, trade conditions in foreign countries, "where associations, combinations, or practices of manufacturers, merchants or traders, or other conditions, may affect the foreign trade of the United States." In general, these were analogous to the powers of the old Bureau of Corporations; they were an aid to legislation and to the formation of public opinion, but had no direct relation to the enforcement of the law.

More directly concerned with the anti-trust laws were certain advisory powers conferred upon the Commission. Upon application by the Attorney General, the Commission was authorized to investigate and make recommendations "for the readjustment of the business of any corporation alleged to be violating the anti-trust acts in order that the corporation may thereafter maintain its organization, management, and conduct of business in accordance with law." On its own initiative, or upon application of the Attorney General, the Commission could investigate the manner in which any final decree in an anti-trust suit was being carried out, and to report its findings and recommendations to the Attorney General. And it was provided that in any suit brought by the Attorney General under the anti-trust laws, the court, if satisfied that the Government was entitled to relief, could refer the suit to the Commission "as a master in chancery," to ascertain and report an appropriate form of decree. The report was advisory only, however; "the court may adopt or reject such report, in whole or in part, and enter such decree as the nature of the case may in its judgment require."

Finally there was an apparently sweeping power, the precise scope of which will be considered in a later chapter, to require corporations (other than banks or common carriers) to file annual or special reports or answers to questions, "furnishing to the Commission such information as it may require as to the organization, business, conduct, practices, management and relation to other corporations, partnerships, and individuals" of the corporation in question. The reports must be in the form prescribed by the Commission, and may be required to be under oath. A "civil" penalty of $100 a day was imposed for failure to file such a report, and a heavy criminal penalty for the making of a false report.

In two subsequent statutes the powers of the Federal Trade Commission have been in one case expanded, in the other case restricted.

The Webb Export Act, approved April 10, 1918, applied to any "association" (*i.e.*, "any corporation or combination, by contract or otherwise, of two or more persons, partnerships, or corporations") engaged solely

in export trade. It was provided that nothing contained in
the Sherman Law should be construed as rendering illegal
such an association, or any agreement made or act done
by it in the course of export trade, "provided such association, agreement, or act is not in restraint of trade
within the United States, or is not in restraint of the
export trade of any domestic competitor of such association," and that the association does not enter into any
agreement or conspiracy to "artificially or intentionally"
enhance or depress prices, or substantially lessen competition in the United States. It was also provided that
Section 7 of the Clayton Act should not be construed to
forbid the acquisition by a corporation of stock in corporations engaged exclusively in the export trade, "unless
the effect of such acquisition or ownership may be to
restrain or substantially lessen competition within the
United States." To obtain the benefit of these exemp-
tions, export associations were required to file their
articles of incorporation or association with the Federal
Trade Commission, and make periodic statements, and
to furnish such additional information as might be called
for. If the Commission believes that an association is
operating in restraint of trade within the United States,
or in restraint of the export trade of a domestic competitor, or that it is artificially or intentionally enhancing or
depressing prices or substantially lessening competition
in the United States, it can make an investigation, and
"if it shall conclude that the law has been violated, it may
make to such association recommendations for the readjustment of its business, in order that it may thereafter maintain its organization and management and
conduct its business in accordance with law." If the
recommendations are not complied with, they may be referred to the Attorney General for such action as he may
deem proper.

In addition, the law provides that the prohibition

against "unfair methods of competition," and the remedies provided in the Federal Trade Commission Act shall extend to unfair methods "used in export trade against competitors engaged in export trade, even though the acts constituting such unfair methods are done without the territorial jurisdiction of the United States."

Finally, on August 15, 1921, the Packers and Stockyards Act became law, in which wide powers were given to the Secretary of Agriculture over the operation and practices of meat packers, stockyards, and livestock commission houses. Section 406 (b) takes away from the Federal Trade Commission all power or jurisdiction so far as it relates to any matter over which jurisdiction is conferred by the Act on the Secretary of Agriculture.

It will be apparent from this review of the legislation of 1914, that in so far as the proponents of supplemental anti-trust legislation had hoped to clarify the law of restraints and monopolies by substituting specific rules of conduct for general principles, they had largely failed. The draftsmen of the Federal Trade Commission Act avowedly chose a phrase embodying a general principle, while the unlawfulness of the practices somewhat inaptly described in the Clayton Act is made to depend upon the construction of a phrase at least as indefinite as the standard of the Sherman Law under the rule of reason. Both statutes were rather a victory for those who doubted the efficacy of legislative codification, and placed their reliance instead upon the development of rules and precedents by the gradual process of interpretation and decision of controversies by administrative and judicial tribunals.

CHAPTER II

THE COMMISSION'S PROCEDURE

ALL formal proceedings before the Federal Trade Commission must be set in motion by a complaint issued by the Commission, and served on the person complained of, embodying the Commission's charges and setting a day for a hearing.[1] No one else can initiate a complaint. An individual aggrieved by an act of unfair competition or by a practice condemned in the Clayton Act may of course bring the matter to the Commission's attention and request that a complaint issue, but he does not thereby become a formal party to the proceeding. He has no remedy if the Commission refuses to issue a complaint, and no control over the prosecution of the case if a complaint is issued.

The Federal Trade Commission is authorized to file a complaint only when it "shall have reason to believe" that Section 5 of the Trade Commission Act or Section 2, 3, 7, or 8 of the Clayton Act has been or is being violated. The phrase seems to imply, not necessarily a firm conviction, but at least a provisional belief, and it is necessary to consider in the first place how this belief is to be acquired.

So far as the statute is concerned, there seems to be no limitation upon the means by which the Commission may acquire "reason to believe" that the law has been violated. The information might, it would seem, be acquired by personal observation of the commissioners or from the daily press. Indeed, there seems to be no procedure by which the sufficiency of the Commission's "reason to believe" can be put in issue, either upon the adequacy of

[1] Federal Trade Commission Act, Sec. 5.

the belief as to the facts, or upon their legal effect.[2] In practice, however, the Commission has found it necessary to organize its sources of information, and to set up, through subordinates, a sifting process by which a certain amount of preliminary investigation is done before the Commission decides whether or not it has reason to believe that there has been a violation of law. The first step is generally an "application for a complaint" by someone who claims that the law is being violated. While anyone may apply to the Commission to institute proceedings, the rules of practice require that the application be in writing, and "contain a short and simple statement of the facts constituting the alleged violation of law and the name and address of the applicant and of the party complained of."[3] The Commission has stated that it will not exercise the functions of a detective bureau. It will not consider an anonymous communication, or a mere suggestion that a certain concern or industry could profitably be investigated. "The Commission insists upon having a definite applicant in each case."[4] A large number of letters and inquiries are of course summarily disposed of. They may complain of conduct which is clearly lawful or beyond the Commission's jurisdiction, in which event the writer is so informed and the file closed. Where it appears that the law may have been violated, the application, perhaps after further correspondence to put it in proper shape, is docketed as a formal "application for the issuance of a complaint."

The application is then assigned to an investigator. The Commission has, of course, no authority to delegate the making of decisions to subordinates. It is not authorized to issue a complaint merely because an investigator believes that the law has been violated. The be-

[2] *Post,* p. 57.
[3] Rules of Practice, No. II.
[4] Annual Report, 1921, p. 36.

lief must be that of a majority of the five members of the Commission. The Commission may, however, appoint "such attorneys, special experts, clerks, and other employees as it may find necessary for the proper performance of its duties," and it can use these employees as advisers and as sources of information upon which a belief can be predicated. The usual routine is to assign an examiner, under the direction of the Chief Examiner, to make an investigation, either by correspondence or in the field. The examiner is generally an attorney, and he is expected to direct his attention to the elements of fact necessary to sustain a complaint, as well as to practical questions of testimony and proof which will be encountered if a complaint is issued. The result of the investigation is embodied in a report, which contains a recommendation either that the application be dismissed or that a formal complaint issue. The file is reviewed by the chief examiner or assistant chief examiner, "to make sure, first, that the investigation is complete, and, second, that a correct conclusion, both as to the law and the facts, has been reached."[5]

The file is then transmitted to the "board of review." This is an extra-legal body with purely advisory powers. Originally, the Commission established two such boards, a "law board of review," composed of attorneys, and a "joint board of review," composed of representatives of both the legal and the economic staff. The chairman of the law board was also chairman of the joint board. The joint board was expected to consider questions of mixed law and economics, while pure questions of law were reserved for the law board.[6] The dual organization, however, proved unsatisfactory, and was replaced in 1917 by a single Board of Review, composed of two lawyers and an economist. This advisory body analyzes the evidence

[5] 1921 Annual Report, p. 35.
[6] 1916 Annual Report, pp. 4 and 5.

and the examiner's report, prepares an opinion applying the law to the facts, and submits its report to the Commission with a recommendation as to the action to be taken. The clerk of the Commission assigns the application, by rotation, to one of the Commissioners, who in turn files a memorandum with a written recommendation. Upon this recommendation and the accompanying file, the whole Commission then decides whether it "has reason to believe" that there has been a violation of any law which it has jurisdiction to enforce.

As yet the proceedings are only preliminary. The person complained of may not even know that he is being investigated, although the usual procedure seems to be to notify him at once and give him a chance to explain or justify his conduct.[7] There is as yet no formal party to the proceeding.

The next step is the issuance of a complaint. Where the proceeding is under the Clayton Act, it is said that such a complaint must issue as a matter of course, if the Commission "has reason to believe" that there has been a violation of law. In the Federal Trade Commission Act there is a further requirement, that "it shall appear to the Commission that a proceeding by it in respect thereof would be to the interest of the public." The meaning and effect of this clause has been much disputed. The Circuit Court of Appeals in the Second Circuit considers that it is designed to characterize the kind of unfair competition which the Commission has jurisdiction to prevent. "Only unfair practices which affect the public, as distinguished from individuals, are within the jurisdiction of the Commission."[8] Upon this view, the clause is not merely procedural, but affects the substantive principle of law

[7] 1921 Annual Report, p. 35.

[8] Federal Trade Commission v. Gratz, 258 Fed. 314. See also New Jersey Asbestos Co. v. Federal Trade Commission, 264 Fed. 509; Gulf Refining Co. v. Same, 282 Fed. 81; Mechem, 21 Mich. Law Rev. 139.

embodied in the statute. It follows that if the Commission issues an order prohibiting a practice which does not "affect the public," the order may be set aside by the reviewing court. It is difficult to reconcile this view with the language of the Act. Section 5 contains first an unqualified declaration that "unfair methods of competition in commerce are hereby declared unlawful." In the next paragraph the Commission is empowered and directed to prevent the use of "unfair methods of competition in commerce." The method of prevention is described in the third paragraph: it is to file a complaint, whenever the Commission has reason to believe that any person, partnership, or corporation has been or is using any unfair method of competition, and if it appears to the Commission that "a proceeding by it in respect thereof would be to the interest of the public." The intention appears to be to characterize the proceeding, rather than the method of competition. It seems more in harmony with the text to hold that all unfair methods of competition are to be considered unlawful, but that the Commission may exercise a certain discretion in determining when it is wise to institute proceedings. This discretion might depend largely upon practical considerations, upon the prevalence and seriousness of the offense, the extent to which it can be effectively dealt with by other agencies, the extent to which persons injured thereby have an adequate remedy in the courts, and the limitations upon the Commission's own activities arising out of limitations of power, of personnel, and of appropriations. Moreover, there seems to be no reason to disregard the words "if it shall appear *to the Commission* that a proceeding would be to the interest of the public." Upon this interpretation it is apparent that persons against whom complaints have been issued would acquire no rights by virtue of the clause in question. A firm or corporation under investigation might endeavor to persuade the Commission that it would not be to the public interest to issue a complaint. If a complaint had been issued, the respondent might appeal to the Commission to dismiss it on the ground that it had been unprovidently issued, there being no public interest. But it could not be asserted that the Commission had no jurisdiction or legal right to issue the complaint, nor could the Circuit Court of Appeals set aside an order on the ground that in its opinion the public interest was not affected.[9]

The complaint itself is the first step in the legal proceeding, and its importance has been greatly enhanced by the decision of the Supreme Court in the Gratz case. The Supreme Court has held that unless the complaint sets forth sufficient facts to show on its face a violation of law, an order based thereon will be set aside, even where, apparently, the order was fully warranted by the evidence.[10] The complaint, therefore, is the foundation for the whole proceeding.

The drafting of the complaint is done in the office of the Chief Counsel, but the complaint is not issued until it has been approved by the Commission. It follows that

[9] This seems to be the view taken by the Commission, 1920 Annual Report, p. 61. *Cf.* Mechem, 21 Mich. Law Rev. 139: "It would seem that the determination of public interest is an administrative function only, not open to judicial review, except, perhaps, where such determination is so arbitrary as to be beyond the powers of the Commission and to work a denial of due process." *See* also Standard Oil Co. *v.* Federal Trade Commission (C.C.A. 3d), 282 Fed. 81, 85 (1922), where the question was raised but not decided.

[10] Federal Trade Commission *v.* Gratz et al., 253 U.S. 421 (1920). The court said: "If, when liberally construed, the complaint is plainly insufficient to show unfair competition within the proper meaning of these words there is no foundation for an order to desist—the thing which may be prohibited is the method of competition specified in the complaint. Such an order should follow the complaint; otherwise it is improvident and, when challenged, will be annulled by the court" (p. 426). Justices Brandeis and Clark dissented from this view.

before a case comes before the Commission in its judicial
capacity, it will already on two separate occasions have
familiarized itself with the subject matter of the controversy; first, when it considers whether or not it "has
reason to believe" that the law has been violated, and a
second time when it approves the form of the "charges"
which it is preferring against the alleged wrongdoers.

Service of the complaint is by the Docket Section, in
the name of the Secretary of the Commission. The statutory provisions governing the service of complaints,
orders, and other processes are liberal. Service may be
by personal delivery of the document in question to the
person to be served, or to a member of the partnership
to be served, or "to the president, secretary, or other
executive officer or a director" where the respondent is
a corporation. Or a copy of the paper in question may be
left at the principal office or place of business of the party
to be served. In either case, "the verified return by the
person so serving said complaint, order, or other process
setting forth the manner of said service shall be proof
of the same." Service may also be by registering and
mailing a copy of the paper in question addressed to the
respondent at his principal office or place of business, in
which event "the return post-office receipt for said complaint, order or other process registered and mailed as
aforesaid" is considered proof of service.[11] The usual
practice is to make service by registered mail, and for all
that appears this innovation upon common law procedure
seems to work satisfactorily.

One point is worth a passing comment. The statute requires that the complaint contain "a notice of a hearing
upon a day and at a place therein fixed at least thirty days
after the service of said complaint." And it provides that

[11] *See* eighth paragraph of Sec. 5 of the Federal Trade Commission
Act, and the corresponding paragraph of Sec. 11 of the Clayton Act.

the respondent "shall have the right to appear at the place and time so fixed and show cause why an order should not be entered . . ." In practice the Commission seems to have quite frankly evaded this requirement. The form of complaint sets, it is true, a date for a hearing (generally forty days from the time of service), but the physical state of the Commission's docket is such that it is said to be practically impossible to reach the case within so short a period. The complaint is therefore always accompanied by a supplemental statement explaining that the date of hearing is "nominal only," and that in fact no hearing will be held until a subsequent date of which the respondent will be duly advised; in effect, that the complaint does not really mean what it says. In view of the unqualified statement in the statute that the respondent "shall have the right to appear at the place and time" fixed in the complaint, an interesting question might perhaps be raised if a respondent were to insist upon a hearing on the day set. It is to be noted that the statute contains no express authority to adjourn a hearing to a later date. However this may be, the practice is clearly established, and is doubtless in many cases welcomed by busy attorneys for respondents, who would otherwise have but a brief time for the preparation of what may be a complicated and important case.

The draftsmen of the statute apparently had it in mind that the complaint would be the only formal pleading, and that the next step would be the appearance of the respondent, at the time and place set, with his witnesses and attorneys, to "show cause" why an order should not issue. The rules of practice of the Commission provide, however, that within thirty days from the service of the complaint (unless the time is extended by the Commission) the defendant shall file an answer, containing "a short and simple statement of the facts which constitute the ground of defense." The answer must "specifically admit or deny or explain each of the facts alleged in the complaint, unless the defendant is without knowledge, in which case he shall so state, such statement operating as a denial.'' The supplemental notice accompanying the complaint is at pains to explain that the thirty days allowed for this purpose must be strictly adhered to. In practice, however, additional time is frequently granted upon a proper showing.

The answer is the only defensive pleading or motion permitted under the Commission's rules. No demurrer, or motion to dismiss, will be entertained, whether upon jurisdictional grounds or on the ground that the facts alleged do not constitute a violation of the act. Such has been the repeated ruling of the Commission,[12] and under the appellate procedure provided in the act, there seems to be no way by which a complaint can be set aside for insufficiency in law. Only one method is provided in either statute for court review in a proceeding by the Federal Trade Commission, and that is by petition to the Circuit Court of Appeals to review an order of the Commission, and both statutes provide that "the jurisdiction of the Circuit Court of Appeals of the United States to enforce, set aside or modify orders of the Commission shall be exclusive." It is true that there is no express denial of jurisdiction to enjoin proceedings under a complaint, but the court decisions to date agree that such a jurisdiction would be inconsistent with the purposes of the act.

The cases may be briefly reviewed. In a case against a ship chandler, for commercial bribery, the respondent endeavored to secure an injunction from a federal district court, to prevent the Commission from proceeding under the complaint, and from compelling the production of records and documents. The bill alleged that the act was unconstitutional, but the court held that the regular

[12] There appear to have been occasional exceptions, however. *See* Mechem, *op. cit.*, p. 138.

statutory procedure amply protected respondent's rights, and denied the injunction.[13]

In a proceeding against the Chamber of Commerce of Minneapolis, its officers and directors, the respondents made a formal motion to dismiss the complaint, because the law was unconstitutional, the Commission without jurisdiction, as well as "biased and prejudiced," and because the complaint did not state a cause of action. An order was entered by the Federal Trade Commission denying the motion, and from this interlocutory order respondents filed a "petition for *certiorari*" in the Circuit Court of Appeals, asking that the order be certified for review and determination. The petition was dismissed, and the reasons for the decision are admirably stated in the following excerpt:

In our judgment certiorari, as such, will not lie, because this court has no power to issue the writ as original process, and because, further, we have not here presented a case where the writ is desired, as in the nature of an auxiliary process in aid of jurisdiction acquired; nor is it necessary for the protection of appellate jurisdiction before such jurisdiction is actually obtained, which otherwise might be defeated, nor to make the jurisdiction effectual, nor because of the absence of any other remedy. The writ, as asked, partakes largely of the nature of a writ of prohibition, but such is not justified by the circumstances in this case under any power conferred by statute upon Circuit Courts of Appeals.

What is really sought by petitioners is that this court should halt inquiry at the threshold, exercising, in effect, the powers of a court of original jurisdiction, in which a cause is pending, to rule *in limine* upon the propriety of the action and whether it should proceed further. The procedure invoked is similar, in effect, to that prevailing in a court of original jurisdiction which has control of the successive steps of pleading, practice, trial, and final judgment or decree. But it must be remembered that

[13] T. C. Hurst & Son *v.* Federal Trade Commission et al., 268 Fed. 874 (1920).

this court has no original jurisdiction of this nature. Its functions, under the act before us, are confined to a review of certain acts of the Federal Trade Commission, which are specifically defined by the Congress. This act creates powers not otherwise conferred upon Circuit Courts of Appeals, and such courts are limited strictly to the powers thus specified. It was not intended that the Circuit Courts of Appeals should be drawn into original conduct of these investigations. If this court is to exercise plenary power and control in determining at the outset what party shall be dealt with, what investigation shall be made, and what recommendation submitted, then it has, in effect, been constituted an original trial tribunal of controversies of this nature. This was in no wise contemplated, nor would it comport with the legitimate practical functions of a court of this nature.

The act itself clearly specifies when the jurisdiction of the Circuit Courts of Appeals may attach and to what extent that jurisdiction may be exercised. The power of the court is limited to the enforcement of the final orders of the Commission to cease and desist, upon the application of the Commission, and to review of such orders at the request of the party against whom such orders are made, and in such cases it has power to enforce, affirm, modify, or set aside as it may deem proper.[14]

Not only does the Commission refuse to entertain motions to dismiss, but it declines to hear motions for bills of particulars, or for an order that the complaint be made more specific. The reason stated in the 1918 Annual Report[15] is that ample opportunity is given to respondents who are surprised by the testimony to prepare their defense and give testimony in rebuttal. An interesting defense of the practice is contained in the record of the hearing in Federal Trade Commission *v.* Joseph Simmonds.[16] In this case the complaint charged that certain

[14] Chamber of Commerce of Minneapolis et al. *v.* Federal Trade Commission et al., 280 Fed. 45.

[15] Page 54.

[16] 2 F.T.C.D. 11 (1919), Docket No. 210. *See* pp. 10-11 of transcript of testimony.

representations had been made "within the year last past." There was a motion for a bill of particulars, and a hearing on the motion before the full Commission. Counsel for respondent stated that he had in good faith searched all the advertising matter of the respondent, and had found no representations of the kind alleged, and that his attempt to get the information from the Federal Trade Commission's attorney had been futile. He asked, therefore, that the time and place of the alleged advertising be specified. The request was refused, and the reasons were given by the Chairman of the Commission, in words which I quote as they appear in the transcript:

The Chairman: The fundamental difficulty, perhaps, with a bill of particulars here is stated something like this: The formal complaint with the Commission is made up after *ex parte* hearings by those who are complaining against some prospective respondent which has been brought to our attention, and some examination by the staff of the Commission as to the charges made. It is not desirable that we should know too much or know anything more than is necessary for us to know in this preliminary matter, because we have to sit as judges later in the matter; and it is that desire on our part not to have disclosed to us either side of the case, . . . and yet it is up to the Commission, and it is the Commission's duty, when such representations are made by the staff and by the processes of the Commission, as merely give us reason to believe that there may be an unfair method of competition, or that it has been indulged in, to hear and determine the matter. . . .

Now the fact that complainants, in their statements to the Commission, in their charges that are lodged with the Commission and investigated by the staff of the Commission,—the fact that that is their version, the version of the complaint, of what the acts are, it makes it difficult for the Commission to lay down a bill of particulars, and then be bound to sustain that particular statement of the acts complained of. We are taking, to a degree, a partisan statement of the case as a foundation for the complaint, and to accept that and then offer it as the bill of particulars would bind the attorneys of the Commission to sustain that particular statement of the acts, whereas the attorneys for the Commission are not the attorneys for the complainant. . . .[17]

It will be noted that two reasons are given: first, that a specification of detailed charges would familiarize the Commissioners too much with the case, and thus tend to make them prejudge the issues in advance of trial; and second, that since they cannot vouch for the accuracy of the precise facts upon which the complaint is based, they do not care to be bound by embodying them in a bill of particulars. It does not seem, however, that either objection raises any insuperable difficulty. Once the complaint is issued, the Commission's duty as a prosecuting agency is at an end. The matter is in the hands of its counsel, who prepares the case for trial and presents the testimony. Thenceforward the Commission acts judicially, and there is no reason why it should not in this capacity reexamine the complaint upon motion, and if it seems to be lacking in some important detail, order counsel to indicate what he expects to prove. As to the second contention, the answer is twofold: first, that there is no reason why the Commission should consider itself bound by the specification of details by counsel, so long as no injustice is done to respondent; and second, that if justice to the respondent requires that he be informed when and where the alleged acts took place, he should be so informed, even if the range of proof available to the Commission's attorneys should be thereby restricted.

It should be noted that motions by the Commission's counsel to strike out portions of the respondent's answer, on the ground that they do not in law constitute a defense, are frequently made and granted.

The case is now at issue, and the next step is the trial

[17] Transcript of testimony, pp. 10-11.

of the facts. The Commission itself, of course, does not hear the testimony. Sometimes a commissioner, but more often an examiner, is appointed by formal resolution to hold hearings at a convenient time and place.[18] The examiner is a member of the examining division of the Legal Department, and is appointed on the recommendation of the Chief Examiner. At the same time the Chief Counsel designates one or more trial attorneys, to represent the Commission in its prosecuting capacity. Notice is given of the time and place set for trial,[19] and the hearing is conducted as if it were a proceeding before a master in chancery. It is invariably held in public, and the testimony (but not the arguments) taken down stenographically and preserved as part of the official record.

The trial counsel of the Commission assumes the burden of going forward with the evidence. Curiously enough, the Trade Commission Act and Clayton Act contain no reference to the presentation of testimony in support of the Commission's complaint. The person complained of is given authority to appear and show cause why an order should not be issued, but there is no express requirement that the Commission prove its case. Were it not for a later provision, it might be thought that the issuance of a complaint, based upon the Commission's "reason to believe" that the law had been violated, itself created a *prima facie* case, and that the burden was on the respondent to "show cause" why a complaint should not issue.[20] Indeed, a close inspection of the phraseology of Section 5 reveals that there is not even an express re-

[18] Authority to receive evidence through examiners is expressly conferred in the first paragraph of Sec. 9 of the Federal Trade Commission Act.

[19] Rule VIII of the Rules of Practice requires that not less than five nor more than ten days' notice be given. Notice is served in the manner provided for service of complaints, *i.e.,* generally by registered mail.

[20] *See* Annual Report, 1918, p. 54.

quirement that the Commission find, from the testimony
at the trial, that the respondent has been guilty of the
acts charged in the complaint. The only requirement is
that it "be of the opinion that the method of competition
in question is prohibited by this act." Taken by itself, the
language suggests that the "hearing" has to do only with
questions of law. However, the later paragraph which
provides for review of the Commission's orders by the
Circuit Court of Appeals, provides that the findings of
the Commission as to the facts, "if supported by testimony," shall be conclusive. The word "testimony" suggests evidence presented at a formal hearing rather than
information acquired by private investigation, and the
implication is, although it is not clearly stated, that the
Commission must find from the testimony whether the
facts alleged are true, and that the finding will be sustained only if it is supported by affirmative testimony.
In practice the formal record upon which an appeal is
based does not include the "application for a complaint,"
or any of the preliminary reports of investigators, but
only the complaint, the transcript of formal testimony
and exhibits, the findings and order, and the incidental
motions and orders, so that the practical result is to in-
sure reversal of the order if the testimony does not support the findings or the findings do not justify the order.

As to rules of evidence in hearings before an examiner,
it is difficult to speak with assurance. Unless the word
"testimony" is taken to mean "testimony which would
be competent under rules of evidence prevailing in courts
of law or equity," the statute is silent upon the subject.
Rule IX of the Rules of Practice provides that "objec-
tions to the evidence before the Commission, a commissioner, or an examiner shall, in any proceeding, be in
short form, stating the grounds of objection relied
upon . . .," but it is not stated what the grounds may
be, nor who shall pass upon the objection. In the 1918

Annual Report it is said that the examiner passes on the admissibility of the evidence presented, but that before testimony is finally closed, a party may have a ruling reviewed by the Commission. Such preliminary hearings upon the admissibility of evidence appear to be rare, however. In practice, evidence is generally admitted under objection, and at the final argument on the merits, the objection will be considered. At the same time it must be remembered that both the counsel and the trial examiner are apt to be men whose training was obtained in trials at common law or equity, and in most cases the record is not easily distinguishable from the record of a court trial. The objection that testimony is "incompetent, irrelevant and immaterial" appears almost as frequently; the hearsay rule is as often invoked and as often disregarded; and the "best evidence rule" as often misapplied. These are merely incidents of the hearing, however. So far as I have been able to find, the Commission itself has never refused to give effect to testimony on the ground that it is technically incompetent, nor have questions of the law of evidence played any part in the cases on appeal. As has been pointed out, the rules of evidence grew out of the practical exigencies of trial by jury, and are probably superfluous in an administrative proceeding. They are particularly ill adapted to the type of cases with which the Commission is concerned. Where a jury has to decide whether the prisoner was near the scene of the murder at a given time, it is of course important that they be not influenced by second-hand gossip. But where there is an issue before a commission of experts as to the economic effect of the sales policy of a company, it seems unreasonable that the sales manager of the company, who has just completed, through his local agents, an extensive investigation of the matter, should not be permitted to present in his own way the result of that investigation, without being pulled up at every sentence by an objection based on the hearsay rule or the rule as to documentary evidence. Principles of due process do not require a rigid adherence to technical rules, and it should be possible for the Commission to consider the source of testimony, as well as its import, and to give it greater or lesser weight according to its apparent reliability.

One rule of exclusion should be noted, however, as it is rigidly applied in the trial of cases before examiners. The Commission refuses to permit witnesses to be questioned as to the identity of the person who supplied the information upon which the complaint was based. Even a witness who volunteers the information is halted abruptly by the examiner. Thus in a case against a small rubber manufacturer, alleged to be simulating a trade name of B. F. Goodrich & Co., counsel for respondent asked a series of questions designed to show that the complaint had originated with the legal department of the Goodrich Company. The evidence was tendered in support of the contention that no public interest was involved. The examiner held that the questions were incompetent, observing that "The Commission has issued an order covering that point very specifically."[21] In another case the examiner made this formal statement:[22]

And the examiner is also instructed to indicate that the Commission will not permit witnesses in the course of trials of these formal cases to disclose the identity of the applicants before they have specific authority from the Commission to do that; and the Examiner has been instructed by the Commission that he will instruct witnesses on his own motion, and without waiting for objection by the attorneys, not to answer questions from Respondent's counsel which are calculated to elicit this information.

[21] Docket No. 788, Transcript, p. 107.

[22] Federal Trade Commission v. Sunlight Creameries, Docket No. 623, Transcript, p. 4.

On another occasion[23] the statements upon which the complaint was based are referred to by the examiner as "privileged communications to the Commission about which he [the witness] was incompetent to testify at a public hearing."

The Commission's desire to shield informants and to keep open the channels of confidential communication can be appreciated, yet it seems doubtful whether the position could be sustained, should a case arise in which the testimony was relevant to a material issue. Surely a respondent is entitled to present any evidence which is competent and relevant, nor is the genius of our law friendly to the policy of encouraging secret accusations by persons who are afraid to testify or submit to cross-examination in public.

The statute makes provision for compelling the attendance of witnesses and production of documentary testimony, and whatever the scope of those provisions may be as far as the general investigating or advisory powers of the Commission are concerned, there seems to be no reason to doubt that they are effective and adequate in connection with the hearings before examiners. Any member of the Commission may sign and issue subpœnas requiring the attendance of witnesses, from any part of the United States, at any designated place of hearing.[24] The Rules of Practice provide that "subpœnas for the production of documentary evidence (unless directed to issue by a Commissioner upon his own motion) will issue only upon application in writing, which must be verified and must specify, as near as may be, the documents desired and the facts to be proved by them." Neglect or refusal to attend and testify, or to answer any lawful

---

[23] Federal Trade Commission v. Taiyo Trading Co., Inc., Docket No. 536, Transcript, p. 146.

[24] Federal Trade Commission Act, Sec. 9. Rule VII of Rules of Practice.

inquiry, or to produce documentary evidence, in obedience
to a subpœna, is punishable by imprisonment of not more
than a year, or by fine of not less than $1000 nor more
than $5000, or both.[25] Moreover, district courts may by
contempt proceedings compel the appearance of contu-
macious witnesses.

A series of court decisions relates to the Commission's
power to compel the production of books and records and
to call for special or periodic reports, and several of
these cases are now pending in the Supreme Court. They
do not, however, arise in connection with a formal complaint under either the Federal Trade Commission Act
or the Clayton Act. Section 6 of the Federal Trade Commission Act authorizes the Commission to gather information concerning certain kinds of corporations in
interstate and foreign commerce, and to require such
corporations, "by general or special orders," to file annual or special reports or answers to specific questions,
and the question involved in the cases to which I refer is
whether this authority can be exercised except in connection with a specific complaint that the law has been
violated.

Thus the Commission ordered a number of coal companies to submit monthly reports showing production,
sales, financial condition, and similar facts. The Maynard
Coal Company refused to comply, and the Commission
notified the company that it would take steps to recover
the forfeiture provided in Section 10 of the Federal Trade
Commission Act. The company sued for an injunction,
and the Supreme Court of the District of Columbia held
that the Commission had no authority to demand the information, since it related to intrastate commerce as well
as to commerce among the states.[26]

[25] *Ibid.,* Sec. 10.
[26] The Maynard Coal Co. *v.* Federal Trade Commission, 3 F.T.C.D.
555.

In another case,[27] the answer of the respondents reveals a peculiar state of facts. It seems that in 1918 the Navy Department ordered from the Basic Products Company 250 tons of "Syndolag," a patented article made according to a secret process. About 65 tons were delivered, and tentatively billed at $30 a ton, the balance of the order being canceled. The Navy Department called for a statement of costs of production, so that a fair price could be fixed, but the company refused to give it, offering, nevertheless, to accept in settlement any price the Navy might determine. The Navy persisted in its demand, although the company offered to refund the whole amount previously paid. The matter was then referred to the Federal Trade Commission, which formally demanded that its examiners be given full access to the books and records of the company. The company refused, and the Attorney General, at the request of the Federal Trade Commission, applied in the Federal District Court in Pennsylvania for a writ of mandamus. The application was refused, however, on the ground that the information did not relate to any transaction in interstate commerce, and was not sought in aid of any power granted to the Commission. The court observed:

An incident of such investigation is the ascertainment of trade secrets. It is plain that the cost of manufacturing a patented product to which the manufacturer has the exclusive right may be a trade secret, a species of property of great value. This is also true of refinements of method in producing the same. The act prohibits the disclosure of trade secrets. The assumption that no such disclosure will be made disappears before the expressed intention to give the information to the Navy Department. We have, then, a contemplated search and seizure, and a contemplated taking of private property for public use, without due process of law, which are violative of the fourth and fifth amendments of the Constitution.[28]

[27] U.S. *v.* Basic Products Co., 260 Fed. 472 (1919).
[28] *Ibid.,* p. 482.

Cases against two tobacco companies[29] and a number of grain companies[30] are at the present time awaiting decision in the Supreme Court. In the tobacco cases, in response to a Senate resolution, and also as a result of complaints of unfair practices, the Commission requested the American Tobacco Company and the Lorillard Company to produce for inspection certain records and correspondence. The companies refused and the Commission applied to the district court for a writ of mandamus, demanding access to all papers and telegrams received from or sent to jobbers in the year 1921. The district court denied the application, taking the position that subdivision (b) of Section 6 must be read in the light of the searches and seizures clause of the Federal Constitution, and that the Commission's demand was therefore unauthorized, since it did not show probable cause for claiming that the law had been violated, and was too sweeping in scope. In the grain cases, the information was sought in connection with a general investigation of the relation between prices at the farm and export prices, and the court held that the powers conferred in Section 6 could not be used in connection with such a general investigation, but only where some conduct of the particular corporation in question was being investigated.

In the District of Columbia, an injunction restraining the Federal Trade Commission from demanding information regarding costs of production from steel companies was sustained by the Court of Appeals.[31] The decision goes mainly on the ground that the information did not relate to interstate commerce, but the court observes that

[29] Federal Trade Commission v. P. Lorillard & Co. et al., 283 Fed. 999 (1922).

[30] Federal Trade Commission v. Baltimore Grain Co., 284 Fed. 886 (1922).

[31] Federal Trade Commission v. Claire Furnace Co., 285 Fed. 936 (1923).

"the investigation seems to be more in the nature of a news-gathering expedition, in hope of securing something of public interest for publication or possibly subject matter for future legislation by Congress."

Curiously enough, the act nowhere gives to respondents the right to procure the issuance of subpœnas in aid of their defense. The Commission alone is given authority to issue subpœnas, and the act does not say whether the authority is granted to the Commission in its prosecuting or its judicial capacity. The rules of practice, also, contain no express reference to compulsory testimony on the respondent's behalf. In practice, however, the Commission places its compulsory powers at the service of the respondents, as well as of its own trial counsel, and the notice of trial contains as a matter of routine a notice that the respondent may secure the issuance of the Commission's subpœnas, on application to the Secretary. Statutory authority is also given to order the taking of testimony by deposition,[32] and the rules of practice contain elaborate regulations for such a proceeding.[33] In practice, however, this method of taking testimony appears to have been rarely used.[34]

There is no argument or opportunity to file briefs before the trial examiner. He is, however, required to prepare, within ten days after receipt of the stenographic report of testimony, proposed findings of fact and a proposed order. Copies of the proposed findings and order are then served on the parties or their attorneys, who may within ten days file written exceptions. The Rules of Practice require that "said exceptions shall specify the particular part or parts of the proposed findings of fact or proposed order to which exception is made, and said exceptions shall include any additional findings and

[32] Sec. 9, Federal Trade Commission Act.
[33] Rule XIII.
[34] Mechem, 21 Mich. Law Rev. 135.

any change in or addition to the proposed order which either party may think proper.'' The case is then set for oral argument before the full Commission (or at least a quorum of three members), and at the conclusion of the argument a time is fixed for filing of briefs by both parties. The case is then taken under advisement, and in due course the findings are adopted by the Commission in their final form.

As to the form and content of the findings, I shall have much to say in the succeeding chapter. As to the order, some comments may be made at this point.

Under the Clayton Act and Trade Commission Act, all that the Commission's order can do is to direct the respondent to "cease and desist" from the unfair method or other practice in question, or if the order concerns Section 7 or 8 of the Clayton Act, to divest itself of the stock held or rid itself of the directors chosen contrary to law. The act does not expressly confer any general power, of the kind possessed by a court of equity, to compel restitution, or otherwise to so mold the decree as to do substantial justice under the circumstances. Of course, no damages can be awarded, or mandatory order entered. Where, therefore, the unfair act has already accomplished its purpose, and there is no occasion for repeating it, the Commission cannot give relief. The Commission seems to take the position that it can, in certain cases, where necessary to make a negative decree effective, embody in it some positive features, just as the Supreme Court in the Standard Oil case[35] found that the mere existence and operation of the defendant company, in view of its history and origin, was a continuing violation of the Sherman Law, and directed that the decree embody mandatory terms of dissolution. In two cases under Section 7 of the Clayton Act, to which I shall re-

[35] Standard Oil Co. *v.* U.S., 221 U.S. 1 (1911).

turn later,[36] the Commission found that after the respondent had purchased the stock of a competing company, it took a paper conveyance of all the property of its new subsidiary. Merely to order the company to "divest itself of the stock held" in violation of law, as authorized by Section 11 of the Clayton Act, would obviously be useless, since the corporation would retain the assets which it had acquired as a consequence of the illegal acquisition of stock. The Commission therefore ordered a reconveyance of the assets, and directed that thereafter the stock of the company be disposed of. In the absence of an authoritative court decision, however, it is by no means clear that the order in question was within the Commission's power.

Another limitation on the Commission's authority, as it has been defined by the Supreme Court, is that the order can prohibit only the method of competition or other practice charged in the complaint.[37] If some other unlawful practice is revealed by the testimony, a new or amended complaint must, it seems, be filed and the statutory procedure followed as though a new proceeding were involved.

The limitation suggests, however, a more difficult question. Must the order be limited to the precise misrepresentation, or unfair conduct, or improper practice, described in the complaint and established by the findings, or may it prohibit the general practice of which the specific conduct in question is an example? The question is one of great practical importance, and also one of considerable difficulty, as a few examples will show.

Suppose that the complaint charges, and the findings establish, that respondent has sold, under the name "silk," a product composed of 40 per cent silk and 60 per

[36] *Infra,* p. 320.
[37] Federal Trade Commission *v.* Gratz et al., 253 U.S. 421 (1920).

cent cotton. What should the order prohibit? Under the statute, it must prohibit the method of competition charged in the complaint, but the question is what that method is. Is it the practice of misbranding, so that an order could be issued prohibiting misbranding in general, regardless of the product or of the nature of the misleading brand? Or is it, to go to the other extreme, the practice of selling as silk a product composed of 40 per cent silk and 60 per cent cotton? On the latter view, the Commission must restrict its order to the precise practice charged, and respondent could avoid the effect of the order by varying the percentage of cotton and silk. Such an order would of course be useless. Some of the Commission's misbranding cases appear to prohibit the application of the misleading brand only to the precise product found to have been used in the past.[38] More often, however, the orders prohibit the sale under the name or brand in question, of any product not composed of the material indicated thereby. The use of the word "silk," for instance, is forbidden unless the material is made wholly of the cocoon of the silkworm, or the word "manila" unless the rope in question is made exclusively of manila fibre. In the Winsted Hosiery case, the only misbranding case which has reached the Supreme Court, the order, in the form in which it was sustained by the court, was somewhat more elaborate:[39]

---

[38] *E.g.,* Federal Trade Commission *v.* Solomon M. Hexter et al., 2 F.T.C.D. 41 (1919), (selling as "Sol Satin," the product theretofore advertised under that name). F.T.C. *v.* Palais Royal, 4 F.T.C.D. 305 (1922), (selling as "ivory," a product made out of nitrated cellulose). F.T.C. *v.* The Spongeable Linen Collar Co., 2 F.T.C.D. 212 (1920), (using the word "linen" to describe collars composed largely of celluloid).

[39] F.T.C. *v.* Winsted Hosiery Co., 3 F.T.C.D. 189 (1921). *Cf.* the order in F.T.C. *v.* Star Provision Co. et al., 3 F.T.C.D. 393 (1921): "From selling or offering for sale in interstate commerce any compound,

IT IS NOW ORDERED, That the respondent, the Winsted Hosiery Co., its officers, agents, representatives, servants, and employees, do cease and desist from employing or using as labels or brands on underwear or other knit goods not composed wholly of wool, or on the wrappers, boxes, or other containers in which they are delivered to customers, the word "Merino," "Wool," or "Worsted," alone or in combination with any other word or words, unless accompanied by a word or words designating the substance, fiber, or material, other than wool, of which the garments are composed in part (*e.g.*, "Merino, Wool, and Cotton"; "Wool and Cotton"; "Worsted, Wool and Cotton"; "Wool, Cotton and Silk"), or by a word or words otherwise clearly indicating that such underwear or other goods is not made wholly of wool (*e.g.*, part wool).[40]

An analogous question is presented where the complaint and findings cover only a single instance of the unfair practice involved, as, for example, the payment of secret commissions to buyers of a single customer, or false and disparaging advertising concerning a single competitor. Assuming that the evidence is sufficient to show that a "method of competition" has been used, can the order forbid all commercial bribery by the respondent in question, or all false statements concerning competitors? The Commission seemingly takes the view that the payment of secret commissions to an employee of a single customer is sufficient to establish a practice of commercial bribery, and to warrant an order to cease and desist from paying such commissions to any employees of any customer or prospective customer.[41] Indeed, in

mixture, or combination of linseed oil with mineral oil or other substances which is labeled or branded as 'linseed oil' unless the name or names of such other oil, to wit, mineral oil, or such other substances, be also displayed upon such labels or brands, in conjunction with the words 'linseed oil' and in letters of the same size, shape, and prominence as said words 'linseeed oil' " (p. 400).

[40] *Ibid.*, pp. 197-198.

[41] Federal Trade Commission *v.* Baeder, Adamson Co., 4 F.T.C.D.

one case[42] the findings show not only a single customer, but a single instance in which an offer of a bribe was alleged to have been made to an officer of the customer. The offer was found to have been made by a salesman, contrary to instructions, and was not accepted. The incident was considered sufficient, however, to warrant a general order to cease and desist from using commercial bribery as a method of competition. In many of the "passing off" cases, the order merely prohibits the use of the particular name or trade mark complained of.[43] In others the order prohibits simulation, by any means, of the trade name or mark of a specified competitor.[44] In one case,[45] a single instance was deemed sufficient to warrant an order to cease from passing off respondent's goods as the goods of any one of respondent's competitors. Cases of trade boycotts involve the same problem. Sometimes the order directs respondents to stop boycotting only the particular concern found to have been boycotted in the past.[46] In one case the order covers the particular concern, as well as "others engaged in similar

129 (1921). *Cf.* F.T.C. *v.* The Oakes Co., 3 F.T.C.D. 36 (1920). Commercial espionage against a single competitor. The order prohibits the practice in general.

[42] F.T.C. *v.* Rockford Varnish Co., Docket No. 41. The complaint, findings, and order are not published, the case being merely referred to in a footnote at 1 F.T.C.D. 105. The case is reviewed *post,* p. 135.

[43] *E.g.,* F.T.C. *v.* Universal Motor Co. et al., 3 F.T.C.D. 387 (1921); F.T.C. *v.* The Great Republic Tire & Rubber Mfg. Co., 3 F.T.C.D. 6 (1920); F.T.C. *v.* Hygrade Knitting Co., 4 F.T.C.D. 402 (1922); F.T.C. *v.* The Sweater Store, 2 F.T.C.D. 67 (1919).

[44] *See* F.T.C. *v.* The Good Wear Tire & Tube Co., 2 F.T.C.D. 216 (1920); F.T.C. *v.* Juvenile Shoe Co., Inc., 5 F.T.C.D. 105 (1922), Affirmed, C.C.A. 9th, 289 Fed. 57 (1923); F.T.C. *v.* Louise, 4 F.T.C.D. 323 (1922); F.T.C. *v.* Ginso Chemical Co., 4 F.T.C.D. 155 (1921).

[45] *See* F.T.C. *v.* The Electric Appliance Co., 2 F.T.C.D. 335 (1920).

[46] *E.g.,* F.T.C. *v.* McKnight-Keaton Grocery Co. et al., 3 F.T.C.D. 87 (1920).

business.''[47] Where there was clearly a general practice of boycotting certain classes of jobbers, the order of course properly covered boycotts of all those within the class.[48] One order, however,[49] directed a respondent to cease and desist from ''hindering or preventing any person, firm, or corporation in or from the purchase of groceries, provisions, or the like commodities direct from the manufacturers or producers thereof, in interstate commerce, or attempting so to do.''[50] The findings showed that respondent had tried to induce a single manufacturer to cease patronizing a single retailer. On petition to review, the Circuit Court of Appeals found that no unfair method of competition was involved, but it had this to say as to the order:[51] ''Although the charge made against petitioner was with reference to said Basket Stores Co., the order above set forth is as broad as the business world, and in any event would have to be modified if it were to be sustained in any particular.''

The examples show that the Commission has constantly to steer a course between Scylla and Charybdis in drafting its orders. If the order is too general, it goes beyond the practice which respondent is found to have used. If it is too narrow, it can be evaded by a slight modification of the practice. An order to cease circulating an advertisement, the precise text of which is set forth, is too specific to be of any value,[52] while an order to cease defrauding or misleading purchasers by writing ''any letter or other communication containing any false, misleading or de-

---

[47] Federal Trade Commission *v.* Wholesale Grocers Asso. of El Paso et al., 3 F.T.C.D. 109 (1920).

[48] F.T.C. *v.* The Wholesale Saddlery Asso. of the U.S. et al., 1 F.T.C.D. 335 (1919).

[49] F.T.C. *v.* Raymond Bros.-Clark Co., 3 F.T.C.D. 295 (1921).

[50] *Ibid.,* p. 301.

[51] Raymond Bros.-Clark Co. *v.* F.T.C., 280 Fed. 529 (1922).

[52] *See* F.T.C. *v.* Plunkett Chemical Co., 3 F.T.C.D. 53 (1920).

ceptive statement or representation'' is of doubtful validity.[53] It is little more than an injunction to be honest.

With the issuance and service of the order, the case is complete. The Commission has, however, added an interesting postscript to the statutory procedure. The order generally directs that respondents shall, within a designated period after the service of the order, file with the Commission a report in writing ''setting forth in detail the manner and form in which they have complied with the order to cease and desist.'' Such a report is of course a valuable check on the effectiveness of the order. Since there is no express statutory authority to issue such an order, it must be based upon the general authority in subsection b of Section 6 of the Trade Commission Act, to require corporations to make special reports or answers in writing to specific questions asked by the Commission. As I have indicated,[54] the legal effect and scope of this subsection is still in doubt.

A simple appellate procedure is provided. If the respondent fails to obey the order, the Commission is authorized to apply to the Circuit Court of Appeals in the proper circuit, ''for the enforcement of its order.'' Likewise any person against whom an order has been issued may obtain a review by petitioning the court to set the order aside. In either event the Commission is required to certify and file with the court a transcript of the entire record, including all the testimony, and thereupon the court is given power ''to make and enter upon the pleadings, testimony and proceedings set forth in such transcript, a decree affirming, modifying, or setting aside the order of the Commission.''[55] There is a curious omission

[53] *See* Federal Trade Commission *v.* Boston Piano & Music Co., 3 F.T.C.D. 168 (1920), par. 3 of Order.

[54] *Supra,* p. 67.

[55] As to printing of the record, see National Harness Mfg. Asso. *v.* F.T.C., 261 Fed. 170 (1919).

in the wording of both statutes at this point. It will be
recalled that the orders of the Commission are not self-
enforcing. The respondent incurs no penalty by violating
them, and the only method of enforcement is by application to the Circuit Court of Appeals, as described above.
The only authority expressly given to the Circuit Court
of Appeals, however, is to enter an order "affirming,
modifying, or setting aside" the order of the Commission. The argument might be made that an order which
is not compulsory does not gain any added efficacy by
the affirmance of an appellate court. However, the proceeding is referred to in the statutes as an "application
for the enforcement" of the order, and undoubtedly the
implication is that the Circuit Court of Appeals can compel obedience to the order when it is affirmed, or, to put
the matter differently, that the order, when affirmed, becomes the order of the court, which has inherent power
to punish a violation by contempt proceedings. The question does not appear to have been raised in any reported
case, nor have there been, so far as I can ascertain, any
contempt proceedings for the enforcement of orders of
the Commission affirmed by a Circuit Court of Appeals.

The law provides that "the findings of the Commission
as to the facts, if supported by testimony," shall be
conclusive. The court is not authorized to take additional
testimony, but it may, on application of either party, send
the case back to the Commission for additional testimony,
on a showing that the new testimony is material and that
there were reasonable grounds for the failure to adduce
it in the proceedings before the Commission.

Apart from the normal statutory procedure which I
have outlined, the Commission has devised a special
procedure which is both interesting to the student of
administrative practice, and seemingly effective in accomplishing results. It frequently happens that a particular practice proves to be so prevalent in a given trade,

and so generally complained of, that some form of mass action seems necessary to cope with it. The immediate occasion may be a deluge of complaints from persons in the trade, or perhaps more formal representations by a trade association. To meet such a situation, the Commission has devised what is now known as a Trade Practice Submittal. The Commission itself, in a formal statement to the package macaroni industry in 1920, described very clearly its nature and purpose:

This trade practice submittal consists of an invitation, which is in no sense a summons, for the whole industry or its representatives, to meet together in the presence of the Commission and discuss the merits and demerits of practices which have been complained of to the Commission and any other practices which may be brought to the attention of the meeting.

At the end of the discussion, each of the practices which have been examined are taken up separately, are submitted to the industry for an expression of opinion as to their fairness or unfairness, their usefulness or harmfulness. The Commission does not participate in the meeting except to ask questions which will tend to bring the whole matter clearly into the record.

If the practically unanimous opinion of the representatives of the industry condemns a given practice, the Commission receives that expression of the industry as being founded on expert knowledge, business experience and peculiar familiarity with the industry, with respect to the condemned practices, and likewise the sanctioning of a practice by the industry, even though the propriety of that practice has been questioned by application for the issuance of a complaint, is similarly regarded as being the expression, based upon the experience of the industry and its business judgment.

Such a practically unanimous expression on the part of a representative body of an industry is given great weight by the Commission in considering such practices. It should be understood that it represents no decision or judgment on the part of the Commission and is in no sense binding upon any one not present at the meeting. Nor indeed is it binding upon any one who is present at the meeting, but who dissents from the majority opinion. The effect is that the weight of opinion of the industry has been communicated to the Commission and that thereafter the Commission will feel it to be its duty in case complaints are made to it of a continuance of the condemned practices on the part of any member of the industry, to issue its formal complaint, after inquiry and the public interest determined, in order that by means of a formal and orderly proceeding with an opportunity for subsequent court review, the judgment of the industry may be subjected to the final test of the courts. Also in case of a division of opinion on any given practice, the Commission considers the question to be so much in doubt that it should be left entirely open to be challenged, if any one desires to challenge it, and made the subject of a more formal proceeding.

To sum up then, the trade practice submittal amounts to a request on the part of the Commission to a given industry that it give its opinion with respect to the fairness or unfairness of any trade practices which have grown up or are growing up and that this opinion is received by the Commission as the best and most authoritative judgment then obtainable, but that this judgment may be challenged by any member of the industry and thereafter be made the subject of a more minute examination in a proceeding around which are thrown all the safeguards of a proceeding in court.[56]

At the conclusion of the conference, the Commission generally summarizes in a written report the action taken by the meeting, and circulates the report among the members of the trade. The text of the reports, including in some cases the formal statement summoning the conference, have been made public, and are available in a pamphlet of mimeographed sheets entitled "Trade Practice Submittals."

The reports constantly emphasize that the action taken at a "trade practice submittal" is advisory only, and is not binding either on the Commission or on the members of the trade who did not participate in the meeting and

[56] Federal Trade Commission, Trade Practice Submittals, 1919 to 1923, pp. 21-22.

subscribe to the action taken. At the same time the reports carry a clear intimation that the agreement of the industry, at least if it is unanimous or nearly so, will carry great weight with the Commission in any formal proceedings that may arise. It is sometimes referred to as "prima-facie law merchant for the industry."[57] In one report it is stated that "until testimony to the contrary is produced, however, the Commission will regard as conclusive, the judgment of the trade in declaring such practices to be in fact unfair."[58] In a subsequent report, the position seems to have been modified: "The expression of the industry as here given," says the report in the submittal of the package macaroni industry, "is advisory to the Commission with respect to the issuance of a complaint, but upon a trial of the complaint, the respondent will come in entirely without prejudice on the part of the Commission and any practice which is challenged will be examined from the beginning."[59] Sometimes, however, the Commission will expressly refuse to accept a trade practice submittal as conclusive or as "dispositive of the issue," and may reserve its decision,[60] or even express affirmatively, though tentatively, an opinion contrary to that expressed by the trade.[61] Indeed, in view of the present construction of the Sherman Act,[62] it is obvious that an embarrassing situation might arise if a meeting should get out of bounds and discuss some forbidden topic. The Commission took occasion to point out, in calling the package macaroni submittal, that "a sub-

[57] *See* Trade Practice Submittals, p. 2, Report of Meeting of the Creamery Industry.

[58] *Ibid.*, p. 6.

[59] *Ibid.*, p. 27.

[60] *See* the submittal on Gold Mounted Knives, *ibid.*, p. 44.

[61] As in the Sheffield Silver Plated Hollow Ware submittal, *ibid.*, p. 40.

[62] American Column Co. *v.* U.S., 257 U.S. 377 (1921).

ject which is not deemed to be proper to be discussed is any question which bears on prices or price fixing.'' No objection seems to have been raised, however, to a vote of the meeting that no packages should be sold containing less than eight ounces,[63] or to a vote of the oil industry of the middle western states, that the minimum annual rental for leased gasoline pumps, tanks, and equipment should not be less than 10 per cent of the selling price.[64] Doubtless such a situation calls for tact and good sense. I shall refer more in detail, in later chapters, to some of the trade practice submittals. In general, they indicate not only an expert familiarity with the problems with which they are concerned, but a sound judgment and a public point of view. As a means of bringing the Commission in direct contact with the trades, and of procuring concerted action in eliminating unfair practices, the trade practice submittal seems to be a valuable adjunct to the formal statutory procedure.

Such, in outline, is the Commission's procedure. To find out how it works, how well it is calculated to secure satisfactory results in the different types of cases which have arisen, and what the Commission has made of it in practice, a thorough study of the decisions will be necessary. It will be necessary to consider not only the quality and content of the complaints, findings, and orders, but the manner in which cases of different kinds have been handled, the practical results which it has been possible to achieve, and the contributions which the Commission has been able to make toward the development of substantive law and procedure. To such a study the succeeding three chapters of this book will be devoted. In the meantime, in order to focus attention upon the issues which seem material, some tentative generalizations may be permitted.

[63] Trade Practice Submittals, p. 25.
[64] *Ibid.*, p. 61.

Clearly from the point of view of organization, the Commission's most important and most difficult task is that of maintaining a distinct separation between its prosecuting capacity and its judicial capacity. This is essential if its decisions are to be fair and just, but it is important also in connection with the thousand and one incidental matters that come up for disposition in the course of the proceeding. In a well-conducted criminal trial, the prosecuting attorney is under the constant check of an impartial judge. If his conduct is oppressive, if he browbeats witnesses, if he makes unfair comments, he courts a rebuke. Even in a civil litigation, any improper conduct, any attempt to create false inferences or to suppress known facts, is likely to receive unfavorable comment from the court. Every attorney who has had trial experience will appreciate how important it is, quite apart from the justice of the final decision, that the details of the trial be administered in a fair and impartial spirit. A trial in a proceeding before the Federal Trade Commission is, as I have said, much like a trial in an important equity suit. There is the same atmosphere of combat, the same strategy in examination and cross-examination, the same amenities and acerbities of counsel, and the same need for constant and even-tempered fairness on the part of the presiding officer.

It seems to me that there is some ground for criticism in the fact that the examiner who presides at the trial in formal proceedings is an employee of the division of the Commission which was responsible for the investigation leading up to the issuance of the complaint. It will be recalled that the complaint is issued on the basis of a report by a member of the examining division of the legal department, who is responsible directly to the Chief Examiner. The report is approved by the Chief Examiner before it goes to the Board of Review and the Commission. Subsequently the Commission appoints, on the recommendation of the Chief Examiner, and out of his division, an examiner to conduct the hearings. Some intangible factors must be recognized. The Commission is a large organization, with examiners and attorneys at salaries varying from $1200 to $8000,[65] and obviously promotions as well as dismissals are matters of constant occurrence. To a large extent an examiner's livelihood and chance of promotion may depend upon the recommendation of the Chief Examiner. It seems almost inevitable that an examiner should be to some extent influenced in the conduct of a case by the fact that his superior officer is the responsible head of the division which gathered the facts leading up to the complaint. If the examiner were selected from an independent panel, not connected with the examining division or the trial division, but responsible solely to the Commission, his standing as an independent and unbiased presiding officer would, it seems to me, be greatly enhanced.

This is a matter of organization, and of course organization is only a part of the task. The other part is the maintenance of a standard and tradition of impartiality which can be the result only of constant watchfulness and unvarying example on the part of the officers and members of the Commission. It is a difficult task, for inevitably in an organization of several hundred men there will be personal friendships, and a feeling of group loyalty, which will make it almost impossible to preserve at all times the impartiality of a court trial. Inevitably, also, there is a shifting around of personnel. A man may be a trial counsel one day and an examiner another, and it will be hard for him to cast off, as examiner, the point of view acquired as advocate. How far impartiality is achieved in practice, I cannot attempt to estimate. Doubtless much depends upon the calibre of the particular

[65] Figures based on 1921 Annual Report. No figures given in 1922 Report.

examiner, upon his temperament as well as his personal and professional standards. In later chapters the quality of the Commission's output will be studied, and it will throw some light upon the fairness of the reports and findings.

In the meantime, however, mention must be made of a surprising practice revealed by an examination of the official dockets in a fairly large number of cases. I have assumed in the previous discussion that the findings were in fact prepared by the examiners who preside at the trials and hear the testimony, but it appears that this is not always the case. In a large number of cases it appears from internal evidence that the findings, at least in the form in which they were finally adopted by the Commission, were dictated by the trial counsel who prosecuted the case, rather than by the examiner who heard it judicially. The findings consist of typewritten sheets, and generally, according to the custom of stenographers, the sheets contain in the upper left hand corner the initials of the dictator. In the cases of which I have examined the official dockets, I have compared these initials, wherever they appear, with the names of the examiners and trial counsel or, as the case may be, with the name or initials of the counsel who appears to have represented the Commission in the preparation of the stipulation of facts. In thirty-two cases, where there was no trial, the counsel who dictated or signed the stipulation appears to have dictated the findings.[66] In ten cases the counsel who represented the Commission at the trial or argument appears to have dictated the findings.[67] As long as this prac-

[66] E.g., in Federal Trade Commission v. Louis Philippe, Docket No. 771, W. R. Choate and W. B. Wooden were at different times examiners. C. S. Moore was counsel for the Federal Trade Commission. The findings bear the typewritten symbols: CSM-FOB—1-8-19.

[67] E.g., in Federal Trade Commission v. Alben-Harley, Docket No. 523, Walter B. Wooden was designated as examiner to hear the testi-

tice is pursued, it is of course idle to endeavor to preserve the judicial independence of the trial examiner.

The second reflection suggested by the present chapter, is that the Federal Trade Commission is not primarily built for speed. Where promptness is essential, a one-man executive is generally provided. The traditional method of administration is through a department head, operating through bureau or division chiefs, and even during the war, when traditions were not highly regarded, single executives, such as the Director General of Railroads, the Food and Fuel Administrators, and the Labor Administrator, occupied, with some exceptions, the most important key positions. A single executive can make up his mind quickly and act at once, while in the case of a board it is necessary to bring a number of minds to focus instead of one, there are likely to be delays and postponements, and the result is often a compromise not easily made the basis for effective executive action.

The Federal Trade Commission Act became law September 26, 1914. The Commission was organized March 16, 1915. The first formal complaint was issued on February 18, 1916, and up to the end of the second fiscal year (June 30, 1916) only five complaints had been issued.[68] The first order (which was on an agreed statement) was not issued until August 19, 1916, more than seventeen months after the Commission was organized.[69] The second order, also on agreed facts, was made two months later.[70] These were the only orders to cease and desist issued during the calendar year 1916. The first order in

mony. Edward L. Smith appeared throughout as counsel for the Commission. The findings contain the following typewritten symbols: ELS-GS, 2-25-21.

[68] See 1916 Annual Report, pp. 10, 11.

[69] F.T.C. v. Circle Cilk Co., 1 F.T.C.D. 13 (Docket No. 3).

[70] F.T.C. v. A. Theo. Abbott & Co., 1 F.T.C.D. 16 (Docket No. 2).

a contested case was on May 25, 1917,[71] and the published decisions indicate that during the whole calendar year 1917 only four cases were finally disposed of by orders to cease and desist, of which all but one were on agreed statements or answers admitting the allegations of the complaint, or were otherwise uncontested.[72] Of course, during some of this time the Commission was busy on other matters, but so far as the business of issuing complaints and making orders was concerned, there was for the first year and a half a virtual state of paralysis, and it is generally understood to have been due to the inability of the members of the Commission to agree in certain fundamental matters of interpretation.

The procedure of the Commission also is not designed primarily with a view to obtaining a quick decision on the merits and a prompt remedy. In part this is due to mandatory provisions of the statute, in part, doubtless, to administrative conditions. It should be borne in mind that the proceeding really begins with the application for a complaint, and is not finally completed until the Commission's order has been acquiesced in by the respondent, or, if it is contested, until it has been affirmed by order of the Circuit Court of Appeals. The preliminary investigation, the examiner's report, the decision of the Board of Review, the issuance of the complaint, the time allowed for answer, the hearing on the merits, and then the filing of briefs and deliberations of the Commission, all these matters consume time, however necessary they may be to a just decision by due process. Just how much time is

[71] Federal Trade Commission v. A. B. Dick Co. et al., 1 F.T.C.D. 20 (Docket No. 4).

[72] The other three are: F.T.C. v. Muenzen Specialty Co., 1 F.T.C.D. 30 (Docket No. 7), (answer admitting allegations); F.T.C. v. Bureau of Statistics of The Book Paper Mfrs. et al., 1 F.T.C.D. 38 (Docket No. 17), (by consent); F.T.C. v. National Binding Machine Co., 1 F.T. C.D. 44 (Docket No. 10), (by stipulation).

taken on the average, cannot well be shown statistically, since the public records of the Commission do not show when the application for a complaint was received. From the table on the opposite page, however, an estimate can be formed of the time which usually elapses between the filing of the formal complaint and the issuance of the order disposing of the case.

The last annual report of the Commission shows that it is fully aware of the situation, and that it is attributed mainly to the large volume of work compared with the "limited force and funds" available. The Commission says:[73]

Along with the steady increase in the "hang over" of work, there has been unavoidably a corresponding lengthening of the time which applications have had to await their turn before work upon them could be commenced. It is desired that the investigation of all complaints shall begin as soon as they are docketed, but for a long time past this has been a physical impossibility, with the force of men available under appropriations made. At the close of the fiscal year there were 231 docketed applications which had been on hand, upon an average, 6 months and 13 days each; and 123 branch applications, the average age of which was 4 months and 8 days. Complaints regarding delays in carrying out investigations are being received. If no new applications should be received for four months, the time would scarcely suffice to dispose of cases now on hand. If the present rate of increase is maintained, there will be about 800 undisposed-of assignments on hand at the close of the next fiscal year.

In this connection it seems proper to point out that this part of the commission's work is not optional with it. A duty is laid upon it to maintain a free tribunal where applicants' complaints can be promptly investigated and heard. Delay is often a denial of justice, in the class of cases which come before the commission.

In part, doubtless, the delay is due to the rigid procedure to which the Commission is bound. It seems to be less flexible than is, for instance, the procedure in an

[73] 1922 Annual Report, p. 38.

TABLE SHOWING TIME ELAPSED BETWEEN ISSUANCE OF COMPLAINT AND FINAL DISPOSITION IN 479 CASES.

	Cases finally disposed of during—																Total Number of Cases	Average Time Elapsed
	1st Month	2nd Month	3rd Month	4th Month	5th Month	6th Month	7th Month	8th Month	9th Month	10th Month	11th Month	12th Month	2nd Year	3rd Year	4th Year	5th Year		
Orders issued after trial or hearing	..	..	1	3	3	3	4	5	3	11	5	4	43	4	..	..	89	13 months and 1 day.
Orders issued by consent or on stipulation	8	55	39	30	59	8	10	8	7	5	5	2	25	10	..	..	271	5 months and 14 days.
Dismissed or discontinued after trial or hearing	..	..	..	1	2	0	4	1	1	0	0	0	15	5	1	1	31	17 months and 13 days.
Dismissed or discontinued without trial or hearing	..	1	10	2	6	3	1	0	2	0	1	3	18	17	11	13	88	23 months and 22 days.

The table covers all the cases as to which data are available in the published records of the Commission. It is compiled from the tables of Proceedings Pending and Disposed Of, in the Annual Reports of the Commission, and the tables of Cases Dismissed, in the published volumes of the Commission's decisions. Unfortunately the dates upon which complaints were issued are missing in certain cases in the 1917 and 1918 Annual Reports, and no dates are given in the 1922 Annual Report.

equity suit in the federal courts. Especially is this so
since the decision of the Supreme Court, already referred
to, in the Gratz case.[74] The court held, upon a construction of Section 5 of the Federal Trade Commission Act,
that regardless of the evidence or findings, an order will
be reversed if the complaint does not set forth facts sufficient to show a violation of the law. The decision rested
on a strict construction of the words of the statute. Section 5 of the Federal Trade Commission Act provides
that if the Commission has reason to believe the law has
been violated, it may issue a complaint "stating its
charges in that respect." The respondent is authorized
to appear and show cause why an order should not be
entered requiring him to cease and desist "from the violation of law so charged in said complaint." If the Commission is of opinion that "the method of competition
in question is prohibited by this act," it shall make a
report and issue an order requiring the respondent to
cease and desist from using "*such method* of competition." Upon the principle followed in the Gratz case, it
would seem, (1) that the complaint itself must state facts
sufficient to show that the law has been violated, and (2)
that the order must cover the precise practice alleged in
the complaint. No provision is made for amendment of
the complaint to conform to the proof. Upon this construction of the law, it would seem that in the event of
a material variance between complaint and proof, the
complaint must be dismissed and the whole proceeding
begun again from the beginning. Of course a court of
equity under similar circumstances would permit the
complainant to amend his pleadings to conform to the
proof, provided no injustice is done to the opposing party.
Even as compared with a suit in equity, therefore, the
procedure of the Commission tends to be formal and
rigid, and of course this is to a much greater extent true

[74] Federal Trade Commission *v.* Gratz, 253 U.S. 421.

when it is compared with an administrative procedure where speed is an essential requisite, such as the procedure for establishing quarantine lines against plant diseases and insect pests, or for excluding fraudulent matter from the mails.

If neither perfect justice, nor promptness and speed were the guiding considerations in devising the Commission's procedure, the reader may well ask what they were. Why was an administrative procedure adopted, instead of leaving the matter to the courts according to the traditional method? It seems to me that there were, fundamentally, two reasons, one growing out of the nature of the interests which the legislation was designed to protect, and the other based upon the nature of the problems likely to be encountered in performing the task.

The legislation was designed to protect the public interest in free and fair competition. It was felt that this paramount interest might not be adequately represented by private litigants or by the usual prosecuting agencies. In a sense, of course, a court represents the public interest in administering a statute, but it has no continuing duty to see that the law is enforced. It is the court's duty to decide cases as they come before it, but if no indictments or civil actions are brought, and the law becomes a dead letter, the court cannot be blamed. An administrative body, on the other hand, has a continuing responsibility for results. It must ferret out violations, initiate proceedings, and adopt whatever proper methods are necessary to enforce compliance with the law. As to the Department of Justice, it is already overburdened with other work, and moreover it is its traditional policy to act as a litigating department, rather than as an agency charged with discovering violations of law. Full responsibility was therefore placed in a specialized commission, directly charged with obtaining the results which Congress desired.

From this point of view, the Federal Trade Commission is in effect a specialized prosecuting agency, authorized to initiate and conduct proceedings in the public interest in a specialized and limited field. Since the Commission's order can be made effective only through the courts, it is perhaps more correct to say that it is an agency endowed with the faculty of creating, of its own volition, controversies over which the Circuit Courts of Appeals can take original jurisdiction in proper proceedings.

This is only half the story, however. The Commission is also endowed with the faculty of making, under certain conditions, findings which the courts must respect if they are supported by testimony. This faculty alone differentiates the Commission from a mere prosecuting agency, and gives it in a limited way a judicial character. The reason for conferring upon the Commission this typically judicial function must have been that Congress expected that the problems which would be encountered would be of a technical and specialized character, calling for experience and training which a court might not possess, but which could be found in a commission especially selected for the purpose, and authorized to employ technical experts as well as lawyers for its guidance. It was doubtless the belief of Congress that the Commission could perform more satisfactorily than a court the task of making findings of fact in the special field over which it was given jurisdiction.

The precise nature of this task of making findings must be considered with some care, since it is, to the student of administrative law, the most significant of the Commission's functions.

It is only the "findings of fact" of the Commission which are binding upon the courts, if supported by testimony. Questions of law, it is assumed, will be disposed of by the courts without regard to the Commission's conclusions. There is an unfortunate ambiguity about the words, which will occur to anyone familiar with administrative practice, and which is heightened by the context in which they appear. A brief analytical digression will bring the ambiguity to light.

Whether or not a man was walking along the sidewalk on a certain street of a certain afternoon is a question of fact. Whether a coal hole on the sidewalk was or was not covered is a question of fact. Whether or not the man fell into the coal hole is a question of fact. In each case, the fact is ascertainable by observation; there can be no question of judgment or opinion. As a matter of law, however, the liability of the person or corporation chargeable with the condition of the coal hole may depend upon whether or not it was reasonably guarded. This will depend upon two questions. It will depend upon the physical character, location, and surroundings of the hole, and it will depend upon whether those physical factors conform to the standard of reasonableness which the law demands. The former is a question of fact, but what is the latter?

When we speak of conformity to a standard, we use language which suggests a question of physical fact. If an architect sets a standard of seven feet six inches as the height of a door, it is a question of observation and measurement (disregarding the question of immaterial variances) whether or not the contractor has complied with the standard. The court which instructs a jury in a negligence case, however, does not give the jury a standard of this kind. It does not say "the coal hole was adequately protected if it was surrounded by a railing at least two feet high and if its location was marked by a flag by day and a lantern by night." It asks the jury to decide what is a reasonable protection. Sometimes, it is true, the court will try to be more explicit, and will ask the jury to ascertain, first, what standards, under the circumstances, reasonable men would observe, and second, whether in this case the defendant observed them. Again the language suggests a finding of fact, but it must be obvious that no finding of fact is really involved. The "reasonable man" is only a personification of the juror's own judgment of what is right under the circumstances. It is a phrase which tends to put the juror in the proper objective frame of mind, but what he is really asked to do is to exercise his judgment as to what conduct may, in cases of the kind presented, be reasonably required.

Is it then a question of law? In a refined analytical sense perhaps it is, for it is a rule of conduct which, when ascertained and acted upon by a jury, will, for the purposes of the case in issue, be enforced by the sanction of the state. In the same sense an amortization table, an algebraic formula, or a rule of accounting may become a rule of conduct endowed under special circumstances with the force of law. Such a classification is not very helpful. A person charged with the duty of deciding a question of law, is expected to decide it by applying a technique of legal reasoning in which lawyers are trained; a technique of reasoning by precedent, by analogy, by the application of general principles, and a certain adherence to logical form. No such task is expected of a juror. He is merely asked to use his good sense. He is asked to go through a mental process which each one of us goes through a hundred times a day, and which anyone but a lawyer affected by the historic exigencies of trial by jury would accept for what it is, a simple exercise of judgment upon a practical question of conduct.

In a negligence case of the kind suggested, the judgment of twelve average men may be in a majority of cases quite satisfactory in applying a standard of reasonable conduct. Where, however, the standard is of such a character that it can be applied only by men of expert knowledge and experience, the decision of a jury is notoriously unsatisfactory. This is true in part because the mere ascertainment of the physical facts may require a specialized training. It is especially true where the formulation and application of a standard of conduct call for the exercise of a practical judgment which can be acquired only by long experience. No one in his senses would care to submit to twelve men picked at random the question whether a bridge is safe for heavy traffic. That is an engineering question, and a decision rests upon accurate observation and measurement, upon the correct application of rules which only a trained professional engineer can understand, and finally upon a capacity for sound judgment which can be achieved only after years of practical contact with similar problems. It is this need in certain cases for officials or tribunals capable of applying standards of conduct in specialized fields, which is responsible for a great part of the modern development of administrative law. The authority of the Secretary of War (exercised through the Chief of Engineers of the Army) over bridges which obstruct navigable waters,[75] and over harbor lines;[76] the authority of the Secretary of Agriculture over grading of cotton[77] and grains,[78] over insect pests[79] and animal diseases,[80] over commerce in food and drugs;[81] the control of the Interstate Commerce Commission over rates, practices, car service, safety devices, and financial matters affecting carriers;[82] the analogous control of the Shipping Board over the merchant

[75] 34 Stat. at L. 85.
[76] 30 Stat. at L. 1151.
[77] 39 Stat. at L. 479.
[78] 39 Stat. at L. 482.
[79] 37 Stat. at L. 317.
[80] 32 Stat. at L. 791.
[81] 34 Stat. at L. 768.
[82] Act to Regulate Commerce, as amended by Title IV of Transportation Act, 1920, 41 Stat. at L. 474.

marine;[83] the Immigration Office in its relation to questions of health and physical condition of immigrants;[84] these are only a few of the instances in which the need for professional and expert judgment was a predominating motive in the adoption of administrative rather than judicial methods of enforcement.

Here again a decision will often depend not only upon the finding of the appropriate official as to the existence or non-existence of a physical fact, but upon his judgment from the practical or professional viewpoint as to the propriety or probable consequences of conduct. Whether or not we call the decision one of fact or law is not very significant. When the Interstate Commerce Commission decides that a certain level of freight and passenger rates will, as nearly as may be, bring to the carriers in a rate group an annual net railway operating income of 6 per cent of the value of the carriers' property, it is certainly not deciding a question of fact, since the question lies in the future. Nor is it sensible to say that what is likely to happen six months later is a question of law. The Commission is merely doing what every board of directors of a business corporation must do— exercise its best judgment, in the light of existing facts and past experience, in determining what is likely to happen in the future, and what is likely to be the practical consequence of one course of action or another. The same may be said of the decision of an immigration inspector, as to whether or not an alien seeking admission is likely to become a public charge; or of the decision of the Comptroller of the Currency, as to whether or not a closed bank can safely be permitted to reopen; or the decision of the Commissioner of Navigation as to whether or not a ship is sufficiently manned and officered to enable it to proceed to sea without danger.

[83] 39 Stat. at L. 728.
[84] 34 Stat. at L. 901.

An administrative officer, however, like a jury, may in a given case act upon an erroneous interpretation of the law which gives him authority; or he may base his decision upon factors to which he was not intended by the legislature to give weight; or he may adopt a procedure which deprives interested persons of the opportunity to bring relevant facts or arguments to his attention. To meet such cases, court review must be provided, unless some paramount social interest renders it impracticable. Unless the very purpose of administrative action is lost sight of, however, the review will be restricted to questions of this character, and will not extend to any issue of fact or conduct which was entrusted to the official in question on account of his supposed technical experience or capacity for sound practical judgment. It would be absurd for a court to consider *de novo* the engineering questions involved in a determination of the Chief of Engineers of the Army that a bridge is an unreasonable obstruction to navigation, or of the medical authorities in the Bureau of Immigration that an alien has a communicable disease, or of the Interstate Commerce Commission that a rate is likely to bring a return of 6 per cent. Whether these are analytically questions of law or questions of fact, the very purpose of the legislature was to create a competent expert tribunal to decide them, and this purpose is clearly defeated if a court proceeds to substitute its lawyers' judgment for the judgment of such a tribunal.

In most statutes creating administrative agencies there is express or implicit recognition in the statute itself of this obvious limitation of the proper scope of judicial review. In the case of the Interstate Commerce Commission, the Supreme Court itself, with but slight aid from the text of the law, has created in a notable series of cases a category of "administrative questions," upon which it will refuse to substitute its judgment for the judgment of the Commission, and into which, indeed, courts may not inquire until the Commission has made its ruling.[85] These cases do not rest upon any supposed distinction between questions of fact or law; generally they are neither, but merely judgments of a practical character. They do not rest upon any statutory limits on the right of review. They rest on a statesmanlike comprehension of the purpose and function of administrative enforcement, and of the importance of expert decision upon questions of great economic importance.

The Federal Trade Commission was conceived to be a body of men especially qualified to pass on questions of competition and monopoly. It was, moreover, given authority to employ experts and examiners; and it has a large staff of economists, accountants, and specialists in various fields. It also has a chief counsel and a corps of attorneys. To what extent is it authorized by law to exercise an administrative discretion in deciding questions entrusted to its jurisdiction? To what extent should its rulings be guided by a practical judgment, and to what extent by the customary technique of legal reasoning? What is the practice in this regard? And to what extent have the courts respected the administrative functions, if any, of the Commission?

Both the Trade Commission Act and the Clayton Act provide that the Commission's findings of fact, "if supported by testimony," shall be conclusive. The phrase leaves it in doubt whether mere physical conditions or occurrences are referred to, or whether there is a larger range of questions involving judgment in the formulation

[85] Texas & Pacific Ry. Co. *v.* Abilene Cotton Oil Co., 204 U.S. 426; Baltimore & Ohio R. R. Co. *v.* Pitcairn Coal Co., 215 U.S. 481; Morrisdale Coal Co. *v.* Pennsylvania R. R. Co., 230 U.S. 304; Northern Pacific Ry. Co. *v.* Solum, 247 U.S. 477; Director General *v.* Viscose Co., 254 U.S. 498. *See* also Great Northern Ry. *v.* Merchants Elevator Co., 259 U.S. 285.

and application of standards, upon which the Commission's conclusions must be respected. Although analytically not questions of fact, such matters of judgment may well be referred to, somewhat loosely, as questions of fact, just as a standard of due care in a negligence case or a question of preference or discrimination under the Interstate Commerce Act is sometimes said to be a question of fact. The substantive provisions of the two statutes must be considered, to ascertain whether we can discover from the character of the issues involved, whether there was any intention to confer on the Commission the power to exercise an administrative judgment, or whether it is confined to a strict application of legal reasoning to physical facts.

The words "unfair methods of competition" do not of themselves suggest any such power. They suggest an ethical criterion rather than one dependent on expert knowledge or experience, and the spirit of American institutions has not been friendly to the creation of a class of administrative or political specialists upon questions of ethics. Where a legal criterion has an ethical content, as in the law of fraud, we have preferred to leave the decision to a jury, or to the legal reasoning of a court. It is obvious, however, that a question of unfair competition may require business judgment or economic knowledge of a specialized character. Even where competitive methods are unfair because they involve the element of misrepresentation the question is not always purely ethical. The findings of the Commission suggest that a method of competition may be unfair because of its practical effect in misleading customers, although no intent to deceive existed. To a certain extent an external standard seems to be implied, and such a standard must of necessity embody a practical compromise. In cases which do not involve misrepresentation, and especially in the cases which involve methods of competition held to be unfair

because of their tendency improperly to hamper or restrain competitors, or to lessen competition, questions of
economic or business judgment are constantly involved.
It is true that they are the kind of questions which the
courts have for a generation been considering under the
Sherman Law, but dissatisfaction with the courts was, as
we have seen, one of the principal motives which actuated
Congress in setting up an administrative tribunal.

In the Clayton Act, the language more clearly suggests
a non-legal criterion. The phrase ''where the effect may
be . . . to substantially lessen competition or tend to
create a monopoly in any line of commerce,'' qualifies, in
one form or another, all the prohibitions over which the
Commission has jurisdiction, and it implies an exercise
of economic or business judgment rather than a finding
of law. This is true whether the phrase be taken to refer
to the probable effect of the price discrimination, tieing
contract, or other practice, under the particular circumstances of the case at issue, or whether it refers to a
general economic tendency inherent in the practice under
any circumstances.[86] Upon either interpretation, the question involved seems particularly appropriate to the exercise of administrative judgment. Experience with the
Sherman Law has shown the futility of the attempt to
find a strictly legal solution of the problem of monopoly
and restraint of trade. The language of the Clayton Act
seems to be a recognition of this experience, and the
power of enforcement conferred on the Trade Commission strongly suggests the inference that Congress expected the Commission, with the aid and advice of the
experts and examiners which it was authorized to employ,
to exercise in its enforcement an administrative judgment not necessarily guided by technical legal reasoning,
and entitled as such to respect by the courts.

Such being the apparent expectation of Congress, the

[86] *See supra,* pp. 40 ff.

next question to consider is how far the Commission has availed itself of the opportunity offered. If we may take the somewhat oratorical pronouncements of its 1919 Annual Report at face value, the Commission itself has not been inclined to minimize its own powers. "Previous to the creation of the Commission," the report says, "the courts had ruled upon various forms of unfair practices. Their decisions are designated as cases arising under the common law. But upon the creation of the Commission it was empowered to leave the shores defined by the common law and, taking the knowledge of those decisions with it, to embark on an uncharted sea, using common sense plus the common law for its compass."[87] The report adds: "The legislative mandate thus far defined is broad enough to challenge the interest of the most ambitious, but when it is realized that the Commission must substitute a constructive measure for a destructive measure, revive an economic principle, or remove an uneconomic factor, the task devolving upon the Commission and its legal department must appear almost overwhelming. Were it not for the efficient service of the economic department, the work imposed would be impossible. Once, however, the facts are investigated, established, and classified by the latter, the legal question becomes much simplified."[88]

In the decisions of the Supreme Court, on the other hand, there is language which suggests a different point of view. "The words 'unfair method of competition,'" said the court in the Gratz case,[89] "are not defined by the statute, and their exact meaning is in dispute. It is for the courts, not the Commission, ultimately to determine what they include." And in the Curtis Publishing Com-

[87] 1919 Annual Report, p. 45.
[88] *Ibid.,* p. 46.
[89] Federal Trade Commission *v.* Gratz, 253 U.S. 421 (1920).

pany case:[90] "We have heretofore pointed out that the ultimate determination of what constitutes unfair competition is for the court, not the Commission; and the same rule must apply when the charge is that leases, sales, agreements, or understandings substantially lessen competition or tend to create monopoly." The implication is that both statutes set up a legal standard, rather than a standard dependent upon expert practical judgment, and perhaps that the Commission is only a "fact finding" body in a very restricted sense, with authority to make conclusive findings only as to the existence or non-existence of physical facts. All questions of economic or business judgment would thus be for the court to decide, and there would not be, as there is in the case of the Interstate Commerce Commission, a range of "administrative questions" which are not in the strict sense questions of fact, but which are so peculiarly within the competence of the administrative tribunal that its conclusions, within reasonable limits, are respected by the courts.

The question is of great importance, for if the Commission is, by these decisions, shorn of all power to exercise administrative discretion in matters of unfair competition or of restraint of trade and monopoly, it has become little more than a subordinate adjunct of the judicial system. Perhaps, on the other hand, the language which I have quoted will be held to mean merely that it is for the courts to decide, ultimately, the limits within which practices may reasonably be held by the Commission to be unfair, or to substantially lessen competition or tend toward monopoly. This is substantially the view taken of the corresponding provisions of the Interstate Commerce Act.[91]

I will leave the subject for the present, and return to

[90] Federal Trade Commission v. Curtis Pub. Co., 260 U.S. 568 (1923).

[91] *See* cases cited in note 85, *supra,* p. 98.

it in a later chapter. For the problem is one which does not involve merely the formal construction of the language of a statute. It is necessary to inquire to what extent the problems with which the Commission deals from day to day do in fact involve the exercise of expert judgment, and to what extent the findings of the Commission indicate that expert judgment, rather than legal reasoning, has been used. In subsequent chapters, a review of the Commission's findings will be made, both with regard to their form and general qualities, and in relation to the different types of controversies in which they have been made. From such a review it will be possible to obtain a clearer picture of the elements and scope of the problem.

CHAPTER III

FINDINGS OF FACT

THE published decisions of an administrative tribunal, like those of a court of justice, should fulfill two important objects. They should constitute the authentic public record of what was done by the tribunal in a particular case, and they should afford an accessible collection of precedents by which its probable action in other cases can be forecast. The latter function is perhaps the more important of the two, especially where the tribunal is administering laws as general in their terms, and as important to the business world, as the Clayton Act and the Trade Commission Act. It was by the gradual accumulation of precedents and the slow evolution of principles tested by concrete cases, that the application of those statutes was to be determined. To the five published volumes of Federal Trade Commission decisions we therefore turn, to obtain an estimate of the character and quality of the Commission's findings, and to ascertain how successful the Commission has been in giving content and vitality to the laws which it is administering.

The published report of a decision of the Federal Trade Commission is made up of the full text of the Commission's complaint, and of its formal findings of fact, conclusions of law, and order. The answer of the person complained of is not published, nor is there any summary of the respondent's contentions or of the evidence presented on his behalf. It does not seem to me that this method of presenting the facts is fair to the respondent. It will be recalled that the Commission is itself the complainant in each case, and that it may not file a complaint until it "has reason to believe" that the person complained of has violated the law. In a provisional way, it is compelled to prejudge every case that comes before it. The authors of the statute apparently believed that a just decision would nevertheless be assured by the provision made for hearings, and for opportunity to present evidence on behalf of the respondent. Yet the evidence so presented, and the contentions of the respondent, are buried in the official files at Washington, where only the curious inquirer can discover them. One who has not the time or opportunity to search the original docket, will naturally gain an opinion of the case from the published decision, and here he will find only the accusations of the Commission as complainant, and the conclusions of the same Commission as judge. He will have no opportunity to ascertain from a survey of the evidence and of the opposing contentions, whether or not the conclusions are warranted, or appear to have been arrived at fairly and impartially.

In defense of the Commission's practice, it may be admitted that 90 per cent of the answers in these cases are probably not worth printing. Sometimes the answer is no more than a formal paper, three or four lines in length, advising the Commission that the respondent herein "now comes" and denies each and every allegation of the complaint. More often it is a long, wearisome document, full of the verbose ambiguities so dear to the expert pleader, formally admitting, denying, or professing lack of information or belief as to each allegation, *seriatim*, of the complaint. Only rarely does it serve to narrow the field of controversy or throw light on the issues as they appear to the respondent. I have read, at random, perhaps a hundred of these answers as they appear in the Commission's dockets, and the result has been to confirm a scepticism as to the value of lawyers' pleadings in cases of this sort. Occasionally, it is true, there is a striking exception. It sometimes happens that an officer of a respondent company, treating the complaint as a business communication, turns to his stenographer and dictates, out of his own experience and knowledge of the situation, a letter giving the facts and arguments which in his opinion justify the practice complained of. Such a letter is sometimes docketed as an answer, and it is apt to be refreshingly direct and informative, as compared with the run of lawyers' pleadings. Probably the respondent's attorney would consider it an unfortunate indiscretion. These are, however, exceptions, and, as a general rule, it may be conceded that little would be gained by encumbering the published reports with the text of the formal answers.

It is not necessary to set forth the pleadings textually, however, to give a fair statement of the respondent's side of a case, and the Commission's failure to do so detracts greatly from the value of its published decisions. They are not only, for this reason, one-sided and unfair to respondents, but their usefulness as precedents is greatly impaired, for unless we know what facts or arguments were presented in defense, it is generally impossible to judge correctly the scope and application of the Commission's decision.

It should be observed, moreover, that formal findings are made and published only in those cases in which the decision supports the charges of the Commission's complaint. Where the complaint is disproved, or the facts alleged are found not to constitute a violation of law, the complaint is dismissed by formal action of the board, but the text of the decision is not made public. In each volume of decisions there is an appendix containing a tabular list of "cases in which orders of discontinuance or dismissal have been entered." The table shows the docket number and the name of the respondent, the nature of the commodity (*e.g.*, "razors" or "shoes" or "drugs and druggists' sundries"). In another column there is a brief indication of the nature of the charge, such as "false and misleading advertising" or "harassing competition" or "commercial bribery (money and gratuities)." The next column shows whether the dismissal or discontinuance was upon trial, or stipulation, or on respondent's answer. The final column is headed "Reason for discontinuance or dismissal," but the entry in this column rarely goes beyond such scant phrases as "failure of proof" or "evidence not sufficient to support an order," and in the majority of cases the entry is "no reasons assigned."

This failure to give to adverse decisions the same publicity as is given to decisions supporting the complaint is perhaps based upon a literal interpretation of the statute. Section 5 of the Trade Commission Act requires a "report in writing" only where the Commission, upon hearing, is of the opinion that the method of competition in question is prohibited by the statute. Yet the authority conferred in Section 6 (f), "to provide for the publication of its reports and decisions in such form and manner as may be best adapted for public information and use," is surely sufficient to warrant a detailed public statement of the facts and reasons warranting dismissal. To fail to make such a statement is manifestly unfair to the person complained of. If charges have been made which prove to have been erroneous, the respondent is entitled to an unequivocal and detailed exoneration. A mere dismissal of the case with "no reasons assigned" is not sufficient. And of course the reports suffer greatly, as a storehouse of precedents, from the fact that only decisions favorable to the Commission are published. Surely it is important that the business world should know what it may lawfully do, as well as what is found by the Commission to be unlawful.

The next point that will occur to the student of the Commission's published reports is the form which the "findings of fact" assume. Although the statute calls for a "report in writing," upon the facts of the case, there is no narrative statement of the kind usually included in the opinion of a court or commission. Instead there are formal "findings," in numbered paragraphs, couched generally in the artificial legal phraseology of a common law pleading, and designed apparently to embody the Commission's ultimate conclusions upon the major issues of fact or judgment thought to be involved, rather than to set forth the happenings or events or economic considerations out of which the controversy arises.

Formal "findings" are a notoriously unsatisfactory means of conveying information. Almost any controversy, and especially an economic or business controversy of the kind that comes before the Federal Trade Commission, has a history, and a setting. To understand the business or economic significance of a practice, we must know something of its origin, of the objects and purposes of those who pursue it, of the persons who object to it and their reasons, and of its practical effect. We need a descriptive and narrative report, couched in simple and direct language. Even a statement of the simplest occurrence suffers when it is couched in "legal" phraseology. To say that "for more than one year last past said respondent has given and offered to give employees of his customers and prospective customers, as an inducement to influence their employees to purchase . . . from the respondent, without other consideration therefor, gratuities consisting of liquors, cigars, meals, theater tickets and other personal property," carries conviction only if we have full confidence in the judgment of the person whose conclusion it embodies. If the examiner would only tell us what happened, his finding would carry more weight. It would be better to say: "The evidence seems clearly to establish that the giving of gratuities on a large scale to employees of customers, was a settled practice of this respondent. Five of his salesmen took the

stand, and of these all admitted that they customarily
handed out cigars to buyers, took them to theater enter-
tainments, and treated them to drinks, and that expenditures of this sort were included in their expense accounts.
Two of them admitted receiving express instructions
from the head salesman not to be too moderate in making
disbursements of this sort. The chief accounting officer
produced the books of the company, and verified entries
for 'spending money' over $100 a week during the buying
season. The president of the company, it is true, denied
that any formal instructions to 'treat' buyers were ever
issued, and denied any intention to exert improper influence on employees of customers, yet in view of the
acknowledged and long standing practice his denial cannot be given great weight. We conclude that the charges
of the complaint in this respect are fully sustained by the
evidence.'' Such a statement would show the elements
from which the Commission's conclusion was reached,
whereas the bare formal ''finding'' which I have quoted,
does little more than to stimulate curiosity. Yet it is the
phraseology in which the great majority of the ''commercial bribery'' cases of the Commission are couched.[1]

To ''find'' that a moving picture booking agency ''has
employed and used the following unfair method of competition within three years last past and prior to February 1, 1918: (a) Cancellation of contracts for the
exhibition of certain moving-picture films made and
entered into by and between certain of its competitors
similarly engaged and the producers of moving-picture
films;'' or that the same agency ''(d) by divers threats

---

[1] See Federal Trade Commission v. The New Jersey Asbestos Co.,
1 F.T.C.D. 472, and the opinion of the court on petition to review,
264 Fed. 509, where "findings" substantially in the form above given
were disregarded as embodying "mere conclusions." More recent "findings" are apt to be more elaborate and specific than the earlier ones, but
the form remains substantially the same.

and different methods of intimidation has induced the owners and operators of certain moving-picture theaters to pay this respondent a sum equal to 10 per centum of the cost of all moving-picture films of various producers booked *directly* from said producers or exchanges," leaves the reader in the greatest doubt as to what has happened.[2] Yet the docket, if we have the time and patience to examine it, reveals an interesting and significant story of the attempt of a powerful booking agency (under the leadership of an officer who had since died) to force independent theatres at Atlantic City and Philadelphia to book pictures exclusively through it. The precise terms of the "exclusive" contract which it tried to enforce, the attempt to persuade producers to boycott the independents, the point at which persuasion becomes coercion, and advice or suggestion becomes a threat, the extent of the economic power which made the threat effective, these were issues upon which, certainly, the judgment of the Commission might be expected to be helpful; yet the formal findings of which I have given a fair sample do not even suggest that such questions exist.

The Commission finds that "respondent . . . through and by its agents, servants and employees, has wilfully caused certain of its trucks to collide with automobiles owned and operated by said competitors . . . (and) that such collisions were calculated and designed to and did so damage the machines of the competitors as to hinder, delay and embarrass said competitors in the conduct of their business."[3] In the absence of any detail as to time, place, or circumstances, a finding of this kind is of little use. Was this a settled practice of the head office of the company or a personal row between truck drivers? Did it happen once or twice or constantly? By whom were

[2] Federal Trade Commission *v.* Stanley Booking Corp., 1 F.T.C.D. 212 (1918). See Docket No. 140.

[3] F.T.C. *v.* American Agricultural Chemical Co., 1 F.T.C.D. 226.

the collisions "calculated and designed" to injure competitors, or is this an allegation of law upon the theory of presumptive intent? Upon these issues neither the reader of the Commission's reports nor the reviewing court can get any assistance from the findings, yet they would seem to be of some importance.

It does not satisfy our legitimate thirst for facts to learn that "numerous agents and representatives of respondent . . . while acting within the scope of their employment with the purpose, intent and effect of stifling and suppressing competition in the manufacture and sale of pumps, tanks . . .," etc., and "for the purpose of embarrassing, harassing and restraining competitors of respondent, . . . have by divers means and methods induced and procured and attempted to induce and procure a large number of . . . customers . . . to cancel and rescind orders . . . placed with competitors." Yet that is all there is to the "findings of fact" in the Milwaukee Tank Works case.[4] This is not a report of facts, but a conclusion as to the existence of a practice, and even the practice is not so described that we can gain any conception of its scope, its effect, or of the means used in carrying it out.

Many similar cases could be cited. In one case there is a bare finding that "the respondents . . . entered into, engaged in, carried out, and conducted, a combination, conspiracy, understanding or 'pool' among themselves as to which of said respondents should receive particular printing contracts submitted to them or brought to their attention for the purpose of bidding on the same and for formulating their respective bids so that the selected member of said 'pool' would receive the business."[5] There are no further details as to the nature or incidents of the alleged conspiracy. In a series of price maintenance

[4] 1 F.T.C.D. 272.

[5] F.T.C. *v.* Blakely Printing Co. et al., 1 F.T.C.D. 277.

cases, the only substantial findings concerning the practice are (1) that respondent "for more than one year prior to" a given date, "indicated the resale prices at which same should be resold and endeavored to have those prices maintained," and (2) that respondent for the same period "refused to sell and did not sell its said products to jobbers, wholesalers or retailers who sold the same below such indicated prices."[6] The findings in some of the "passing off" cases merely inform us that the respondent made "certain statements" which were false and misleading and which "were calculated and designed" or which "tend" to deceive the public into believing that his product is that of a competitor.[7] In a misbranding case[8] the charge was that respondent advertised as "pure linseed oil equivalent" a product which it called "Flaxol." Upon the vital issue of the falsity of the claim, the only finding is that Flaxol "is not the equivalent of" linseed oil. The ingredients and properties of the preparation are not given, and no facts are stated in support of the conclusion. Another respondent[9] was found to have sent out letters and circulars "containing statements to the effect that certain competitors of respondents were and are financially irresponsible, which statements were and are false and misleading and known by the respondents so to be . . ." The statements are not given, nor the facts which render them false. In the same case it is found "that the respondent has made false and injurious statements to prospective customers con-

[6] Federal Trade Commission v. Auto Strop Safety Razor Co., 1 F.T.C.D. 418. The same bare allegations, with slight changes, appear in F.T.C. v. Clayton F. Summy Co., 1 F.T.C.D. 413. See F.T.C. v. Chester Kent & Co., Inc., 1 F.T.C.D. 149.

[7] See F.T.C. v. Geographical Publishing Co., 1 F.T.C.D. 235 (1918); F.T.C. v. Malzo Coffee Co., 2 F.T.C.D. 58.

[8] F.T.C. v. International Flaxol Co., 3 F.T.C.D. 64.

[9] F.T.C. v. Muenzen Specialty Co., 1 F.T.C.D. 30 (1917).

cerning the material of which certain competitive cleaners are constructed and the cost of production of said cleaners.'' The statements themselves are not given. In the Sears, Roebuck case, the formal finding is that respondent circulated advertisements ''which were calculated to lead the trade and the general public to believe that competitors were charging more than a fair price for the same,'' and other advertisements ''in which it was represented that respondent's competitors did not deal justly, fairly and honestly with their customers.''[10] What the advertisements were can be ascertained only by examining the docket, or the opinion of the Circuit Court of Appeals on petition to review.[11]

The typical way in which a violation of Section 2 of the Clayton Act is set forth, is by substantially repeating (without more elaboration) the language of the statute. Often all that appears is a finding that ''the respondent . . . for several years last past in the course of interstate commerce has discriminated in price between different purchasers of [the commodity in question] which commodities were sold by respondent for use, consumption or resale within the United States . . . and that the effect of such discrimination may be to substantially lessen competition and tend to create a monopoly.''[12] The typical finding that Section 3 of the Clayton Act has been violated, takes substantially this form: That the respondent for several years last past has sold or made contracts for the sale of (a given commodity), and is now selling

[10] Federal Trade Commission v. Sears, Roebuck & Co., 1 F.T.C.D. 163.

[11] 258 Fed. 307.

[12] See F.T.C. v. Wayne Oil Tank & Pump Co., 1 F.T.C.D. 259. There are other findings relating to unfair competition, but the finding upon which a violation of Section 2 was based was substantially as quoted above. And see F.T.C. v. The Eli Lilly & Co., 1 F.T.C.D. 442, Part II of findings. Part I relates to charges of unfair competition, and indicates that a price maintenance case is involved.

or making contracts for the sale of (said commodity) and
has fixed and is now fixing the price charged therefor,
or discount from or rebate from such price, on the condition, agreement, or understanding that the purchasers
thereof shall not use or deal in the goods, wares, merchandise, supplies, or commodities of a competitor or
competitors of respondent, and that the effect of such
sales and contracts for sale, or such condition, agreement,
or understanding may be and is to substantially lessen
competition and tend to create a monopoly.[13]

In the Standard Car Equipment Company case,[14] there
is an interesting example of the manner in which a formal
finding can be made to conceal a serious conflict in the
evidence. From the docket, it appears that the case involved a dispute between the Pennsylvania Tank Line
and its former president. He organized a car construction
company, and, according to the allegations of the complaint, had been for more than a year last past, systematically and on a large scale, enticing away employees
of his competitor, although he had no occasion for their
services, all "with the effect of stifling and suppressing
competition in interstate commerce" in the leasing of
tank cars. Hearings were had, and the examiner submitted tentative findings that respondent had "enticed
away the entire office force" of the Pennsylvania Tank
Line at St. Louis, and had persistently, systematically,
and on a large scale, enticed away employees of the Petroleum Iron Works Company, an affiliated concern. The
proposed findings gave the names of eight employees
enticed from the Pennsylvania Tank Lines, and twenty-
one from the offices of the Petroleum Iron Works, with
the exact date, in each case, of the alleged enticement.

[13] *See* F.T.C. *v.* Standard Oil Co. of Indiana, 2 F.T.C.D. 26, 33;
F.T.C. *v.* B. S. Pearsall Butter Co., 5 F.T.C.D. 127.
[14] Federal Trade Commission *v.* Standard Car Equipment Co., 1
F.T.C.D. 144 (1918), Docket No. 9.

The respondent filed formal exceptions, and a brief in support, raising, by reference to the transcript of the testimony, serious doubts as to the accuracy of the proposed findings. Some of the employees named had, it was claimed, resigned of their own volition and applied for work without any solicitation from respondent. One had testified that he had been dismissed. Another was said never to have been in respondent's employ at all, and yet another to have resigned to take a job with an electrical contractor, only subsequently joining respondent's force. As to virtually all of the persons mentioned, an issue of fact was raised, which, it would seem, the "report in writing" of the Commission should have analyzed and met. The following, however, is the revised version of the finding as it was adopted by the Commission:

Par. 2. That within three years last past respondents, for the purpose and with the effect of unduly harassing and embarrassing a competitor in the manufacture, sale, and leasing of tank cars in commerce as aforesaid, maliciously enticed away employees of said competitor.[15]

In some of the cases one is appalled at the amount of time, labor, and money obviously expended in the investigation and trial of the facts, and at the meagre quality of the resulting findings. Thus in a case against an automobile company,[16] alleged to be selling its securities by means of fraudulent representations, both complaint and findings charge, in a series of formally phrased paragraphs, that respondent has made false and misleading statements "concerning" the plan of organization, resources, assets, and financial standing of the company, and the manufacture, design, and production of its cars. The following is a typical paragraph:

That during said period respondent Samuel C. Pandolfo, as

[15] 1 F.T.C.D. 148.
[16] F.T.C. v. Pan Motor Co., 2 F.T.C.D. 407 (1920), Docket No. 273.

fiscal agent of said company, at divers times has made, published, advertised and circulated false and misleading statements, representations, predictions, and promises relating to the design, production, and manufacture of a certain motor tractor, described as the "Pan Tank-Tread Tractor."[17]

It is not stated what the representations are, nor in what respect they were false. The findings are practically worthless. Yet the docket shows that testimony was taken in this case for three days at Denver, two days at Monte Vista, Colorado, and four days at Minneapolis. The testimony covered 1056 typewritten sheets, besides two large volumes of exhibits. A year and a day elapsed between the filing of the complaint and the entry of the order. If the case was important enough to warrant so expensive and long-drawn-out a proceeding, surely it was worth while to devote a little painstaking care to the preparation of a real statement of facts.

The use of stock phrases to describe frequently recurring situations is noticeable in the reports, and is one of the unfortunate consequences of the formal character of the "findings." The time element is generally indicated by a finding that "for more than one year last past," or "for more than two years last past," respondent has done the acts complained of. The phrase leaves it in doubt whether a continuous practice is involved, or occasional acts spread over a period of more than two years, or whether there was only an isolated occurrence. The use of this phrase seems to have originated in the Reliance Varnish Works case,[18] and it reappears with distressing regularity in the findings in subsequent cases.[19] A good illustration of the ambiguity of the phrase is in the Sears,

---

[17] *Ibid.*, 424, par. (f).

[18] 1 F.T.C.D. 98.

[19] *See* F.T.C. *v.* Twin City Varnish Co., 1 F.T.C.D. 190, 192; F.T.C. *v.* The Royal Varnish Co., 1 F.T.C.D. 194, 197; F.T.C. *v.* The Printers' Roller Co., 1 F.T.C.D. 240; F.T.C. *v.* Blakely Printing Co. et al., 1

Roebuck case. The complaint in this case was filed February 26, 1918, and charged that certain advertising practices had been carried on "for more than two years last past." The findings were made June 24, 1918, and recited that the sales of sugar below cost as a "leader" had taken place "for a long time prior to August, 1917, and continuously during such period." All the other acts were found to have been performed "for more than two years last past" (apparently meaning for two years prior to the findings?). The stipulation, however, upon which the findings were based, shows that the advertisements complained of were issued principally in March and April of 1916, and that none were more recent than August, 1917. The dissenting judge in the Court of Appeals thought this fact of sufficient relevance to warrant a reversal.

Sometimes the finding is merely that the respondent "within the last three years," or "prior to" a given date, "has given and offered to give" commercial bribes, or committed some other unfair act, again without specification of time or place or indication whether a single or many occurrences are referred to.[20] On the other hand, a

F.T.C.D. 277, 282, par. 4; F.T.C. v. Wall Rope Works, Inc., 1 F.T.C.D. 468, 470, par. 2; F.T.C. v. Standard Soap Mfg. Co., 1 F.T.C.D. 480, 483, par. 2; F.T.C. v. Rome Soap Mfg. Co., 1 F.T.C.D. 484, 487, par. 2; F.T.C. v. Engineering Supply Co., 2 F.T.C.D. 62, 65, par. 2; F.T.C. v. Federal Color and Chemical Co., 2 F.T.C.D. 71, 75, pars. 3 and 4; F.T.C. v. Woodley Soap Mfg. Co., 2 F.T.C.D. 78, 80, par. 2; F.T.C. v. Twin City Printers' Roller Co., 2 F.T.C.D. 102, 104, par. 2; F.T.C. v. Marine Supply Co., 2 F.T.C.D. 107, 110, par. 3; F.T.C. v. Royal Easy Chair Co., 2 F.T.C.D. 139, 142, par. 3; F.T.C. v. Carter Paint Co., 2 F.T.C.D. 181, 183, par. 2.

[20] See Federal Trade Commission v. Essex Varnish Co., 1 F.T.C.D. 138; F.T.C. v. The American Printers' Roller Co., 1 F.T.C.D. 244, 247; F.T.C. v. Baltimore Hub-Wheel & Mfg. Co., 1 F.T.C.D. 395, 398 ("That each of the respondents . . . during the past two years has corresponded with a manufacturer" and demanded that he cease giving a discount to certain dealers); F.T.C. v. The Hoover Suction Sweeper Co., 1 F.T.C.D.

stock phrase that often appears where the examiner
wishes to emphasize the frequency of an occurrence, is
"systematically and on a large scale." The phrase seems
to have originated in the complaint in the Botsford Lumber case,[21] and perhaps appropriately described the conduct of some of the respondents in that case, but the
phrase, by itself and without further specification, suggests a formal pleader's allegation rather than a mirror
of actual happenings.[22]

A favorite stock phrase, apparently used to fit almost
any state of facts, is the allegation that certain acts were
done "with the intent, purpose and effect of stifling and
suppressing competition in interstate commerce" either
generally, or in the sale of designated articles. The
phrase suggests conduct involving some element of restraint of trade or of monopolizing methods,[23] but it is

476, 479, par. 3 ("within the year last past has given"); F.T.C. v. The
Utah Bedding & Mfg. Co., 2 F.T.C.D. 185, 187 ("has within the last
three years sold and offered to sell . . ."); F.T.C. v. Flood & Calvert,
3 F.T.C.D. 205, 207, par. 2 ("for several years last past have given"
bribes to ships' captains); F.T.C. v. John R. Adams & Co., 3 F.T.C.D.
209, 211, par. 2 (same); F.T.C. v. Marine Equipment Co., Inc., 3
F.T.C.D. 227, 229, par. 2 (same), and all the ship chandlers' bribery
cases to 3 F.T.C.D. 245; F.T.C. v. Seymour Chemical Co., 4 F.T.C.D.
69, 71, par. 3 ("during the years 1918, 1919, and 1920 have given"
bribes, etc.), and see F.T.C. v. Russell Grader Mfg. Co., 5 F.T.C.D. 77,
where the finding was merely that respondent had "in many instances"
done the act in question. Since the charge was bribery of public officials,
it would seem that names, dates, and other details should have been
given.

[21] 1 F.T.C.D. 60.

[22] See use of the phrase in findings in F.T.C. v. George Muench, 1
F.T.C.D. 370, 373, par. 2; F.T.C. v. F. E. Atteaux & Co., Inc., 2
F.T.C.D. 82, 85, pars. 2 and 3.

[23] It was so used in F.T.C. v. American Agricultural Chemical Co.,
1 F.T.C.D. 226, 232; F.T.C. v. Wayne Oil Tank & Pump Co., 1 F.T.C.D.
259, 266, par. 4; F.T.C. v. Milwaukee Tank Works, 1 F.T.C.D. 272,
275, par. 3; F.T.C. v. Western Sugar Refinery et al., 2 F.T.C.D. 151,
159, par. 8; F.T.C. v. Gratz, 1 F.T.C.D. 249.

most frequently used in cases involving commercial bribery, or misrepresentation, or even in simple "passing off" cases.[24] Sometimes the phrase is "with the intent, purpose and effect of harassing and embarrassing its competitors and destroying their trade," as in the Sears, Roebuck case—a seemingly exaggerated characterization of a practice of selling sugar below cost for advertising purposes.[25] The purpose of such a "finding" seems to have been to meet, argumentatively, the contention that the Commission had no jurisdiction over cases of mere fraud or misrepresentation, but that its powers related only to cases involving some kind of an assault upon competitive conditions, of the kind encountered in Sherman Law cases. It resembles, in this respect, the "finding" to be found in many of the later commercial bribery cases, that "the cost of making such expenditures becomes a part of the expense incurred by respondent in distributing its products and is added to the price charged the purchasing public for such products,"[26] or similar language, the purpose being to meet the conten-

[24] See F.T.C. v. Wayne Oil Tank & Pump Co., 1 F.T.C.D. 259, 267 (misleading statements by salesman regarding "a competitor"); F.T.C. v. Gartside Iron Rust Soap Co., 1 F.T.C.D. 310, 314, par. 3 (misleading statements that "certain competitors" were financially irresponsible); F.T.C. v. The Lasso Pictures Co., 1 F.T.C.D. 374, 378, par. 3 ("passing off" old moving picture films as new ones); F.T.C. v. Ward Baking Co., 1 F.T.C.D. 388, 390, par. 2 (giving away free bread as an advertisement); F.T.C. v. Ringwalt Linoleum Works, Inc., 1 F.T.C.D. 436, 440, par. 6 (selling as "linoleum" a product made of felt paper saturated with asphaltum).

[25] 1 F.T.C.D. 163, 169. The phrase, with immaterial variations appears also in F.T.C. v. Berk Bros., 2 F.T.C.D. 377, 380, par. 4.

[26] See F.T.C. v. Sealwood Co., 4 F.T.C.D. 65, 67, par. 3; F.T.C. v. Beckwith-Chandler Co. et al., 4 F.T.C.D. 108, 112, par. 4; F.T.C. v. United Chemical Products Corp., 4 F.T.C.D. 220, 223, par. 5; F.T.C. v. The Model Market, 4 F.T.C.D. 225, 228, par. 12; F.T.C. v. Ernst Bischoff Co., Inc., 4 F.T.C.D. 230, 233, par. 6; F.T.C. v. E. E. White, 4 F.T.C.D. 313, 315, par. 4, and numerous other cases.

tion that the Commission had no jurisdiction over these
cases because they did not "affect the public."[27] Yet it
is difficult to conceive that such a phrase could be given
any effect as a finding of fact. The phrase about "stifling
and suppressing competition" is little more than an epithet, and, in some of the cases, is ludicrously inappro-
priate. Witness the solemn "finding" that the respondent, by setting up a "Sweater Store" in the city of
Washington, in simulation of the name of another store,
"stifles and suppresses competition in the sale of men's
and women's wearing apparel and knitted goods in
the District of Columbia."[28] The "finding" as to the
effect of commercial bribery upon the price of the product
may be relevant, but it is generally so phrased that it is
impossible to tell whether it refers to something which
the testimony shows has actually happened, or whether
it is no more than an economic conclusion of an argumentative character. This is especially so where the
"finding" takes the following form: "That as a result
of the payment of such sums of money to employees as
aforesaid, the respondent adds to its cost of doing business the amount of money given by it as shown by these
findings, and the price of its product to its customers is
its cost of doing business plus its profit."[29] An argument
against the relevancy of such a finding may be that the
economic conclusion which it embodies suggests a corol-
lary: that the employees who receive the bribes may in
the long run be content with lower wages, and that therefore the costs of the purchasing company may be reduced,
with a corresponding reduction in prices. It seems, however, that the public interest in the rooting out of this
disgraceful practice does not depend upon a showing that

[27] *See* New Jersey Asbestos Co. *v.* F.T.C., 264 Fed. 509 (1920).

[28] F.T.C. *v.* The Sweater Store, 2 F.T.C.D. 67, 70, par. 3.

[29] *See* F.T.C. *v.* Ernst Bischoff Co., Inc., 4 F.T.C.D. 230, 233, par.
4; F.T.C. *v.* The Model Market, 4 F.T.C.D. 225, 228, par. 12.

a few cents may be saved in the price of what the public buys.

It is a striking fact that ambiguous and inadequate findings are most often en'countered in cases in which there are agreed statements of fact. Sometimes the vice seems to lie in the Commission's summary or interpretation of the agreed facts, a matter to which I shall return shortly. Frequently, however, the ambiguity is in the agreed statement itself. It is often apparent from the record that the stipulation is the product of compromise between attorneys. Doubtless a word is objected to and a substitute is suggested, and there is a deadlock which is finally solved by the use of an ambiguous or colorless phrase. It seems to be especially true of economic or business controversies that a litigation upon an agreed statement of facts is likely to turn upon the construction of phrases rather than upon inferences or judgments based upon actual facts. In the Wayne Oil Tank & Pump case, and the Stanley Booking Corporation case, previously referred to,[30] the unsatisfactory character of the findings merely reflects an unintelligible or inadequate agreed statement. Even where the agreed statement is detailed and elaborate, one gains the impression that while it may represent an agreement of attorneys as to phraseology, it fails nevertheless to reveal that thorough comprehension of the facts which can only be gained by hearing witnesses, by questioning them, and by examining at first hand the documentary evidence involved.

The danger that an agreed statement may represent a compromise between attorneys rather than a picture of actual events and circumstances is illustrated by the Botsford Lumber Company case.[31] Complaint was filed against more than a hundred lumber dealers in the middle

[30] *Supra,* pp. 114, 110.
[31] 1 F.T.C.D. 60.

western and intermountain territory, charging a conspiracy to suppress the competition of mail order houses. It was alleged that through the medium of a trade periodical, a campaign had been conducted of which the object was to encourage sending to the mail order houses spurious requests for estimates and catalogues, with the object of causing them expense and embarrassment. The answers in general denied participation in any such conspiracy, denied that the trade periodical was the organ or representative of the respondents, and in so far as they admitted sending for estimates and catalogues, claimed it was for the legitimate purpose of obtaining information as to the prices the competing mail order houses were making, and not to cause them expense or embarrassment. After negotiations between counsel, however, all but a few of the respondents signed a stipulation of which the gist is in the following paragraph:

4. That each of the stipulating respondents individually, and some of them without concert or conspiracy with any one or more of the others, some of them with the purpose or intent of causing such mail order houses annoyance and delay in the transaction of their business, and damage and expense, and some of them without any such purpose or intent, and some of them with the purpose or intent of furnishing the information thus secured to the respondent Platt B. Walker for publication in the Mississippi Valley Lumberman, and some of them without such purpose or intent, has done or caused to be done one or more of the acts charged in paragraphs 8 and 10 of the complaint in this proceeding and for the purpose of this proceeding it is further agreed that each stipulating respondent consents that an order and decree may be entered against him or it within substantially, the terms hereinafter set forth.

Another paragraph admitted that "some of stipulating respondents" have "systematically and on a large scale," and "some" have occasionally and at infrequent inter-

vals, written to mail order houses for estimates and catalogues; that one object of these inquiries was to secure
information as to prices; but that "some" of the stipulating respondents "knew or are chargeable with knowledge" that the requests would cause expense and delay
to the mail order houses.

Obviously the stipulation contains no admission by any
respondent that he has been guilty of any specific act of
wrongdoing, but it contains a clause declaring that each
respondent "does hereby waive all and every right each
has to object to an order based upon this stipulation on
the ground of indefiniteness or lack of precision in designating or stipulating the particular act or acts which
each respondent has done." The Commission's trial
counsel commented upon the clause at the final argument
as follows: "Frankly and plainly the purpose of that
waiver . . . is that in view of the fact that the specific act
is not designated, not charged against a specific respondent, it takes a waiver of this sort to make the order valid
against all of the respondents against whom it will be
entered." Whether or not the legality of the order was
saved by the waiver, it would seem that it should have
been beneath the dignity of an administrative tribunal
to act upon an agreed statement, of this character, obviously devised by astute attorneys with the sole view
of giving the Commission a paper victory without con-
ceding any facts against any particular respondent.

An agreed statement of facts may be a convenient
means of shortening a trial and avoiding expensive litigation, but an agreed statement of economic conclusions is
seldom conducive to a clear understanding. It is not very
helpful to have a complaint, a stipulation, and a formal
finding unanimously agreeing that the effect of a contract
"may be to substantially lessen competition and tend to
create a monopoly," but equally silent as to the sub-

sidiary economic factors which go to make up the conclusion.[32]

The examples which I have given show the "findings" at their worst, and while the percentage of cases of this kind seems to me to be large, I do not want to give the impression that all the reports are of this character, or even that they are typical. Especially in the later volumes there is a noticeable improvement, and a growing tendency to eliminate vague phrases and conclusions, to give names, dates, and figures, and even in some cases to refer to the evidence in substantiation of conclusions.[33] The form of the "findings," however, remains the same. They are still formal pronouncements in legal phraseology rather than simple narrative or descriptive statements of happenings and circumstances. An examiner charged with making formal "findings" is apt to approach the task in the wrong frame of mind. He is apt to begin with

[32] *See* F.T.C. *v.* Chicago Flexible Shaft Co., 1 F.T.C.D. 181, and F.T.C. *v.* B. S. Pearsall Butter Co., 5 F.T.C.D. 127 (1922).

[33] *See,* for instance, the following findings, which appear to be both comprehensive and specific: F.T.C. *v.* Nulomoline Co., 1 F.T.C.D. 400 (sets forth fully the chemical facts involved in a charge of misleading advertising concerning a chemical process); F.T.C. *v.* Berry Seed Co., 2 F.T.C.D. 427 (technical facts regarding kind, origin, and germinating quality of seeds, fully set forth in misbranding case); F.T.C. *v.* Beech-Nut Packing Co., 1 F.T.C.D. 516 (contains detailed description of method of enforcing a price maintenance policy); F.T.C. *v.* Wholesale Grocers Association of El Paso, 3 F.T.C.D. 109 (a commercial boycott described in great detail); F.T.C. *v.* Winsted Hosiery Co., 3 F.T.C.D. 189 (modified findings, made after the case had been remanded to the Commission by the Circuit Court of Appeals; contains excellent statement of trade terms and usage in the sale of woolens and worsteds. The Supreme Court referred to the findings as "clear, specific, and comprehensive." F.T.C. *v.* Winsted Hosiery Co., 258 U.S. 483 (1922); F.T.C. *v.* Royal Baking Powder Co., 4 F.T.C.D. 1 (a misleading advertising practice fully and convincingly described); F.T.C. *v.* Swift & Co., 5 F.T.C.D. 143 (detailed account of acquisition of stock of competitor, found to be in violation of Sec. 7 of the Clayton Act). More could, of course, be added to the list.

the legal conclusion which he wishes to reach. Next he will ascertain from the textbooks and precedents what conclusions of fact are necessary in law to support the result. Finally, if he is conscientious, he will comb the record to ascertain whether it contains evidence supporting the necessary conclusions of fact. A person charged with writing a narrative and descriptive account of a controversy approaches the task from a different viewpoint. His first concern is to set forth as clearly and accurately as possible what has happened and what are the circumstances and surroundings. Having stated the facts, he will endeavor to reach more general conclusions of fact or judgment, and finally he will apply the law to these general conclusions. Throughout, he will be concerned mainly with the fairness and accuracy and impartial character of the report, rather than with its sufficiency in supporting one or another legal conclusion. Even the best of the Commission's findings have an accusatory rather than a judicial tone, which, in the eye of the impartial reader as well as of the reviewing court, must greatly weaken their authority.

In the instances which I have given it has generally been evident on the face of the printed reports that the findings were inadequate and unsatisfactory, whatever the evidence may have been on which they were based. To go further, and attempt to ascertain to what extent, as a matter of substance rather than of form, the findings correspond with the evidence, is of course a task far beyond the scope of this study. Since the evidence is not summarized in the published reports, such a task would involve a study of the original records, including often voluminous testimony and exhibits. This study is concerned, however, with the Commission's technique, and such examination as I have been able to make of original dockets, supplemented by the opinions of reviewing courts, reveals certain defects which appear to be directly attributable to methods which seem to be mistaken. I will review a few such cases, with the caution, however, that only a small percentage of the dockets have been examined, and that the examples which I give may not be representative of the average. I may add, however, that I have examined in all 100 dockets, that the selection was made, of course, without any previous knowledge of what the search would bring to light, and that I have tried so far as possible to select for examination cases representing a large variety of subjects fairly distributed, in point of time, over the period covered by the published reports.

I will begin with a case in which we can test with a fair degree of certainty the quality of the Commission's findings, because it is possible to compare them with an exhaustive review of the evidence in the opinion of an able judge of a reviewing court.[34] A complaint was filed against the Curtis Publishing Company, charging a violation of Section 5 of the Federal Trade Commission Act, and also a violation of Section 3 of the Clayton Act. Upon the first charge, the only allegation in the complaint (aside from formal averments relating to the corporate existence of the respondent and to its business in interstate commerce) was the statement that "with the intent, purpose and effect of stifling and suppressing competition," the respondent refuses and has for several months refused to sell its publications to any dealer who will not agree that he will not sell or distribute the publications "of certain of the competitors of the respondent to other dealers or distributors." Upon the second charge the averments are, as usual, substantially in the language of Section 3 of the Clayton Act, including the formal averment "that the effect of such sales and contracts for sale, or such conditions, agreements or understandings, may be and is to substantially lessen competition and to tend to create a monopoly."

[34] F.T.C. *v.* Curtis Publishing Co., 2 F.T.C.D. 20 (1919).

The findings contain a few more details. It is found that the respondent "has entered into contracts" by which the dealers in question agree not to "act as agent for or supply at wholesale rates, any periodical other than those published by" the respondent, without its written consent; that of such dealers, 447 were regularly engaged as wholesale dealers, and that of these "many" have requested the respondent's consent to engage also in the distribution of "certain publications" competing with respondent, "which permission as to said competing publications has been uniformly denied by respondent." Thereby, it is found, respondent has prevented and now prevents "certain" of its competitors from utilizing established channels for the distribution of publications of "different and sundry" publishers, and that these channels are "in most instances" the most efficient and in numerous cases the only medium for the distribution of such publications. A formal averment that the method of competition "has proved and is unfair" concludes the findings upon Section 5. The findings as to a violation of Section 3 of the Clayton Act are in the identical words of those relating to Section 5, except that the formal conclusion is "that the effect of said contract provision has been and is to substantially lessen competition with respondent's magazines and tends to create for the respondent a monopoly in the business of publishing magazines of the character of those published by respondent."

Even as to the physical facts and occurrences upon which the controversy arises, these findings are vague and lacking in precision. The so-called "finding" that the contract "has proved and is unfair," and that its effect "has been and is" to substantially lessen competition and tend to create a monopoly, is the barest assertion of unsupported opinion; it is impossible to tell whether it is intended to.assert a fact, or an economic judgment, or an opinion of law. Turn now, by way of contrast, to the opinion of Judge Buffington, in the Circuit Court of Appeals, where the case was carried for review.[35] Observing that "an examination of these findings of fact shows that no findings whatever have been made in reference to the greater part of the vast volume of testimony in this case," the court proceeds in an opinion thirty-five pages long to develop from the record what actually had occurred. It seems that the Curtis Publishing Company had developed, in the course of years, a remarkable sales organization composed of young boys, mostly still in school, and employed on a part-time basis. The boys were organized into a league, membership being dependent in part on standing in school, as well as on efficiency in making sales. Local "teams" were organized, in charge of distributing agents, and the educational features of the plan were entrusted to these agents as well as the business features. The plan was remarkably successful from the sales viewpoint, and in its educational aspect won the praise of as high an authority as Ex-President Eliot of Harvard University. It was correspondingly expensive to maintain; in the four years from 1914 to 1917 alone it represented an investment of over $5,500,-000. Naturally a few competitors began to cast hungry eyes on this sales system, and endeavored to persuade district managers to use the Curtis boys in selling their papers as well as those of the Curtis Publishing Company. Some of the district managers were regular news dealers, but the court found from an exhaustive review of evidence that what the competitors were aiming at was the appropriation of the sales system organized at much cost by the respondent. It was to protect itself against these would-be appropriators that the Curtis Publishing Company inserted the clause in its contract, and it was against them alone that it was enforced.

[35] Curtis Publishing Co. *v.* Federal Trade Commission, 270 Fed. 881 (1921).

All this elaborate testimony appeared in the official records of the Commission. It was doubtless the view of the Commission that it did not constitute in law a defense to the complaint; hence it was ignored in the findings.

Another feature of this case must be mentioned. Under the terms of Section 3 of the Clayton Act there is a violation of law only if the transaction constitutes a lease, sale, or contract of sale. A mere consignment to an agent is not within the language of the section. Upon their face, the contracts between the Curtis Publishing Company and its retail distributors purported to be mere contracts of agency, contemplating sale on consignment. Whether they were what they purported to be, or whether, instead, they were disguised contracts of sale, was therefore a crucial issue in the case, so far as the charge under the Clayton Act was concerned. It is impossible to conceive that this issue was not clearly in the examiner's mind when he prepared his findings. Yet this is what he found: "That in the course of such commerce the respondent has made sales of its magazines to *or entered into contracts for the sale of the same with* certain persons, partnerships or corporations." The use of the word "or" negatives the force of the first part of the finding; the italicized phrase is a masterpiece of ambiguity. The text of the contract is not given nor are its terms set forth except as above stated. Both the Circuit Court of Appeals and the Supreme Court subsequently held that the contracts contemplated an agency rather than a sale. The case strongly suggests that the examiner purposely used an ambiguous phrase to smooth over a defect in the proof.

A case against a well-known mail order house illustrates the same weakness.[36] The complaint was issued on May 4, 1920, and charged that Montgomery Ward & Company "has been within two years last past, and still is,"

[36] Federal Trade Commission *v.* Montgomery Ward & Co., 3 F.T.C.D. 151 (1920).

offering for sale a liquid roofing cement advertised to contain no coal tar, when in truth and in fact it does contain coal tar, "which respondent has well known." The docket shows that on September 10, 1920, an agreed statement of facts was made, "said agreed statement of facts," the report recites, "being in lieu of evidence, no testimony being taken or other evidence offered herein." The agreed statement[37] sets forth in detail that respondent had been purchasing the liquid cement in question for some time from a Cleveland manufacturer, and that the president of the Cleveland company had told the paint advertisement writer of respondent that the cement contained no coal tar, and had suggested this as a valuable advertising point. On January 14, 1920, a representative of the Federal Trade Commission called on officers of Montgomery Ward & Company, and charged verbally that the product did contain coal tar. Tests were made by respondent, and the presence of coal tar was revealed. The company thereupon returned all the stocks on hand to the manufacturer, and has since sold only a product which contained no coal tar. All this appears at length in the agreed statement, stipulated by both parties, but it does not appear in the published findings. The findings aver that respondent has been, for more than two years last past, offering for sale a liquid roof cement represented to contain no coal tar, "and that said representation was false, because said liquid roof cement did in truth and fact contain coal tar, *all of which respondent knew or ought to have known.*" The falsity and misleading character of the representation are emphasized by repetition in two paragraphs of the findings. Finally there is a statement that "there was no evidence to show that the respondent did in fact know that the said liquid roof cement did contain coal tar," and that on or about January 14, 1920, "being informed by a representative

---

[37] *See* text in Docket No. 610.

of the Federal Trade Commission of said false and misleading advertisement'' the respondent discontinued the
further sale of the liquid cement in question. Nothing
appears as to the source from which the cement was
obtained, nor is the stipulated fact revealed that the representations were made in reliance upon the statement
of the president of the manufacturing company. Whether
or not the order to cease and desist was properly made,
the published findings are obviously unfair to the respondent, and the phrase which I have italicized is both
gratuitous and unjust.

Somewhat similar is the case against Park & Tilford,
as distributor, and Louis Phillipe, Inc., as manufacturer
of a toilet preparation known as ''Creme Angelus.''[38]
The findings are based upon agreed facts embodied in
stipulations of counsel. It seems that the product was
made in New York City, and the whole output sold by
the manufacturer to Park & Tilford, in the same city.
The stipulation recites that ''since January, 1920, the
respondent, Louis Phillipe, Inc., has not sold or shipped
any of said products outside of the City of New York.''
Park & Tilford, however, sell the product in other states.
The contract between the two concerns provided that
Park & Tilford should have full control of the advertising,
as to subject matter, style, and arrangement, the cost,
however, to be divided equally. Some advertisements appeared in the daily press which gave the impression, by
verbal and pictorial representation, that ''Creme Angelus'' contained lemon juice, whereas in fact it contained
no lemon juice, the ingredient being ''oil of lemon,'' made
from lemon rind. The stipulation proceeds:

5. That the following are the circumstances under which the
advertisement quoted in Paragraph 3 was published:

[38] F.T.C. *v.* Louis Phillipe, Inc., 5 F.T.C.D. 136 (1922). *See* Docket
No. 771.

That shortly after Park & Tilford took the exclusive sale of "Creme Angelus" it arranged with the advertising firm of Jules P. Storm & Sons, Inc., of 120 West 41st Street, New York City, which is a reputable concern, to conduct an advertising campaign with reference to said "Creme Angelus." In the course of this advertising campaign copy of an advertisement was sent to Park & Tilford by Storm & Sons which contained the statement that Creme Angelus contained lemon juice. Immediately upon this copy being submitted to Park & Tilford the manager of its druggists' sundries department notified Storm & Sons that all reference to the fact that Creme Angelus contained lemon juice must be stricken from the advertisements. This was done, but through some inadvertence in the office of Storm & Sons, the original copy went out and the advertisement containing the representation that "Creme Angelus" contained lemon juice appeared on two occasions, and on these occasions because of the inadvertence mentioned.

It would seem that this succinct statement, stipulated to by counsel for the Commission as well as by respondent, should have appeared, as such, in the findings. It seems to show clearly that neither respondent had anything to do with the misleading advertisement, unless upon some legal theory of responsibility for the unauthorized acts of an agent or independent contractor. In the published findings, the agreed statement of facts is completely rewritten, and while, perhaps, if critically scanned, the findings contain no statement of fact inconsistent with the stipulation, the impression which they give is very different. Partly this is a matter of emphasis. Thus the stipulated fact that respondent has made no sales outside of the city is omitted from the findings, but appears inferentially in the finding that by the terms of the contract Park & Tilford agreed to purchase the entire output of Louis Phillipe, Inc., delivery to take place at the factory in New York. There is, however, a finding that the respondent, Park & Tilford, "in promoting the sale and distribution of these products, *advertised* the cleansing cream trade-marked 'Creme Angelus,' on the 31st day of October, 1920 as follows:" The text of the advertisement follows. Subsequently there appears the following paragraph:

Par. 6. The advertising campaign of these products was conducted by a reputable advertising agency in the city of New York, under the direction of Park & Tilford. During this campaign Park & Tilford gave directions to this advertising agency to omit from the advertisements statements that "Creme Angelus" contained lemon juice. Through an inadvertence on the part of the advertising agency, twice after notice were statements made that lemon juice was used in the preparations.

There is a finding that the effect of the advertisements has been to mislead purchasers and the general public, and a conclusion that "the practices of said respondents," under the circumstances described, are "unfair methods of competition in interstate commerce."

From the stipulation, as well as from the brief filed by the Commission's attorney, it is apparent that the conclusion and order are based on a theory of *respondeat superior*. In the brief it is stated that: "The claim that the advertisements which contained the positive statement that the preparation contained lemon juice, were inserted contrary to the instructions of Park & Tilford, cannot be relied upon by respondents as an extenuating circumstance, for the reason that the agency which had charge of the advertising was respondent's agent, and respondents are bound by the act of such agent."[39] And the brief points out that while Louis Phillipe, Inc., is not engaged in interstate commerce, it is in law a participant in the illegal act because it paid half the cost of the advertising. A reader of the findings, however, taking

[39] Brief of counsel for Federal Trade Commission, p. 3, Docket No. 771.

them at their face value, hardly gets the impression that the case rests upon such an artificial legal theory. Instead he finds the direct statement that respondent "advertised" the product in the misleading manner indicated, that the advertisements mislead the public, and that "the practices of said respondents" are unfair methods of competition. The only extenuating circumstance revealed by the findings is that sometime during the course of the campaign Park & Tilford directed that the reference to lemon juice be omitted. The essential fact that these instructions were given "immediately" upon receipt of proof of the advertisement, apparently before any advertisement appeared, is not brought out in the findings. It would seem in such a case that the published report of the case should clearly show that respondents have violated the act, if at all, only on a legal theory of *respondeat superior,* and did not themselves participate in the deceptive conduct.

I pass now to a case against a company not so well known as the respondents in the Montgomery Ward and Park & Tilford cases, but nevertheless equally entitled to just treatment on behalf of the Commission. A complaint was filed against the Rockford Varnish Company, of Rockford, Illinois, charging that respondent, with the intent, purpose, and effect of stifling and suppressing competition, for more than one year last past, has been, systematically and on a large scale, giving and offering to give to employees of customers and prospective customers, as an inducement to influence purchases, and "without other consideration therefor," gratuities such as liquor, cigars, meals, theatre tickets, and entertainment. Another paragraph, in similar verbiage, charges secret payments of "large sums of money." The findings set forth that respondent has "in several instances" given foremen finishers of furniture manufacturers meals, cigars, Christmas turkeys, etc., and that "one of

the purposes of said gratuities'' was to induce them to
influence their employers to make purchases from respondent. On one occasion, it is stated, a salesman of
respondent offered to give ''a certain foreman finisher
. . . without the knowledge and consent of his employer
. . . certain sums of money,''—but that the offer was
made without respondent's knowledge or approval, and
contrary to express instructions. There is also a somewhat obscure statement that respondent's relations with
Rockford manufacturers (the nature of which is not revealed) ''were not such as to relieve respondent from
the necessity of competing for the trade of such consumers'' with other varnish companies doing an interstate business. The order to cease and desist covers the
giving of money as well as of other kinds of gratuities.
While the findings are general, and, as to the giving of
money, somewhat weak, they do not differ substantially
from the findings in scores of commercial bribery cases
in the Commission's published reports.

The docket, however, reveals a story which gives the
case individuality and interest. It seems that Rockford,
Illinois, has been for years a furniture manufacturing
centre. The furniture companies are a community affair,
often owned by the workmen themselves or by the de-
scendants of former workmen, many of them of Swedish
origin. Dissatisfied with conditions in the varnish trade,
and especially with the practice of commercial bribery so
generally prevalent, substantially all the companies had
joined in organizing the Rockford Varnish Company,
which undertook to manufacture varnish in Rockford.
From 92 per cent to 95 per cent of the varnish company's
business was local, although it tried at times, on the whole
unsuccessfully, to get some business in adjoining states.
Substantially, it was a community venture, owned and
controlled by the local furniture companies and operated
for their benefit.

It seems that the town of Rockford has always had the "picnic" habit. When the hot weather comes, someone organizes a party to spend a few days "at the lakes," swimming and fishing. The general manager of respondent was often a leader in these outings. He would call up some of his friends, generally among the officers of the stockholding mills, often among their buyers, and suggest a trip to the lakes. The officer in question would gather together a few friends, generally among his employees, contribute his automobile, and the "party" was launched. There was of course nothing secret about the trips, and unless a contrary inference is created by the mere fact that the parties included employees of respondent's customers, there is no evidence in the record of any wrongful purpose. The expenses were generally borne by the participants, although on one occasion the Rockford Varnish Company paid a bill for a dinner at a country hotel, at the rate of 75 cents per guest. On another occasion, again with the full knowledge and acquiescence of their employers, the company sent to the finishing foreman in each stockholding mill a Christmas turkey. The only testimony as to the purpose of these gifts was that of the general manager, who said that since the varnish company was owned by the mills, it seemed a convenient conduit through which such expenses should be met.

As to the offer of money referred to in the findings, the record contains the testimony of the buyer of a Grand Rapids furniture house that a Mr. Franklin, then a salesman of respondent, called on him and offered him a commission of $5 a barrel on all purchases, but that the offer was rejected. The undisputed testimony of the general manager of the Rockford Varnish Company was that he had specifically directed his salesmen never to offer bribes, and that he had never heard of an instance in which the practice was indulged in. It was also an undisputed fact that Franklin's salary was $100 a month, and that his expense accounts, including railroad fares and hotel expenses, averaged only $142 a month. Franklin himself was no longer in respondent's employ, and was apparently not available as a witness.

Whether or not the evidence warranted the issuance of an order to cease and desist, is not here relevant. My point is that the record contained an elaborate and on its face fairly convincing defense, which should have been presented and disposed of in the Commission's "report in writing" upon the facts, before respondent could fairly be held up to the public as a giver of commercial bribes.

A case against an Ohio breeder of hogs is worthy of note, because the findings seem on their face to be unusually full and specific.[40] The complaint is that respondent advertised for sale an alleged breed of swine known as Ohio Improved Chesters, or O. I. C.'s, claiming that they were a distinct breed from the usual Chester Whites and superior thereto, and that two of the O. I. C. breed "weighed 2806 pounds." Especial immunity from cholera was claimed for the O. I. C.'s. In fact, the complaint charged, they were no different from the Chester Whites, and were not peculiarly immune from disease. As to the 2806 pound hogs, the advertisements were said to give the impression that these phenomena were then or recently in existence, whereas in fact two alleged specimens of the year 1868 were referred to. The findings cover nine printed pages, and contain much interesting information of a technical character as to the breeding and genealogy of hogs. It is found that all authors of national reputation on the subject, who have made personal investigations, state that the O. I. C. is only a "strain or type" of the Chester White, and not a separate breed: that in expositions and livestock shows they are so classed, except

[40] Federal Trade Commission v. L. B. Silver Co., 4 F.T.C.D. 73 (1921).

that some fairs, "induced to do so for financial considerations," give the O. I. C. a "special," but not a "separate" classification. The National Association of Swine
Records refused membership to the O. I. C. Swine Breeders' Association, as such, on the ground that the O. I. C.
was not a distinct breed. In support of this conclusion
the findings invoke the cumulative testimony of "eminent
professors of swine breeding," of "practical prominent
hog growers of National reputation," of the Canadian
Government, of federal and state officials, of local veteri-
narians, and of "the general public in and around Salem,
Ohio." The marshaling of evidence is on its face complete
and convincing; in fact, before the opinion of the Circuit
Court of Appeals in this case appeared[41] I had tabulated
the case as worthy of special comment because of its
clear and apparently convincing findings.

The opinion of the Circuit Court of Appeals, however,
reveals the following facts, shown by the evidence, but
not alluded to in the findings: 1. That L. B. Silver and
his successors have claimed since 1870 that the O. I. C. is
a distinct breed. 2. That no one had taken any action to
challenge the truth of this claim until 1916, and again in
1918, when complaints were made to the postal authorities, which, however, failed of their purpose. 3. That it
was claimed by respondent (though not proved, since the
matter rested on tradition) that the original O. I. C. was
a cross between a Chester White and a Mammoth English
hog. 4. That whether or not this was so, "there is no
conflict in the evidence that by careful selection and systematic mating he did accomplish a substantial improvement in the original stock, and that the result of his
efforts was a valuable contribution to progress in swine
breeding." 5. As to what constitutes a distinct breed, the

[41] L. B. Silver & Co. *v.* Federal Trade Commission, C.C.A. 6th, 289
Fed. 985 (advance sheets, September 6, 1923).

court found "a sharp and irreconcilable conflict in the expert opinion evidence." One group of breeders and experts took the view that where the blood line goes back to the foundation stock, there cannot be a distinct breed; another group, that a distinct breed may be established through inbreeding and selection. 6. That the words "breed" and "strain" were used indiscriminately by many breeders, so that it was not of controlling importance whether the O. I. C. is a separate breed or a strain. 7. That at time of the complaint there were registered in the herd book of the O. I. C. Swine Breeders, about 950,-000 hogs, whereas but 90,000 were registered in the books of the three Chester White Associations. The court concluded that regardless of the merits of the controversy, and even giving conclusive effect to the Commission's finding that the O. I. C. was not in fact a distinct breed, the subject was one of long-standing scientific dispute, upon which honest opinions could be entertained on either hand, and that it was not an unfair method of competition to express claims based upon either view of the controversy.

As to the 2806 pound hogs, the opinion reveals that they have been featured in advertising for forty years; that at one time the advertising read "two hogs *weigh* 2806 pounds," but that some years before the complaint was filed this was changed to "two hogs *weighed* 2806 pounds." As to this feature also, therefore, the complaint was vacated. In some other respects it was sustained.

The case speaks for itself. It is obvious, whether the Commission or the Circuit Court of Appeals is right in its ultimate conclusions, that the Commission's findings failed to give an adequate account of respondent's defense, or even to mention the evidence given in respondent's behalf.

A complaint was issued against the Wayne Oil Tank

& Pump Company,[42] a manufacturer of automatic measuring pumps, charging, among other things, that respondent, with the intent, purpose, and effect of stifling and suppressing competition, had by divers means and methods procured customers and prospective customers to "cancel and rescind orders and contracts" placed and made with competitors. The complaint also charged that respondent, with the purpose, intent, and effect of annoying, embarrassing, and restraining its competitors, systematically and on a large scale induced salesmen of its competitors to leave their employment, by offering them employment with the respondent.

An agreed statement of facts was entered into, of which the first three paragraphs contain the formal statements as to corporate organization and interstate business contained in the corresponding paragraphs of the published findings. Paragraph 4 of the stipulation recites that "on numerous and divers occasions" the president, and the sales and credit managers of respondent have directed its sales agents, orally, by letter, and by circular, not to cancel or interfere with orders given to competitors, and "have discharged certain of its sales agents for disobeying such orders and instructions." Nevertheless, numerous sales agents, "while acting within the scope of their employment," with the purpose, intent, and effect of stifling and suppressing competition, have induced customers, "to cancel and rescind orders and contracts." Paragraph 5 of the stipulation sets forth that for the past four years, respondent's contracts with its district managers have, with one exception, contained clauses forbidding the district manager to hire employees away from competitors. It admits that on one occasion a district manager was employed who had within a month previously thereto resigned from the employment of a com-

[42] F.T.C. *v.* Wayne Oil Tank & Pump Co., 1 F.T.C.D. 259 (1918), Docket No. 129.

peting manufacturer of pumps and tanks. It sets forth, however, that within two years last past, district managers have employed and attempted to employ salesmen of a competitor for the purpose of injuring the competitor in the conduct of its business.

In the findings, based solely on this stipulation, there is no reference whatever to the instructions to salesmen not to procure cancellations of orders, nor to the discharge of sales agents for disobeying the instructions. Nor is the clause in the contract with district managers mentioned. Instead there is a finding that respondent "through the acts of numerous of its sales agents, who were acting within the scope of their employment, . . . with the purpose, intent and effect of stifling and suppressing competition . . . has by divers means and methods induced and procured" the cancellation of orders and contracts of competitors; and that respondent "through numerous of its district managers, while engaged within the scope of their employment, has within two years last past employed and attempted to employ salesmen and sales agents of a competitor of respondent, well knowing that such salesmen and sales agents were then in the employment of such competitor." Here again the finding is obviously based upon the doctrine of *respondeat superior,* a doctrine apparently deemed applicable even where the principal has done his best to prevent the commission of the wrongful act by the employee. Yet even if it was right as a matter of law, surely the examiner was not justified in suppressing important parts of the agreed statement of facts, which strongly tended to lessen the gravity of the company's offense, if they were not a complete exoneration, and which showed that the intent to harass competitors and stifle competition was not an actual intent entertained by the management of the company, but an intent imputed to them by a fiction of law.

A complaint was filed against the firm of Korb & Dwyer, dealers in secondhand typewriters and adding machines, charging that they had advertised for sale "several hundred rebuilt, first-class Dalton Adding and Listing machines," whereas in fact they had on hand only a small number of such machines, and had no way of procuring several hundred as advertised. The only machines they had on hand were alleged to be not "rebuilt" but merely "overhauled." Obviously the case turned largely upon the correct technical meaning of the phrases "rebuilt" and "overhauled." The Commission made a finding that "the word 'rebuilt' as applied to secondhand adding machines has a well-known meaning, especially to the adding machine and typewriter trade, so that an adding machine may properly be said to be a rebuilt machine when after several years it is stripped down to its base and then built up, replacing parts that have been worn by new parts, and building into the machine at the same time any refinement and improvements made since it was manufactured."[43] It found that the leading adding machine manufacturers made it a practice not to sell new parts, so that as a practical matter, only the Dalton Company could, properly speaking, "rebuild" its own secondhand machines. It found that the false advertisement was inserted "for the purpose of misleading and deceiving the purchasing public."

Examination of the testimony shows that the definition of a "rebuilt" adding machine was based mainly on the testimony of sales representatives of the Dalton and Burroughs companies.[44] A member of the respondent firm, on the other hand, testified that in his opinion a "rebuilt" machine was one in which wornout parts had been replaced by serviceable parts, *either new or secondhand,* provided they were in good condition. I am not

[43] 4 F.T.C.D., p. 421.
[44] Transcript of testimony, pp. 17, 18, and 21.

suggesting, of course, that the Commission's conclusion upon this point is wrong, although it would seem that the finding would be entitled to more weight if it gave some reason for preferring the testimony of one witness over that of another. But it does seem that a full and fair "report in writing" should have mentioned the fact, fully established by the evidence, that at the time they inserted the advertisement, Korb & Dwyer held an option (secured by a cash deposit) on 600 secondhand Dalton machines from the General Adding Machine Exchange, which was a corporate subsidiary used by the Burroughs Adding Machine Company in disposing of secondhand machines "turned in" for new ones; and that the letter from the Burroughs subsidiary confirming the option referred to the machines as "*600 rebuilt Dalton Adding Machines.*" Yet this important piece of testimony, which strongly tended to impeach the Commission's conclusion that the use of the word "rebuilt" was false and misleading, was not mentioned in the finding.

The reader will have noticed that in several of the cases which I have analyzed, the evidence consisted exclusively of an agreed statement of facts stipulated by counsel on both sides. Where facts have been formally stipulated it seems elementary that formal findings should set forth the facts as stipulated, or at least that where any portions are omitted for the sake of brevity or because deemed immaterial, the omission should be clearly indicated in the findings. Often the findings are in fact *verbatim* reproductions of the agreed statement of facts.[45]

[45] *See,* for instance, the following: F.T.C. *v.* E. J. Brach & Co., 1 F.T.C.D. 186 (1918), Docket No. 121; F.T.C. *v.* American Agricultural Chemical Co., 1 F.T.C.D. 226 (1918), Docket No. 79; F.T.C. *v.* Baltimore Hub-Wheel & Mfg. Co., 1 F.T.C.D. 395 (1919), Docket No. 197; F.T.C. *v.* Joseph Simmonds, 2 F.T.C.D. 11 (1919), Docket No. 210; F.T.C. *v.* Brown Portable Conveying Machinery Co., 2 F.T.C.D. 143 (1919), Docket No. 235; F.T.C. *v.* Nestlé's Food Co., Inc., 2 F.T.C.D.

Yet in a distressingly large number of cases the examiner seems to have felt himself privileged to rewrite the agreed facts, leave out what is unfavorable to the conclusions which he desires to reach, and even to make additions and alterations which substantially change the meaning or emphasis of the statement. And this is done without any indication on the face of the published findings that the agreed statement is altered. All that appears is the recital in the preamble that counsel for the respective parties have made an agreed statement of facts, and have stipulated that it may be treated as the evidence in the case, and that the Commission has thereupon made its findings. I have given some examples, but more can be added.

A complaint against the Albany Chemical Company[46] charged that upon expiration of The Bayer Company's patent for "aspirin," and the cancellation of the name as a trade mark on the ground that it had become merely descriptive, respondent had procured the registration of the name on its own behalf with numerous state authorities, and was falsely claiming in its advertising that the word was its registered trade-mark property. An agreed statement of facts substantially admitted the charge, but added that the registration of the word "Aspirin" by the respondent was made on advice of counsel; that as soon as the matter was called to the company's attention by the Commission, the practices were abandoned; and that respondent is now as rapidly as possible abandoning the registration of the name.[47] The findings follow the agreed statement in substantially the

171 (1919), Docket No. 274; F.T.C. *v.* The Good Wear Tire & Tube Co., 2 F.T.C.D. 216 (1920), Docket No. 403; F.T.C. *v.* The Aeolian Co., 3 F.T.C.D. 124, Docket No. 268 (1920).

[46] F.T.C. *v.* Albany Chemical Co., 3 F.T.C.D. 369 (1921).

[47] *See* Paragraph 14 of Agreed Statement of Facts, Docket No. 700.

same language, except that the defensive matter above summarized is wholly omitted.

In another case[48] a maker of "rebuilt" auto tires was charged with advertising that the tires were guaranteed to give 4000 miles' service, and would be replaced at half price if they failed to do so, the implied representation that they would in fact run 4000 miles being alleged to be false and misleading. I give in parallel columns the paragraph of the stipulation, and of the findings relating to this charge:

Par. 4 of Stipulation.	*Par. 6 of Findings of Fact.*
That a circular was distributed under the name of Akron Tire Co., Inc., containing an advertisement representing substantially that if a tire failed to give service of 4000 miles, such tire would be replaced at one-half the price paid; that the advertisement tended to create the belief and impression among users of automobile tires that the said tires sold by respondents could be expected to give a service of 4000 miles; that *many* of them did give such service; and those which did not, were replaced by respondents on the receipt from the customer of one-half of the original purchase price.	That a circular was distributed under the name of the Akron Tire Co., Inc., containing an advertisement representing substantially that if a tire failed to give service of 4000 miles, such tire would be replaced at one-half the price paid; that *some* of the tires did give this service, and that those which did not were replaced for one-half the original purchase price, but that the advertisement tended to create the belief and impression among users of automobile tires that the said tires sold by respondents could be expected to give a service of 4000 miles.

It will be noticed that by a rearrangement of clauses the emphasis is completely changed. One is tempted to

[48] F.T.C. *v.* Akron Tire Co., Inc., 2 F.T.C.D. 119 (1919), Docket No. 253.

ask by what warrant the examiner felt himself entitled to change the word "many," which I have italicized in the stipulated facts, to the word "some," similarly italicized in the findings. Although the stipulation above quoted obviously destroys the Commission's case upon this point, an order was nevertheless entered to cease and desist wording its advertisements so as to give the impression that its tires could reasonably be expected to give a service of 4000 miles.

In a commercial bribery case[49] the complaint was issued May 13, 1921. The answer was an informal letter of the vice-president of the company, admitting that his company had once indulged in the practice, but stating that he was in thorough accord with the Commission's attempt to root it out, and maintaining that he had succeeded in stopping the practice, so far as his company was concerned, in the summer of 1920. Paragraph 4 of the agreed statement concludes as follows: "That the respondents assert that since June, 1920, such practices by this company and its salesmen have been discontinued and that since that time they have not used such practices in connection with their business." The findings set forth in detail the stipulated facts as to wrongdoing in 1919, but omit all reference to the claim that the company had of its own initiative discontinued the practice almost a year before the complaint was issued.

In a case against a mail order lumber house[50] it was charged that respondent had circulated as an advertisement a misleading account of certain proceedings by the Federal Trade Commission against some lumber dealers.[51] The stipulated facts admit that the report was

[49] F.T.C. *v.* Beckwith-Chandler Co. et al., 4 F.T.C.D. 108 (1921), Docket No. 769.

[50] F.T.C. *v.* Gordon-Van Tine Co., 1 F.T.C.D. 316 (1919), Docket No. 220.

[51] *See* the case discussed on its merits, *infra,* p. 210.

a gross misrepresentation of the order, but go on to say
that the advertisement was "unauthorized and undig-
nified" and that "distribution of the circular was immediately stopped for that reason when the fact of its
existence became known to the officers of respondent."
Specifically, it is agreed in the stipulation that the distribution stopped on August 1, 1918, being nearly four
months before the complaint was issued. The findings
give the text of the circular, state that it is false and misleading, and a gross misrepresentation, but fail to reveal
the stipulated fact that it was unauthorized, and was discontinued as soon as its existence became known to respondent's officers. Instead there is a finding, totally
unsupported by anything in the stipulation, that the advertisement "was calculated and designed to, and did,
deceive the trade and general public."

Paragraph 6 of the stipulation in this case contains a
list of representations admitted to have been made by respondent, ending with the statement that such representations "were not wholly true, and did unfairly tend to
mislead purchasers and the general public." The representations are set forth in five separate sub-paragraphs
lettered (a) to (e), respectively. The same paragraph,
lettering and all, appears in Paragraph 5 of the findings,
but carefully edited by deleting all matters favorable to
respondent. Thus sub-paragraph (a) admits a representation that "the United States Government vouches for,
and guarantees the reliability, honesty and business
methods of respondent," but adds, in parenthesis, that
"no representations to this effect have been made since
February, 1916."[52] This latter sentence does not appear
in the corresponding sub-paragraph of the findings. Instead there is interpolated a clause, not included in the
stipulation, "that such statements carry the impression

[52] The complaint was issued November 25, 1918, and the findings
made February 6, 1919.

that the Post Office Department censors respondent's advertising matter." The stipulated matter omitted flatly contradicts the statement in the beginning of Paragraph 5 of the findings, that the representations have been circulated "for more than two years last past." Sub-paragraph (e), in the stipulation, admits a representation that respondent saves for purchasers from $200 to $500 per building as compared with prices of "regular" dealers. The stipulation adds, in parenthesis, "Respondent has received numerous letters from its customers, many of which have come unsolicited, in which letters statements are contained that in certain cases such savings have been made." In the corresponding sub-paragraphs of the findings the matter in parenthesis is omitted. The concluding sentence in the stipulation, admitting that the statements "were not wholly true," is completely rewritten in the findings, and much strengthened and elaborated.

In the same case there is a finding that respondent, "for more than two years last past, did offer to pay to local contractors, builders, and carpenters a bonus or so-called commission without the knowledge of the purchaser or consumer, as an inducement to influence such contractors or builders to push or favor the sale of respondent's lumber and building materials over those of its competitors."[53] The phraseology is like that of a commercial bribery case. The only evidence to support it, however, is Paragraph 5 of the stipulation, which shows that offer of a commission was made on a printed form of cash certificate, that the payment of such commissions is a common practice, and that "only two (2) per cent of the allowances were paid to contractors without the knowledge of consumers."

A case against a manufacturer of underwear,[54] at Ben-

[53] 1 F.T.C.D. 322-323.
[54] F.T.C. v. Bradford Co., 2 F.T.C.D. 207, Docket No. 346 (1920).

nington, Vermont, illustrates the same tendency to take
liberties with stipulated facts. The complaint charged
that respondent, "with the effect of stifling and suppressing competition in the manufacture and sale of underwear
in interstate commerce," had branded as "Men's merino
shirts," and "Men's natural wool union suits," certain
underwear "composed but partly of wool." An agreed
statement of facts was entered into by counsel for the
Commission and for the respondent, which admitted the
practice complained of, and admitted that the brands and
labels "may tend to mislead the purchasing public" into
believing that the goods were made wholly of wool. In
defense of the practice, however, the stipulation set
forth that the custom of using the brands in question is
"general and universal in the trade," and specifically,
"that the word 'Merino' as known in the underwear trade,
signifies a fabric composed of a mixture of wool and
cotton." The stipulation adds "that there are a few
manufacturers of underwear whose products are composed wholly of wool, and are branded and labelled by
them as 'All Wool'." The findings set forth the practice
as admitted in the stipulation, and concede that there has
been for twenty years "a general custom and practice"
to use such labels, throughout the United States, although
the stronger word "universal," in the stipulation is
omitted. The findings, however, omit completely the sentence which stipulates that the word "Merino," as known
in the underwear trade, "signifies a fabric composed of
a mixture of wool and cotton." The stipulated fact
that a few manufacturers of underwear composed wholly
of wool label their produce "All Wool," is altered to
read: "that there are a few manufacturers of underwear
whose products are composed wholly of wool and are
branded and labelled by them as such." Perhaps the
stipulation was improvidently entered into by counsel,
but that is no reason for disregarding altogether an

agreed fact obviously destructive of a part of the Commission's case, or for rewriting a part of the stipulation so as to alter its sense materially.

In the case just mentioned there was at least a reference, though an inadequate one, to the respondent's defense, but in Federal Trade Commission *v.* Brown, Durrell Company,[55] decided as late as April 11, 1923, a long paragraph of the stipulation containing a similar defense, and showing that respondent had abandoned the practice nearly three years before the order was made, was not even referred to in the findings. In another recent case, also,[56] the stipulated fact that the practice had been abandoned "at least six months prior to the issuance of this complaint" was likewise omitted from the findings.

A complaint was filed against a shorthand correspondence school, which used the Pitmanic system, charging that it had circulated false and misleading statements concerning its business and the business of competitors.[57] One charge was that the respondent had circulated a pamphlet entitled "Government Reports on Pitmanic and Gregg Shorthand Writers," and containing false and misleading matter, and statements erroneously purporting to be from government reports. The stipulation conceded that the pamphlet contained what purported to be an extract of a report of a "New York High-School Committee," or the "Shorthand Section, High-School Teachers' Association," and that "this association was and is a private organization composed of individual high-school teachers and was and is not a public organization or governmental agency, *except insofar as shown by the report.*" The stipulation adds: "*The name, function and authority of such committee are stated on*

[55] 6 F.T.C.D. 79 (1923), Docket No. 678.

[56] F.T.C. *v.* Pilling & Madeley, 6 F.T.C.D. 74 (1923), Docket No. 698.

[57] F.T.C. *v.* Draughon Text Book Co., 2 F.T.C.D. 388, Docket No. 511.

pages 5 and 6 of said circular . . ." In the findings the words which I have italicized, obviously damaging to the Commission's case, are omitted. In another folder respondent had said that "the Government stenographers who draw the big salaries, who hold positions paying $5000 or more a year," use the Graham-Pitman method. Referring to this, the stipulation admits that "It is not a fact that the official stenographer for any United States court receives a salary of $5000 or more per year," but qualifies the statement by adding that "some reporters and stenographers who report for Government departments make more than $5000 per year in salaries and fees and other emoluments." The admission as to court reporters appears in the findings, but the qualifying clause, which affords some justification for advertisement complained of, is omitted. Finally, the stipulation embodies more than five pages of matter, showing that respondent had, on hearing of the objections raised by the Federal Trade Commission and the Civil Service Commission, promptly eliminated all objectionable matter from its advertising. All this is likewise omitted in the published findings.

In a misbranding case[58] the findings follow *verbatim* an agreed statement of facts, with one exception. Paragraph 6 of the agreed statement sets forth that *"while the aforesaid trade name and trade mark of 'Sol Satin' so used by the respondents may not have been adopted and used by them in bad faith for the purpose of fraudulently deceiving the public, nevertheless* the use of the word 'satin' . . . tends to deceive and mislead the public into the belief that the said fabric . . . is made either wholly or partly of silk." In the findings the words above italicized are omitted. This is the only respect in which the finding differs from the agreed facts.

[58] F.T.C. *v.* S. M. Hexter & Co., 2 F.T.C.D. 41 (1919), Docket No. 97.

In a proceeding against a small producer of moving picture films[59] the only evidence was an agreed statement stipulated by respondents. The findings recite that the respondents had purchased old films, changed the names and titles, and reissued them "as new and original motion picture films;" that the substitution of new names was done "with the intent, purpose and effect of stifling and suppressing competition in the motion picture industry," and "furthermore," that it was "calculated and designed to and does deceive the general public into the belief" that the films were new. Examination of the stipulated facts shows that the only admission was that the old films were exhibited under new names and titles "without designating and advertising said motion picture films to have been old films and reissues." Nothing appears in the stipulation as to the intent, purpose, and effect of stifling competition, nor as to the calculation and design of deceiving the public.

In a complaint against an Ohio concern[60] the charge was that respondent was selling as "second run" linseed oil and "second run" turpentine, products adulterated with low grade mineral oils. Paragraph 3 of the agreed statement of facts sets forth that there is no such product as "second run" linseed oil, since linseed oil is pressed from flaxseed; that respondent's product is composed of 45 per cent linseed oil, 10 per cent turpentine, and 45 per cent mineral oil; and that "the use of the term 'second run' as applied to linseed oil *may possibly tend* to mislead the purchasing public into believing that linseed oil sold and advertised as 'second run' is a pure product and not an adulterated product." Paragraph 3 of the findings sets forth the same facts, except that the quoted

[59] F.T.C. *v.* The Lasso Pictures Co., 1 F.T.C.D. 374 (1919), Docket No. 222.

[60] F.T.C. *v.* Plomo Specialty Mfg. Co., 2 F.T.C.D. 195 (1919), Docket No. 448.

language is changed to read: "That the use of the term 'second run' *misleads* the purchasing public into believing that linseed oil sold and advertised as 'second run' is a pure product." In Paragraph 4, relating to turpentine, similar changes are made: the stipulated fact that the use of the term "second run" applied to turpentine "may have a tendency" to mislead the public, is changed into a finding that it "misleads" the public. In the same paragraph of the agreed statement, the stipulated fact that respondent "has not represented the turpentine compound sold by it as pure and unadulterated turpentine" is totally omitted from the published findings.

The complaint against a maker of disinfectants[61] charged the circulation of an advertisement purporting to quote an official report of the Public Health Service condemning "drip machines" as toilet disinfectors. In fact the excerpt was from a paper of a private physician, published as a matter of information by the Health Service, but not officially endorsed. The complaint also charged the circulation of letters "to the public" referring to drip cans as frauds. An agreed statement was drawn up, and it was stipulated by counsel that it should be taken "as all of the evidence" in the case. One offending letter and "not more than two or three similar letters"[62] were admitted to have been sent by the Eastern General Manager of respondent, and the misleading circular was admitted to have been sent out from both the Chicago and New York offices. As to the circular, the fact is stipulated that since being informed that "the Government of the United States did not, by publishing the article of Dr. Thomas R. Crowder in the bulletin, intend to endorse all of the statements made by him," respondent had caused

[61] F.T.C. *v.* Plunkett Chemical Co., 3 F.T.C.D. 53 (1920), Docket No. 572.

[62] In the published findings the words "not more than" do not appear. The omission is trivial, but quite characteristic.

all the circulars in question to be destroyed. This is omitted from the findings. As to the letters referring to drip cans as frauds, the agreement recites: "that the respondent himself, whose home, general office and place of business is in Chicago, Illinois, did not know that his agent had sent out the above named letter or letters of a similar character to other persons; that when complaint was made to him (the respondent) that such letters were being sent out he directed his agent not to write or send out any other such letters as the one above mentioned; that the agent has complied with the instructions given by the respondent and has not sent out any such letters since he was so directed." Not a word of this appears in the published findings.

In a case in which it was charged that respondent had sold as "Army and Navy Paints" a product not in fact made for the Government or upon government specifications, the stipulation admitted the facts charged, but set forth that respondent realized immediately afterwards that the advertisement was misleading and gave orders to discontinue it. In response to all inquiries resulting from the advertisement, he sent the prospective purchaser a blank which set forth that the paint was "our special brand." "Said respondent used the aforesaid acknowledgment blanks," continues the stipulation, "to give notice of such facts to the prospective purchasers of said paint." In the findings this is changed to read: "Respondent used said acknowledgment blanks because he realized that the said advertisements were misleading and improper." In this way a fact stipulated as evidence of respondent's good faith was made to appear as a confession of wrongdoing.

A case against the American Hosiery Company[63] is interesting, because it shows that the Commission itself

[63] 3 F.T.C.D. 1 (1920).

had, upon second thought, some compunctions as to the
manner in which stipulations favorable to the respondent
were omitted in the findings. The case involved misbranding of goods composed partly of cotton, and Paragraphs 1 to 4 inclusive of the agreed statement of facts
contained a frank admission of the practice. Paragraphs
5 to 8 inclusive exonerated respondent of any deliberate
intent or purpose to mislead the public; showed that his
descriptive price lists clearly revealed the presence of
cotton in the goods in question; and that the misleading
brands in question had been in general and customary
use among underwear manufacturers for the past twenty
years. The findings, as at first made by the Commission,
included, substantially *verbatim,* Paragraphs 1 to 4 of the
stipulation, but omitted all reference to Paragraphs 5 to
8. Two months later, however, amended findings were
issued, which included all eight paragraphs of the stipulation, adding only the conclusion, not admitted in the
stipulation, "that the tendency of said labels to mislead
the public, entails interference with fair competition."

Finally, mention may be made of two cases against the
Standard Oil Company of Indiana,[64] which throw interesting light upon the Commission's conception of the
nature of an agreed statement and of its findings of fact.
The complaint in one case (Docket No. 85) involved unfair practices in the sale of petroleum products. In the
other case (Docket No. 133) unfair acts against competing makers of tanks and pumps were involved. A variety
of practices were alleged, including division of territory
with other Standard companies, "direct" sales to consumers, and threats of such sales, for the purpose of
"punishing" or intimidating local dealers; loaning tanks
and equipment on condition that they be used exclusively
in handling respondent's product; misrepresentations as

[64] Reported at 2 F.T.C.D. 26 and 2 F.T.C.D. 46, respectively.

to the quality of its products and disparaging statements concerning competitors; causing "cancellation" of orders placed with competitors; and sales below cost. There were also general charges under Sections 2 and 3 of the Clayton Act. In fact, the complaints include most of the offenses that could be brought within the scope of the Commission's jurisdiction. A year after the complaint in No. 85 was issued, public hearings were held, and a stipulation of facts was entered into, to "stand in lieu of testimony, the same as though testified to by competent witnesses, and if approved by the Commission, [it] shall be and constitute all the evidence in the case." The stipulation disposes of a number of the charges of the complaint. Thus Paragraph 4 covers four pages, and is devoted to the charge of selling direct to consumers as a means of punishing retailers. The paragraph admits that the company has established "filling stations" from which sales are made direct to consumers, but sets forth that its officers, if called, would testify that they established such stations only where there was reason to believe that they would be profitable. Paragraph 5, covering three pages, admits that certain witnesses, if called by complainant, would testify that sales agents of respondents had used threats and other unfair methods, but that the sales agents, if called, would deny such testimony. It is set forth that the officers of the company had at various times in good faith issued orders that no such threats or false statements regarding competitors would be tolerated.

A preamble to the findings recites that the "agreed statement of facts" was submitted to the Commission, subject to its approval, by "the attorneys for the respective parties," and that the Commission "approved all the agreed statements of facts *except paragraphs 4 and 5* for the purpose of this proceeding only." These are the paragraphs favorable to the respondent, mentioned above. The findings are devoted solely to the practice of leasing tanks and pumps at nominal rates with "exclusive" covenants. The reader of the Commission's published reports cannot tell whether the serious charges of the complaint, spread at large over seven pages of the printed volume of decisions, have been withdrawn, or disproved, or whether they are perhaps true but for some reason are not pressed. They are simply ignored.

The stipulation in Docket No. 133 contains a full description of the practice of leasing pumps and tanks at nominal rates. The stipulation contains the following: "that the practice of leasing, tanks and their equipments, requires a large capital investment in such outfits and equipments . . . that there have been and are many of the smaller competitors of respondent and its competitors who did not and do not engage in such practices; that many of such smaller competitors have had, and have small capital and assets and would not have been able, and are not now able to invest the capital in pumps, tanks and their equipment that is necessary in conducting either of the above business practices." The same language appears in the findings adopted September 12, 1919. A year later, for some reason that does not appear, the findings were amended by omitting the quoted language. It is not quite clear what purpose was served by striking out of the formal findings a fact admitted in an agreed statement of facts.

I have devoted perhaps an undue amount of space to these comparisons between stipulations and findings, but they will serve to show the extent of the practice of revising stipulated facts, of omitting matters favorable to respondents, and interpolating findings which are thought to strengthen the Commission's case. Of fifty-seven cases involving stipulated facts in which I have examined the original docket, twenty-seven cases have revealed important discrepancies. Most of these cases have been analyzed in this chapter, so that the reader can judge for himself the nature of the alterations. In fifteen more cases there are lesser alterations, omissions, or interpolations, but the revision is on the whole a fair one. In fifteen of the cases examined the findings conform, word for word, to the stipulated facts.

Where the respective attorneys have agreed as to the facts to be embodied in a formal stipulation, it seems only fair to the respondent that the whole stipulation, and nothing else, should go into the findings, or at least that if any part is omitted, or anything added, that fact should clearly appear in the published report. The reader is entitled to know what part of the findings the respondent admits, and what part represents merely the conclusions or interpolations of the Commission. Often the findings, after setting forth in detail the representation or other practice in question, will end with a finding that such representation is "false and misleading" or that such practice is "calculated and designed to harass or embarrass competitors." The preamble recites that the findings are based on an agreed statement, and the reader gets the impression that not only the representation or practice is admitted, but also its falsity or improper purpose. In fact, the characterization does not appear in the stipulation, but is merely the Commission's conclusion from the facts stipulated. There is no reason why the Commission should not draw such a conclusion, where it is warranted, but the report should show that it is an inference, and not an admitted fact.

The unsatisfactory character of many of the Commission's "reports in writing" is, of course, greatly enhanced by the fact mentioned at the beginning of this chapter, that the answers of respondents are not included in the published reports, and that no summary or other indication of respondent's defense is given. Instead, the findings appear in immediate juxtaposition with a complaint, in which sweeping charges are made, bristling with phrases about the intent, purpose, and effect of suppressing and stifling competition, the calculation and design of deceiving and misleading the public, and the intent to create a monopoly. For the use of generalities and stock phrases of this character, frequent enough in the findings, is even more prevalent in the complaints. By way of illustration, of the seventy-one complaints published in Volume I of the Commission's decisions, forty contain at least once the phrase "with the intent, purpose and effect of stifling and suppressing competition," or variations thereof. In one case it is repeated six times,[65] in another nine times,[66] in another twelve times.[67] Where the complaint contains serious charges, and is published in full in the reports, it is all the more important that the published findings should clearly dispose of the charges, by sustaining them or expressly dismissing them. In a number of cases, however, serious charges in the complaint are completely ignored in the findings. I have already mentioned the case against the Standard Oil Company of Indiana.[68] In a more recent case[69] the complaint was against two respondents, one a manufacturer of women's wearing apparel and the other a retailer in the city of Washington. The charge was that some coats had been sold by the manufacturer to the retailer, and by the retailer to the public, on the false representation that they were made of "Salt's Peco Plush," a proprietary brand. The complaint ascribed guilty knowledge to the retailer as well as to the manufacturer. At the trial, the retailer's representative testified that he bought the coats from the manufacturer in good faith

[65] F.T.C. *v.* Allen Sales Service, Inc., 1 F.T.C.D. 459 (1919).

[66] F.T.C. *v.* National Distilling Co., 1 F.T.C.D. 88 (1918).

[67] F.T.C. *v.* Fleischmann Co., 1 F.T.C.D. 119 (1918).

[68] *Supra,* p. 156.

[69] F.T.C. *v.* The Loeb Co., 6 F.T.C.D. 11 (1923).

on the representation that they were made of "Salt's Peco Plush," and expert witnesses were called to show that it was impossible to tell, except by the most minute examination, that the goods were not as represented. The Better Business Bureau, which seems to have originated the charge, exonerated the retailer of any wrong intention. The Commission's attorney endeavored to establish that the retailer had continued the sale even after he had been informed of the fraud, and the examiner's tentative report so found, but upon exception this finding was eliminated. The order finally adopted refers only to the manufacturer. The charge of willful fraud against the retailer is ignored, and it does not even appear that the complaint, as to the retailer, was formally dismissed. Surely a retail merchant who has been charged with dishonesty by a government agency is entitled to an explicit public vindication if the charge is not proven.

In other cases we find the following charges, embodied in the published complaints, not mentioned in the published findings: false representations, by misquotation of public records, as to the contents of a patent claim;[70] false representations that respondent was "closely affiliated" with a competitor;[71] obtaining a patent by means of "false and misleading" statements to the U. S. Patent Office;[72] secret payments of money to employees of customers to influence purchases;[73] refusal to sell organ rolls except to purchasers of respondent's pipe organs;[74] simulation of the name of a competitor;[75] concerted price

---

[70] F.T.C. *v.* Chicago Lino-Tabler Co., 1 F.T.C.D. 110 (1918).

[71] F.T.C. *v.* Standard Car Equipment Co., 1 F.T.C.D. 144 (1918).

[72] F.T.C. *v.* Nulomoline Co., 1 F.T.C.D. 400 (1919).

[73] F.T.C. *v.* Rome Soap Mfg. Co., 1 F.T.C.D. 484 (1919). In this case the complaint charged both payment of money, and giving of gratuities such as cigars, meals, entertainment, etc. Only the latter charge is mentioned in the findings.

[74] F.T.C. *v.* The Aeolian Co., 3 F.T.C.D. 124 (1920).

[75] F.T.C. *v.* National Tailoring Co., 4 F.T.C.D. 215 (1922).

maintenance by competing salt manufacturers;[76] and payment of gratuities and traveling expenses to public officials to induce them to purchase road machinery.[77] There is no valid reason why the Commission should not in all cases, as it has done in some,[78] admit frankly in its findings that some or all of the charges of the complaint were disproved at the trial or withdrawn by the Commission's counsel.

I have analyzed in this chapter a substantial number of cases in which, either from excessive zeal or from a failure to appreciate the true function of a judicial statement of facts, the examiner or attorney who drafted the findings has produced a report which is flagrantly defective when compared with the evidence or the stipulated facts. I repeat again the caution which I have previously expressed, that these cases are in the minority, and that the reader should not jump to the conclusion that all the findings are similarly defective, or that the Commission has a settled policy of impartiality. Doubtless a great deal depends upon the calibre of the examiner or attorney in charge of the case, and there are many cases in which a desire to be fair and impartial is apparent. But the number of the cases in which the findings are manifestly unfair is sufficient to seriously impair the value and reliability of all the findings. And regardless of accuracy and fairness, the formal character of the findings, the use of "legal" phraseology and of ambiguous words and stock phrases, and the frequently obvious attempt to frame

[76] F.T.C. v. Salt Producers' Asso. et al., 5 F.T.C.D. 67 (1922).

[77] F.T.C. v. Russell Grader Mfg. Co., 5 F.T.C.D. 77 (1922). The findings, however, sustained the charge of allowing commissions for the sale of road machinery to firms of local dealers of which public officials were members.

[78] As in F.T.C. v. The Silvex Co., 4 F.T.C.D. 41 (1921); F.T.C. v. The L. B. Silver Co., 4 F.T.C.D. 73 (1921); F.T.C. v. Behrend's, 5 F.T.C.D. 303 (1922).

findings with a view to the legal result desired, rather than as a mirror of events and circumstances,—all these tend to make the findings unsatisfactory and unconvincing, and to explain in some degree the scant respect with which they have been treated by some of the appellate courts.

CHAPTER IV

DECEPTIVE AND DISHONEST PRACTICES

IN previous chapters I have outlined the method by which the Federal Trade Commission arrives at its findings of fact, and have commented on the form and quality of the findings. In this chapter and the next I will attempt a more detailed appraisal of the output of the Commission in the different types of cases which it has handled. The cases will be classified according to the nature of the practice involved, and the inquiry will be, as to each type of practice, what contribution the Commission has made toward the substantive development of the law, and whether the procedure to which the Commission adheres is such as to enable it to deal satisfactorily with the practice in question.

The cases divide themselves conveniently into two major categories: those which involve an element of fraud or dishonesty, and those which involve practices not dishonest, but for some other reason supposed to be restrictive of fair competition. Cases in the first category arise exclusively under Section 5 of the Trade Commission Act, while cases in the second category arise either under that section, or under Sections 2, 3, 7, or 8 of the Clayton Act.

Without attempting any academic catalogue of frauds, some preliminaries may be helpful before turning to the specific dishonest or deceptive practices with which the present chapter is concerned.

When a citizen has been induced to part with his money by false representations, he is the person primarily injured, and it is his protection that has been the main concern of the host of punitive laws and ordinances designed to punish commercial fraud. The criminal law punishes one who obtains money by false pretenses; federal statutes protect consumers against misbranding or adulteration of foods and drugs; against the use of the mails to defraud; against deception by improper grading of certain agricultural staples. State statutes and local ordinances give protection against dishonest advertising, fraudulent weights and measures, and similar forms of commercial fraud. The Federal Trade Commission, however, is not a general censor of business morals. It can take cognizance of a dishonest practice only if it is a competitive practice in the course of commerce as defined in the statute. A fraud which merely injures the person defrauded, without affecting or tending to affect a competitor, appears to be beyond the Commission's jurisdiction. It is concerned with the consumer only because the consumer is in the long run benefited by honest competition. Although the approach is different, the field covered is nevertheless much the same, for it is rare that a deceptive practice in the course of commerce is not a method of competition. Two men are commercial competitors when they are endeavoring to fill the same commercial wants by offering the same or similar goods. Any practice, device, or course of conduct adopted by either to improve his relative position as compared with the other, or to prevent the other from gaining on him, is a method of competition. It may be aimed primarily at increasing his own sales, or it may be aimed at hindering the sales of the competitor. In either event, if the method used is deceptive, it is an unfair method of competition.

Accordingly it is not surprising to find that the Federal Trade Commission has encroached upon many fields already well occupied by other tribunals or administrative agencies. Deception in the course of commerce is the foundation of the jurisdiction of courts of equity in cases involving trade marks and trade names, and "unfair competition" in the narrower sense of the word. The prevention of fraud, no less than the preservation of health, is the basis of the pure food and drugs acts, and of the many similar police measures, both state and federal, already referred to. For this reason it is especially important to estimate fairly the extent to which the Commission is fitted, by its powers and procedure, to deal with such cases, and whether it is expending time and energy upon cases which can more effectively be handled elsewhere.

TRADE MARKS AND TRADE NAMES

I will begin with those cases, familiar to all lawyers, in which a manufacturer or dealer complains that a competitor is simulating his trade mark or trade name, or by some other form of misrepresentation is causing confusion among customers as to the origin or identity of the goods they purchase. The misrepresentation may take one of two forms. It may lead the customer to think that the goods he is buying from the competitor were in fact made by the complainant. Or it may lead the customer to think that the competitor, rather than the complainant, is the manufacturer of all goods sold under the brand in question. In either case good will belonging to the complainant has been wrongfully appropriated and the public has been deceived. The wrong may be aggravated where the competitor sells, under the complainant's brand, a grossly inferior article, thus in effect representing that all articles sold under that brand are equally poor in quality.

Although analytically they are closely allied, in considering available remedies it is necessary to distinguish between cases in which the simulation is of a registered trade mark, and where it is of a trade name or device not registered. Where a mark, affixed to goods sold in interstate or foreign commerce, is eligible for registration and has been registered under the Trade Mark Act, it is protected by a special procedure set forth in that Act.[1] Where there is a dispute as to the right to use a trade mark (in view of its possible interference with another mark previously in use), the question may be adjudicated, in the first instance, according to prescribed procedure, by an examiner in the Patent Office, with a right of appeal to the Commissioner of Patents, and to the Court of Appeals of the District of Columbia. Or it may be determined in a litigation in the district court, between the adverse claimants, the registration being in such cases *prima facie* evidence of "ownership." In such a case the jurisdiction of the district court does not depend upon diversity of citizenship, nor upon the amount in controversy. Where an infringement is found to exist, the infringing mark may be denied registration, or its registration canceled; further use of the infringing mark may be enjoined; where there is guilty knowledge, any wrongful profits derived from the infringement may be required to be accounted for; and damages may be awarded, whether the litigation is on the law or the equity side, up to three times the proven losses sustained by the plaintiff. Infringing labels and wrappers may be destroyed by the court. In addition state courts have concurrent jurisdiction, often aided by special statutory provisions.

Where the mark is one which cannot be registered as a technical trade mark, or where the simulation is of the form, size, color, or other distinctive attribute of the complainant's goods, the statutory procedure is not available. A court of law, however (whether state or

[1] U.S. Rev. Stat., Sec. 4965.

federal), will give damages in a proper case for injury sustained on account of the fraudulent attempt of a competitor to pass off his goods as those of the plaintiff, or the plaintiff's goods as his own. A court of equity will enjoin such conduct, and will generally grant incidental damages. Where diversity of citizenship exists and the amount in controversy is sufficient, the litigation may be conducted in the Federal courts; otherwise the state courts are available.

In a series of "conference rulings," the Federal Trade Commission has held that where nothing further is involved than a claim of infringement of a patent,[2] copyright,[3] or registered trade mark,[4] the public interest does not warrant the issuance of a complaint, in the absence of important countervailing considerations. The rulings refer to the fact that special remedies are provided by Federal law in such cases. They are not, apparently, based upon any doubt as to the Commission's jurisdiction but upon an exercise of discretion in view of the adequacy of other available remedies. In several instances, however, the Commission has carried through to final order cases in which the violation of a registered trade mark appears to have been the gist of the offense charged. A maker of rebuilt automobile tires, for instance, was ordered to cease and desist from using the firm name "Racine Tire Sales Company," or the trade name "Multi-Cord" because they were found to infringe registered trade marks of the Racine Rubber Company.[5] A milliner was ordered to cease doing business in the District of Columbia under the trade name "Louise," because it conflicted with the registered trade name "Marie

[2] Conference ruling No. 74 (1 F.T.C.D. 560).

[3] Conference ruling No. 58 (1 F.T.C.D. 554).

[4] Conference ruling No. 46 (1 F.T.C.D. 548) and No. 68 (1 F.T.C.D. 557).

[5] F.T.C. v. Racine Tire Sales Co., 5 F.T.C.D. 327 (1922).

Louise.'"[6] A chemical company was ordered to cease selling disinfectants under the name "B-D Bacilli-Destroy," because it infringed the registered trade name "B-K Bacilli-Kill."[7] In a fourth case the situation was reversed: the Commission ordered the respondent to cease using a trade mark which he had duly registered in the Patent Office, on the ground that it infringed an unregistered trade name previously adopted and used by a competitor.[8]

A much larger number of cases involve simulation of names of competitors or of their products, not registered as technical trade marks. There are conference rulings in which it was held that where the use of the simulating name had been discontinued, and assurance received that it would not be resumed, it would not be in the public interest to issue a complaint.[9] The mere fact that there is a remedy by a suit at law or in equity, in state courts, and where jurisdictional requisites exist in federal courts, is not, however, considered a reason for refusing to act in such a case. There are twenty-four such cases in the reports covered by this study,[10] and in many of them

---

[6] F.T.C. *v.* Louise, 4 F.T.C.D. 323.

[7] F.T.C. *v.* Ginso Chemical Co., 4 F.T.C.D. 155.

[8] F.T.C. *v.* Hygrade Knitting Co., Inc., 4 F.T.C.D. 402.

[9] Conference Rulings No. 57 (1 F.T.C.D. 554) and No. 65 (1 F.T.C.D. 556).

[10] F.T.C. *v.* Block & Co., 1 F.T.C.D. 154; F.T.C. *v.* Geographical Pub. Co., 1 F.T.C.D. 235; F.T.C. *v.* Genevieve Symonds, 1 F.T.C.D. 424; F.T.C. *v.* Malzo Coffee Co., 2 F.T.C.D. 58; F.T.C. *v.* The Sweater Store, 2 F.T.C.D. 67; F.T.C. *v.* The Universal Battery Service Co., Inc., 2 F.T.C.D. 95; F.T.C. *v.* The Good Wear Tire & Tube Co., 2 F.T.C.D. 216; F.T.C. *v.* Himes Underwear Co., 2 F.T.C.D. 307; F.T.C. *v.* The Electric Appliance Co., 2 F.T.C.D. 335; F.T.C. *v.* The Great Republic Tire & Rubber Mfg. Co., 3 F.T.C.D. 6; F.T.C. *v.* Liberty Paper Co., 3 F.T.C.D. 13; F.T.C. *v.* Franklin Knitting Mills, 3 F.T.C.D. 144; F.T.C. *v.* Federal Press, Inc., 3 F.T.C.D. 345; F.T.C. *v.* Universal Motor Co. et al., 3 F.T.C.D. 387; F.T.C. *v.* Morgan Razor Works, 4 F.T.C.D. 22; F.T.C. *v.* Carbo Oil Co., 4 F.T.C.D. 102; F.T.C. *v.* Hall-Marvin Co.

the records are long and much time seems to have been spent by the Commission's investigators and attorneys in their preparation and trial. Some of these cases seem on the face of the record to concern themselves with matters of but slight public consequence. One case in which a complaint was issued, testimony heard, briefs filed, and a formal decision rendered, involved a family quarrel over the right to use the name "Phillips Old Time Sausage" in the District of Columbia.[11] In another case it appears from the findings that one Sammons operated a "Shade Shop" in the District of Columbia, on premises leased from the respondent, by profession a wall paperer. There was a disagreement, and Sammons threatened to move out, and started to remove his signboard. This incensed the respondent, who drew "a deadly weapon, to wit a revolver," and ordered him to stop. Thereafter he refused to speak to Sammons, and "continued this attitude of hatred and malice" to the point of opening a competing business under the name "Shade Shop." He was ordered to cease and desist from using the misleading name.[12] It is not clear what there was in the case to call for the intervention of a federal administrative tribunal.

An order of the Commission in a simple "passing off" case has been sustained by the Circuit Court of Appeals in one circuit,[13] but the court was of course concerned only with the Commission's legal jurisdiction. The

et al., 4 F.T.C.D. 285; F.T.C. *v.* Planters Mfg. Co., 4 F.T.C.D. 391; F.T.C. *v.* Hygrade Knitting Co., Inc., 4 F.T.C.D. 402; F.T.C. *v.* Paul Balme, 4 F.T.C.D. 410; F.T.C. *v.* The Best Oil Co., 5 F.T.C.D. 92; F.T.C. *v.* Juvenile Shoe Co., Inc., 5 F.T.C.D. 105; F.T.C. *v.* Warewell Co., 5 F.T.C.D. 294; F.T.C. *v.* John McQuade & Co., Inc., 6 F.T.C.D. 1.

[11] F.T.C. *v.* Phillips Brothers & Co., 4 F.T.C.D. 297 (1922). The genealogy of the Phillips family from Civil War days is rehearsed in the findings.

[12] F.T.C. *v.* Alfred Klesner, 5 F.T.C.D. 24 (1922).

[13] F.T.C. *v.* Juvenile Shoe Co., C.C.A. 9th, 289 Fed. 57 (1923).

wisdom of a proceeding by the Commission in cases of this kind seems to me to be open to serious doubt. Where a manufacturer or distributor claims that his goods are being simulated by a competitor, he has full redress in the courts, and can generally be relied upon to take all necessary steps to put a stop to any deception of the public incident to the infringement of his rights. It is not, therefore, a case in which the public interest is likely to go by default. Moreover, the Commission is generally quite unable to give an adequate remedy to the complaining party. To deal effectively with these cases, a tribunal must be in a position to do two things. Where there is a real dispute as to the substantive rights of the parties, where, for instance, each party claims in good faith the right to use a trade name or design, the tribunal must be in a position to render a decision which is just, impartial, and binding on the parties. Where, on the other hand, the rights of the complainant are clearly established, the problem is one of enforcement, and the tribunal must be equipped to compel prompt and complete obedience to its orders, and to secure effective redress for past injuries. The Federal Trade Commission cannot properly perform either of these tasks. It cannot determine disputed substantive rights, for its decisions are rendered in an *ex parte* proceeding, and are obviously not *"res adjudicata"* between the real parties to the controversy. The Commission may solemnly decide, after the most exhaustive investigation and prolonged hearing, that A has the prior right to use a certain trade device, and that B is infringing. The decision may be affirmed by the Circuit Court of Appeals upon petition to review, and by the Supreme Court on *certiorari*. Even then there is nothing to prevent B from instituting a new litigation against A in the courts, trying all the issues of fact over again, and perhaps, by presenting somewhat different evidence, obtaining a decision contrary to that reached in the Commission's case. Nor is the Commission any better fitted for the task of affording protection to private rights which are undisputed or clearly established. Suppose that the manufacturer of a well-known brand of automobile tires finds that a "pirate" concern is fraudulently simulating his name or product, and appeals to the Federal Trade Commission for protection. The Commission will send out an investigator for a preliminary report. The report must be approved by the chief examiner, then by the Board of Review, then by a commissioner, and finally by the Commission as a whole. If the decision is favorable, a complaint will issue, and the respondent has thirty days to file his answer. In due course (perhaps not for several months) the case comes on for hearing and testimony is taken. Time is then allowed for the filing of briefs and reply briefs, and, if the respondent desires, there is oral argument before the Commission. The case is taken under advisement and after further lapse of time a decision is reached and an order issued. Yet even now the pirate dealer is under no legal compulsion to cease his dishonest practices. He can continue with impunity to simulate the applicant's brand. It is only when a petition has been filed in the Circuit Court of Appeals, the transcript remitted to the court, public hearing held, and a decree issued by the court, that the proceeding acquires any "teeth." It will be unusual if such a decree can be obtained, in a contested case, within a year from the date of the original application to the Federal Trade Commission, and during that whole year the applicant may be losing business to the dishonest competitor. As an effective protection against the pirating of trade names or brands such a procedure is of course useless, and it becomes ludicrous when compared with the remedies which an ordinary court of equity can administer in such a case. If instead of appealing to the Commission the manufacturer files a bill in equity in the state or federal court (as the case may be), he can within a day or two, if the case is clear, get a restraining order or preliminary injunction, which can be violated only at the risk of paying a fine or going to jail. Such an interlocutory decree will generally put an end to the matter, and the offender will turn his talents into other channels; but even if the suit is contested the manufacturer can in a proper case be protected by the preliminary injunction during the whole course of the litigation.

Moreover, the Commission has no power to award damages for past infringement, or even for willful infringement after the order has been issued, nor can its order be made the basis for a suit for damages in the courts. In an equity suit in the courts, an award of damages or an order to account for profits derived from the infringement may be made as a part of the decree awarding an injunction.

The argument is sometimes made that there is a legitimate place for the Federal Trade Commission in cases of this sort, as the protector of the weak against the strong. A large corporation, it is said, can hire eminent lawyers and experts, and prolong the litigation until the strength and resources of the small competitor, whose private brand the corporation is trying to appropriate, have been exhausted. The difficulty with this argument is that, in the cases in which complaints have been issued, the object has as often as not been to protect a large, nationally known company against a small but unscrupulous competitor. Among the companies for whose protection such complaints have been issued are the B. F. Goodrich Company,[14] the Universal Battery Company,[15] the Goodyear Tire & Rubber Company,[16] the Vacuum Oil

[14] F.T.C. v. Diamond Holfast Rubber Co., 4 F.T.C.D. 235.

[15] F.T.C. v. Universal Battery Service Co., Inc., 2 F.T.C.D. 95, and F.T.C. v. Universal Motor Co. et al., 3 F.T.C.D. 387.

[16] F.T.C. v. The Good Wear Tire & Tube Co., 2 F.T.C.D. 216.

Company,[17] and the Herring-Hall-Marvin Safe Company.[18] These companies would hardly admit that they were applying, *in forma pauperis,* to have the Government assume the expense of their private litigations. The only other argument I have heard to justify such a proceeding by the Federal Trade Commission was advanced by the complaining witness in the United Allegretti case.[19] It seems that one Allegretti had achieved fame as a maker of candy, and that the witness' company claimed to be the only true heir to the name and business. There were, however, at least eight different concerns, some composed of relatives and others merely of compatriots, in business under the well-known name. "We cannot be in court all the time with the different Allegrettis," said the complaining witness. "It is an impossible thing to do, and for that reason we appealed to the Federal Trade Commission, they are so numerous."[20] Such a bill of peace against the tribe of Allegrettis is perhaps useful, yet it seems doubtful whether the public interest was sufficiently involved to warrant interference in the premises by a government agency possessed of such inadequate powers.

Perhaps, however, a similar argument is applicable to a case against two enterprising taxi drivers in the District of Columbia who had themselves listed in the telephone directory under fifty different names of taxi companies, some closely resembling the names of competitors, others in imitation of concerns in other cities.[21] One of the local competitors secured an injunction in the District of Columbia courts, but the Commission took action on

[17] F.T.C. *v.* Carbo Oil Co., 4 F.T.C.D. 102, and F.T.C. *v.* The Best Oil Co., 5 F.T.C.D. 92 (1922).

[18] F.T.C. *v.* Hall-Marvin Co. et al., 4 F.T.C.D. 285.

[19] F.T.C. *v.* United Allegretti Co., 4 F.T.C.D. 120.

[20] Transcript of Record, p. 80, Docket No. 715.

[21] F.T.C. *v.* Maltby, 5 F.T.C.D. 473 (1923).

behalf of the others, and ordered respondent to cease and desist from listing the same business in the telephone book under more than one name.

What has been said as to trade mark and "passing off" cases applies with equal force to another group of cases, in which the complaint is that the respondent has circulated false statements concerning a specific competitor. A manufacturer of hydrogen peroxide, for instance, obtained from chemists an analysis of a competitor's product, and circulated it in the trade with comments of his own not strictly accurate. The Commission issued its complaint, found that the comments were false and misleading, and ordered respondent to cease and desist.[22] A manufacturer of lightning rods was ordered to cease and desist from circulating "any false or disparaging statement, comment or criticism concerning the business or business method of any competitor," the controversy arising out of a dispute with a named company.[23] Again, a manufacturer of automobile tires and rims was ordered to cease applying the term "pirate" to a competitor who made spare parts designed to fit respondent's rims.[24] These cases are similar to the "passing off" cases in that they involve unfair acts aimed at specific named competitors; that these competitors, in so far as their cases have merit, have adequate remedies at law or in equity; and that the powers and procedure of the Federal Trade Commission are ill adapted to the task of giving effective protection to the interests at stake.

Mention should be made at this point of a case which raises a more difficult problem. In Federal Trade Commission v. Liberty Paper Company[25] it appeared that the Liberty Paper Company was an established and well-

[22] F.T.C. v. John Bene & Son, Inc., 5 F.T.C.D. 314 (1922).
[23] F.T.C. v. St. Louis Lightning Rod Co., 3 F.T.C.D. 327 (1921).
[24] F.T.C. v. Keaton Tire & Rubber Co., 5 F.T.C.D. 335 (1922).
[25] 3 F.T.C.D. 13.

known manufacturer of gummed paper. The respondent was a dealer in paper bags and toilet papers, and proceeded to do business under the same name. He was ordered to cease and desist from using the name "Liberty Paper Company" as a trade name. The facts suggest a line of cases which have given the courts in the United States much trouble. It has always been said that a trade mark will be protected only against unauthorized use upon goods of the same kind. To use the classic example, the mere fact that one man stamps a lion on his iron products will not prevent another from stamping a lion upon his linen goods.[26] It has been supposed that this rule requires that the owner of the trade mark and the infringer be competitors.[27] Yet the injustice of the result has been apparent. A manufacturer sells self-raising flour under the distinctive name "Aunt Jemima." By dint of advertising and persistent use he has induced the public to associate the name with his product, the quality of which is recognized. Suppose, now, that a second manufacturer should begin to sell "Aunt Jemima Pancake Syrup," a third "Aunt Jemima Baking Powder," a fourth "Aunt Jemima Yeast." Obviously, the public would be deceived into thinking that the original Aunt Jemima Company had branched out into allied lines, and the new appropriators of the trade name would be reaping the benefit of the original manufacturer's reputation and good will. It is true that the appropriators would not be directly diverting customers from the owner of the trade name, but the injury would be none the less serious. As long as a man has the exclusive right to use the distinctive trade name to which he has given value, he remains in control of his own business reputation. But as

[26] Ainsworth *v.* Walmsley, L. R. 1 Eq. Cas. 518, 524. Hanover Star Milling Co. *v.* Metcalf, 240 U.S. 403, 414.

[27] Borden's Ice Cream Co. *v.* Bordens Condensed Milk Co., 201 Fed. 510 (1912).

soon as anyone can use the name to describe any conceivable allied though non-competitive article, whether the quality be good or bad, the reputation of the trade name is at the mercy of persons whom the owner cannot control. The argument, therefore, that no property interest of the owner of the trade name is infringed seems unsound.

The weight of authority is now clearly that a vendor of an allied though non-competitive article may be enjoined from appropriating another's trade name.[28] The character of the goods manufactured by the alleged infringer seems relevant only upon the issue of fact, whether or not there is substantial deception. Even the most gullible customer is not likely to think, from the similarity of brands, that a prominent iron manufacturer has branched out into the linen business. But he is likely to think that "Overland" tires are produced by the maker of automobiles of that name,[29] or that "Penslar" cigars are made by the owner of a brand of "Penslar" drugs and chain store supplies.[30]

So far as the jurisdiction of the Federal Trade Commission is concerned, this line of reasoning does not, however, fully meet the situation. If the owner of the trade name and the infringer are not competitors, the latter cannot be guilty of unfair competition toward the former. The Commission has no jurisdiction over mere conversion of property, whether tangible or intangible,

[28] Florence Mfg. Co. v. Dowd & Co., 178 Fed. 73 (C.C.A. 2d) (1910); Aunt Jemima Mills Co. v. Rigney & Co., 247 Fed. 407 (C.C.A. 2d) (1917); Peninsular Chemical Co. v. Levinson, 247 Fed. 658 (C.C.A. 6th) (1917); Willys-Overland Co. v. Akron-Overland Tire Co. (D.C.-Del.), 268 Fed. 151 (1920).

[29] Willys-Overland Co. v. Akron-Overland Tire Co., 268 Fed. 151 (1920).

[30] Peninsular Chemical Co. v. Levinson, 247 Fed. 658 (C.C.A. 6th) (1917).

from one who is not a competitor. If the Commission has jurisdiction over such cases, it must be because the practice is unfair to the competitors of the appropriator, rather than because it is unfair to the owner of the trade mark.

The Liberty Paper case, therefore, falls more appropriately within the class of cases next to be considered. Of the cases previously discussed the distinguishing feature has been an attempt by dishonest means to divert customers from a specific and identified competitor. We turn now to a group of cases in which the deceptive practice is not directed against any ascertainable competitor, but is designed to promote the sales of the person engaging in the practice, at the expense of his competitors generally. Such cases involve totally different legal and practical considerations.

MISBRANDING GOODS OFFERED FOR SALE

In a leading case, it was held by the Circuit Court of Appeals for the Sixth Circuit (Circuit Judges Taft, Lurton, and Day) that a manufacturer could not be enjoined from misbranding his goods, at the suit of a vendor of competing articles which were honestly branded.[31] The facts of the case were peculiar. The plaintiff produced under the name "Aluminum" washboards faced with that material. The plaintiff was, moreover, the only manufacturer of aluminum washboards in the United States, having an exclusive contract with the sole producer of the metal. It was charged that the defendant was selling under the name "Aluminum" a washboard made substantially of zinc, and containing no appreciable trace of aluminum. The district court awarded an injunction, but the decree

[31] American Washboard Co. v. Saginaw Mfg. Co. (C.C.A. 6th), 103 Fed. 281 (1900).

was reversed in the Circuit Court of Appeals, in an opinion of which the gist is in the following paragraph:

Many articles are now being put upon the market under the name of aluminum, because of the attractive qualities of that metal, which are not made of pure aluminum, yet they answer the purpose for which they are made and are useful. Can it be that the courts have the power to suppress such trade at the instance of others starting in the same business who use only pure aluminum? There is a widespread suspicion that many articles sold as being manufactured of wool are not entirely made of that material. Can it be that a dealer who should make such articles only of pure wool could invoke the equitable jurisdiction of the courts to suppress the trade and business of all persons whose goods may deceive the public? We find no such authority in the books, and are clear in the opinion that, if the doctrine is to be thus extended, and all persons compelled to deal solely in goods which are exactly what they are represented to be, the remedy must come from the legislature, and not from the courts.[32]

The case has been followed in the New Jersey District, where the maker of "Linoleum" (a name held not to be registerable as a trade mark, because descriptive of the material rather than of the maker) tried to prevent another concern from selling as "Linoleum" a product of a different and cheaper material.[33]

These cases reveal a situation in which an unscrupulous trader can deceive the public as to the ingredients or character of his wares, can injure the business and reputation of all honest merchants in the same line, and yet cannot be restrained by a court of equity because the injury is not directed against any specific competitor.

It is frequently another characteristic of these cases that the deceptive practice in question has gradually

[32] *Ibid.,* p. 286.

[33] Armstrong Cork Co. *v.* Ringwalt Linoleum Works, 235 Fed. 458 (1916).

come to permeate the trade to such an extent that it is difficult for any one dealer or manufacturer to abandon it while his competitors are permitted to continue the deception. Indeed, so widespread and time-honored have some of these practices become that they have at least given color to the argument that, despite their deceptive origin, they no longer deceive anyone; in other words, that the average purchaser of a product labeled "wool" is fully aware that he is getting mostly cotton.[34]

The task of purging a trade of vicious practices of this character has been energetically taken up by some of the trade associations, as is interestingly described by Mr. Jones in his excellent book.[35] Several of these associations have adopted codes of unfair practices, which specifically condemn misbranding, false and misleading advertising, sale of secondhand or rebuilt products as new, and similar deceptive practices.[36] Some associations visit with expulsion any violation of the code.[37] The work of these associations is doubtless of great value, but its efficacy is impaired by the fact that a private association can at best control only its own members, whereas the wrong-doers are as likely as not outside the association. In such cases, under the doctrine of the American Washboard Company case,[38] there is no remedy at the suit of the honest competitor, nor has the medieval policy of giving to trade or merchant guilds a coercive power over outsiders[39] commended itself to our modern policy as to the relation between corporations and the state.

[34] *See* this argument suggested but disposed of in F.T.C. *v.* Winsted Hosiery Co., 258 U.S. 483, 493 (1922).

[35] Franklin D. Jones, *Trade Association Activities and the Law* (1922), p. 34.

[36] *Ibid.*, pp. 35 ff.

[37] *Ibid.*, p. 39.

[38] *Supra*, p. 179.

[39] Cheyney, *An Introduction to the Industrial and Social History of*

It is here that the Federal Trade Commission has found an opportunity for valuable and effective work. The Supreme Court has sustained fully its contention that injury to a specific competitor is not necessary to its jurisdiction, and that it has full authority to deal with any case in which a deceptive trade practice is used in the course of competition in interstate or foreign commerce.[40] It fills precisely the gap revealed by the American Washboard case. A review of the different groups of cases of this kind disposed of by the Commission will show how extensive have been its activities in this direction.

The typical case is one in which a product is sold under the name of a well-known material, although in fact it contains largely or even exclusively a cheaper material. It was, for example, a widespread practice to sell as "Wool," or as "Merino," or "Cashmere," or under some similar term implying that the raw material was derived from the fleece of sheep, a product of which the principal, if not the only, constituent was cotton. In a group of cases[41] the practice has been held to be mislead-

England, pp. 126 et seq. The extract referred to is reproduced in Oliphant, Cases on Trade Regulation (1923), p. 16, especially p. 20.

[40] F.T.C. v. Winsted Hosiery Co., 258 U.S. 483 (1922). See Sears, Roebuck & Co., v. F.T.C. (C.C.A. 7th), 258 Fed. 307 (1919); Royal Baking Powder Co. v. F.T.C. (C.C.A. 2d), 281 Fed. 744 (1922).

[41] F.T.C. v. Winsted Hosiery Co., 2 F.T.C.D. 202; F.T.C. v. H. E. Bradford Co., Inc., 2 F.T.C.D. 207; F.T.C. v. Moore & Tierney, 2 F.T.C.D. 223; F.T.C. v. G. H. McDowell & Co., 2 F.T.C.D. 228; F.T.C. v. The Faith Knitting Co, 2 F.T.C.D. 233; F.T.C. v. Black Cat Textiles Co., 2 F.T.C.D. 238; F.T.C. v. William Moore Knitting Co., 2 F.T.C.D. 243; F.T.C. v. W. E. Tillotson Mfg. Co., 2 F.T.C.D. 248; F.T.C. v. Hope Knitting Co., 2 F.T.C.D. 253; F.T.C. v. The Lackawanna Mills, 2 F.T.C.D. 258; F.T.C. v. Atlas Knitting Co., 2 F.T.C.D. 264; F.T.C. v. The Broadalbin Knitting Co., Ltd., 2 F.T.C.D. 269; F.T.C. v. Glastonbury Knitting Co., 2 F.T.C.D. 274; F.T.C. v. The New England Knitting Co., 2 F.T.C.D. 279; F.T.C. v. Clarke & Holsapple Mfg. Co., 2 F.T.C.D. 285; F.T.C. v. Root Mfg. Co., 2 F.T.C.D. 290; F.T.C. v. The Rob Roy

ing, and in the Winsted Hosiery case[42] the Commission's position has been confirmed by the Supreme Court. A typical order in such a case is that respondent "cease and desist from employing or using as labels or brands on underwear or other knit goods not composed wholly of wool, or on the wrappers, boxes, or other containers in which they are delivered to customers, the word 'Merino,' 'Wool,' or 'Worsted,' alone or in combination with any other word or words, unless accompanied by a word or words designating the substance, fibre, or material, other than wool, of which the garments are composed in part (*e.g.,* 'Merino, Wool and Cotton'; 'Wool and Cotton'; 'Worsted, Wool and Cotton'; 'Wool, Cotton and Silk') or by a word or words otherwise clearly indicating that such underwear or other goods is not made wholly of wool (*e.g.,* part wool).''[43]

A similar group of cases[44] involves misuse of the words "silk" or "satin," or of similar terms designating a material made of the cocoon of the silkworm, when applied to materials composed wholly or partly of cotton. The "artificial silk" industry is of course recognized as

Hosiery Co., 2 F.T.C.D. 340; F.T.C. *v.* American Hosiery Co., 3 F.T.C.D. 1; F.T.C. *v.* Horn, the Tailor, 4 F.T.C.D. 452; F.T.C. *v.* Grosner's, 5 F.T.C.D. 55; F.T.C. *v.* Rockford Mitten & Hosiery Co., 5 F.T.C.D. 264; F.T.C. *v.* Sulloway Mills, 5 F.T.C.D. 269; F.T.C. *v.* Nolde & Horst Co., 5 F.T.C.D. 284, and F.T.C. *v.* Hub Hosiery Mills, 5 F.T.C.D. 290.

[42] F.T.C. *v.* Winsted Hosiery Co., 258 U.S. 483 (1922).

[43] F.T.C. *v.* Winsted Hosiery Co., 3 F.T.C.D. 189.

[44] F.T.C. *v.* Circle Cilk Co., 1 F.T.C.D. 13; F.T.C. *v.* A. Theo. Abbot & Co., 1 F.T.C.D. 16; F.T.C. *v.* Solomon M. Hexter et al., 2 F.T.C.D. 41; F.T.C. *v.* Simons, Hatch & Whitten Co., 5 F.T.C.D. 183; F.T.C. *v.* Moore & Fisher, 5 F.T.C.D. 239; F.T.C. *v.* The Alamance Hosiery Mills, 5 F.T.C.D. 230; F.T.C. *v.* Hancock Knitting Mills, 5 F.T.C.D. 234; F.T.C. *v.* The Daum, Rogers, Spritzer Co., 5 F.T.C.D. 257; F.T.C. *v.* Behrend's 5 F.T.C.D. 303; F.T.C. *v.* Kahn & Frank, 5 F.T.C.D. 309; F.T.C. *v.* Esco Hosiery Co., Inc., 5 F.T.C.D. 321.

legitimate, but processes by which long staple cotton can be given a finish almost indistinguishable from that of true silk have been brought to such a stage of perfection that deception is greatly facilitated. A typical order prohibits "Using as labels or brands on hosiery sold by it [respondent], or on the containers thereof, the word 'silk,' or any modification thereof, (1) unless the hosiery on which it is used is made entirely of the silk of the silkworm, or (2) unless, where the hosiery is made partly of silk, it is accompanied by a word or words aptly and truthfully describing the other material or materials of which such hosiery is in part composed."

Similar action has been taken against a practice apparently prevalent in certain quarters in the vegetable oil industry, of selling as "linseed oil" or "turpentine," or as "second run" linseed oil or turpentine, or as "boiled oil," an inferior product largely adulterated with a cheap mineral oil.[45] The words "lard oil," "sperm oil," and "fish oil" appear to have been similarly abused.[46] In such a case the Commission ordered respondent to cease and desist "From selling or offering for sale in interstate commerce any compound, mixture, or combination of linseed oil with mineral oil or other substances which is labeled or branded as 'linseed oil,' unless the name or names of such other oil, to wit, mineral oil, or such other substance, be also displayed upon such labels or brands, in conjunction with the words 'linseed oil' and in letters of the same size, shape, and prominence as said words 'linseed oil.' "

[45] F.T.C. v. Consolidated Oil Co. et al., 1 F.T.C.D. 285; F.T.C. v. Plomo Specialty Mfg. Co., 2 F.T.C.D. 195; F.T.C. v. Midwest Linseed Oil & Paint Co., 2 F.T.C.D. 295; F.T.C. v. The Sanitary Turpentine Co., 2 F.T.C.D. 313; F.T.C. v. The International Flaxol Co., 3 F.T.C.D. 64; F.T.C. v. The Star Provision Co. et al., 3 F.T.C.D. 393, and F.T.C. v. Clifford Smith Co., 5 F.T.C.D. 435 (1923).

[46] F.T.C. v. The Star Provision Co. et al., 3 F.T.C.D. 393.

Other cases involve the use of the words "spongeable linen" to describe a cotton fabric with an outer layer of celluloid;[47] of the word "Ivory" to describe an artificial substitute;[48] of the word "Manila" to describe rope not made exclusively of manila fibre;[49] of the initials "M. & J." on a cheap coffee which was not a blend of Mocha and Java;[50] of the words "Seal Plush" (a trade name properly designating an imitation seal made of Tussa silk) to describe a cheap cotton fabric;[51] of the words "engraved in gold" to describe lettering of auto-foil;[52] and of the words "Olive Cream Castile," "Cucumber Cream," and "Almond Cream" to describe a product containing only the ingredients of cheap soap.[53]

An interesting group of cases that may be mentioned here involve the practice, once seemingly common among sponge manufacturers, of "loading" sponges in order to increase their weight. The sponges are soaked in a solution of glucose, glycerin, salt, and similar ingredients, and the sole purpose of the process was found by the Commission to be to obtain a higher price when the product was sold by weight. Orders directed against this practice were issued against twenty-two firms.[54]

Again there may be a direct representation that a product contains, or does not contain, certain named ingredients, as when a distributor of a toilet preparation was found to have advertised that it contained lemon

[47] F.T.C. v. The Spongeable Linen Collar Co., 2 F.T.C.D. 212 (1920).

[48] F.T.C. v. Palais Royal, 4 F.T.C.D. 305; F.T.C. v. Louis K. Liggett Co., 4 F.T.C.D. 423, and Peoples Drug Stores, 4 F.T.C.D. 446.

[49] F.T.C. v. Federal Rope Co., 2 F.T.C.D. 327 (1920).

[50] F.T.C. v. E. E. Gray Co., 1 F.T.C.D. 221 (1918).

[51] F.T.C. v. Bellas-Hess & Co., 5 F.T.C.D. 131 (1922).

[52] F.T.C. v. Union Pencil Co., Inc., 4 F.T.C.D. 51 (1921).

[53] F.T.C. v. Union Soap Co., 4 F.T.C.D. 397 (1922).

[54] F.T.C. v. Lasker & Bernstein, 3 F.T.C.D. 246 (1921), and cases in footnote. Other cases pp. 253-278, inclusive.

juice, when the actual ingredient was oil of lemon;[55] where a company sold as "Graphite Carbon Roof Paint" a product containing neither graphite nor free carbon;[56] or advertised that a roofing cement contained no coal tar, when in fact it did;[57] or where a company advertised that a product named by them "Sal-Tonik," contained sulphate of iron, carbonized peat, charcoal, tobacco, quassia, sulphur, gentian, pure salt, chloride of magnesia, Epsom salts, Glauber's salts, bicarbonate of soda, oxide of iron, mineralized humoides, American Worm Seed, Levant Worm Seed, and Capsicum, when in truth and in fact it was nothing but an impure grade of common salt.[58]

A more difficult case is presented where there is no direct representation as to the character or ingredients of the product, but where a name is used which by inference suggests that the product contains materials which it does not in fact contain. The word "Flaxol" clearly suggests that the oil in question is a product of flaxseed (*i.e.*, linseed oil), and its use to describe a cheap mineral oil was prohibited.[59] The words "Cilk" and "Sylk" have been held to create an implication that the material was genuine silk,[60] and the word "Pinene," to describe a chemical, was found to embody a misleading suggestion that it contained the essential constituent of

[55] F.T.C. *v.* Louis Phillipe, Inc., et al., 5 F.T.C.D. 136 (1922). As to this case, *see supra*, p. 132.

[56] F.T.C. *v.* Consolidated Oil Co., 4 F.T.C.D. 27. (1921).

[57] F.T.C. *v.* Montgomery Ward & Co., 3 F.T.C.D. 151 (1920). As to this case, however, *see supra*, p. 130.

[58] F.T.C. *v.* Guarantee Veterinary Co. et al., 3 F.T.C.D. 402; 4 F.T.C.D. 149. Order affirmed in Circuit Court of Appeals (2d Circuit), 285 Fed. 853 (1922). *See* also F.T.C. *v.* A. A. Berry Seed Co., 2 F.T.C.D. 427 (1920); F.T.C. *v.* American Mutual Seed Co., 3 F.T.C.D. 177 (1921), and F.T.C. *v.* Ginso Chemical Co., 4 F.T.C.D. 155 (1921).

[59] F.T.C. *v.* International Flaxol Co., 3 F.T.C.D. 64 (1920).

[60] F.T.C. *v.* Circle Cilk Co., 1 F.T.C.D. 13 (1916); F.T.C. *v.* Hancock Knitting Mills, 5 F.T.C.D. 234 (1922).

turpentine.[61] The difficulty in these cases is to determine when the name is so changed or qualified as to carry of itself a clear warning that an imitation product is involved. "Artificial silk," of course, clearly indicates that the product is not silk. The words "Seal Plush" apparently do not designate a material containing seal skin, but an imitation made of a certain type of silk, known as Tussa silk.[62] The words "Pyralin Ivory" to designate a composition of nitrated cellulose has been prohibited, although "pyralin" is the trade name for the imitation product.[63] Also on the border line, or perhaps beyond it, seems to be the case in which the use of the term "Silkoline" was held to contain a "literally and palpably false" implication that the product contained silk. In this case the testimony of persons in the trade was unanimous that the name had been well known for at least thirty years as designating a mercerized cotton fabric, but some "ultimate consumers" testified that they thought it contained silk.[64]

A leading case of this kind is Federal Trade Commission *v.* Royal Baking Powder Company.[65] It seems that for more than half a century a brand of "Dr. Price's Cream Baking Powder" had been on the market. Since 1899 the brand had been owned, directly or through a corporate subsidiary, by the Royal Baking Powder Company. Its distinguishing characteristic, much featured in advertising for at least thirty-five years, had been the use of cream of tartar, rather than the cheaper phosphate

[61] F.T.C. *v.* Pinene Mfg. Co., Inc., 5 F.T.C.D. 203 (1922).

[62] *See* F.T.C. *v.* Bellas-Hess & Co., 5 F.T.C.D. 131 (1922), where the order prohibits the use of the words "Seal Plush" to designate a product not made of Tussa silk.

[63] F.T.C. *v.* Louis K. Liggett Co., 4 F.T.C.D. 423 (1922). *See* Trade Practice Submittals, p. 14, and *post,* p. 190.

[64] F.T.C. *v.* Behrend's, 5 F.T.C.D. 303 (1922). See *post,* p. 238.

[65] 4 F.T.C.D. 1 (1921).

or alum compound, as the acid ingredient. Indeed, for years the company had published advertising disparaging the use of "bone acid," or "lime phosphate," and claiming that cream of tartar was the only acid ingredient which should be used in baking powder. In 1919, owing to the increased price of cream of tartar, the company decided to substitute phosphate for cream of tartar. Owing to this change they were enabled to reduce the price by one-half. The name "Dr. Price's Cream Baking Powder" was retained, except that the word "Cream" was put in quotation marks. The label closely simulated the old label in form and appearance, but the phraseology was changed in certain respects. "Standard for 60 years" became "Makers for 60 years." A cornucopia containing grapes was changed to a cornucopia containing flowers. The words "Perfectly Pure," however, became "A pure, phosphate Powder." The propriety of the new label had been attacked by numerous state pure food authorities and in certain cases their conclusions had been sustained by the courts. The company's advertising (quoted at length in the findings) made much of the reduction in price of the well-known brand, but in some cases failed entirely to mention the substitution of phosphate for cream of tartar; in others mentioned it only inconspicuously. The Commission found that the advertising tended to conceal or obscure the change in ingredients, and that about half the retailers in their advertising showed the price reduction but failed to mention the reason. It further found that the use on a phosphate powder of a brand which had become identified for years with a cream of tartar powder was "calculated and designed to deceive and did deceive the public." The order prohibited selling the phosphate powder as "Dr. Price's" unless the word "Cream" was omitted and the word "Phosphate" incorporated in the name; and representing that the new powder was the same as the one sold for years under the old brand.

The company petitioned the Circuit Court of Appeals to set aside the order, but the court found that the findings were amply justified by the evidence, and affirmed the order, on the authority of the Winsted Hosiery Case. "The purpose of the Congress," said the court, "in creating the Federal Trade Commission was aimed at just such dishonest practices, and business concerns that resort to dishonest devices of this nature must understand that they cannot add to their revenues or maintain their business standing by methods of competition which the law brands as 'unfair' and therefore unlawful."[66]

Of course, where recognized marks or grades indicating quality are falsified, the deception is clear, as in Federal Trade Commission v. A. T. McClure Glass Company,[67] where it was found that respondent, a window glass jobber, made it a practice to erase the letters designating manufacturer's grades, and remove the "quality slips," stenciling on the boxes letters designating a higher grade.

The misrepresentation may be as to the place of origin or manufacture of the product, as where a local product was sold as "Sheffield" steel;[68] where matches of Japanese manufacture were sold as "Sakerhets Tandstickor," thus giving the impression that they were made in Sweden;[69] where clothes made in Scranton, Pennsylvania, were sold by a company calling itself "Rochester Tailor-

[66] Royal Baking Powder Co. v. F.T.C., 281 Fed. 744. See, to the same effect, Royal Baking Powder Co. v. Donohue et al., 265 Fed. 406; Royal Baking Powder Co. v. Emerson, 270 Fed. 429.

[67] 2 F.T.C.D. 113 (1919).

[68] F.T.C. v. Sheffield Razor Co., 4 F.T.C.D. 373 (1922); F.T.C. v. Samuel E. Bernstein, 4 F.T.C.D. 114 (1921).

[69] F.T.C. v. Cupples Co., 3 F.T.C.D. 407 (1921); F.T.C. v. The Taiyo Trading Co., Inc., 3 F.T.C.D. 199 (1921).

ing Co.'';[70] or where condensed milk of American manufacture was sold (though without intent to deceive) under
labels which gave the impression that it was made in
Europe.[71] In these cases, it should be noted, the Commission is not troubled by the difficulty which has confronted
the courts in preventing the pirating of geographical
trade names. In view of what was said by the Supreme
Court in the Hanover Star Milling Company case,[72] there
is doubt whether the fraudulent use of a geographical
name can be enjoined, except at the suit of one who can
show that the geographical name has acquired a sec-
ondary meaning designating wares manufactured only
by him. It is not clear that any one of the many Rochester
clothing manufacturers would have a cause of action
merely because a Scranton, Pennsylvania, clothier sold
"Rochester" clothes. The fraud on the public, however,
and the injury to the whole group of Rochester manufacturers, is undeniable, and the Commission's procedure
seems to afford a helpful means by which the integrity
of such a geographic trade name can be protected.

Several trade practice submittals have dealt with misbranding and similar deceptive practices.

The pyroxylin plastics industry was called together in
1920, to consider the prevalent practice of selling as
"ivory", "tortoise shell", "amber", "pearl", "jade",
"jet", or "coral", various artificial and sometimes in-
flammable compounds.[73] The meeting appointed a committee, which submitted a detailed report, carefully distinguishing between proper and improper terminology
in the trade. Thus the use of the word "ivory" in a
substantive sense, as in "Pyralin Ivory," was condemned,

[70] F.T.C. v. Rochester Tailoring Co., 4 F.T.C.D. 309 (1922).

[71] F.T.C. v. Nestlé's Food Co., Inc., 2 F.T.C.D. 171 (1919).

[72] Hanover Star Milling Co. v. Metcalf, 240 U.S. 403. See, however,
Edward S. Rogers, 27 Harv. L. Rev. 139, 141, and cases cited.

[73] Trade Practice Submittals, p. 14.

but its use in an adjective sense, as in "Ivory Pyralin," was approved. In view of the practical difficulties, the committee advised against any rule requiring that all such merchandise be branded to indicate affirmatively its compound character, or its inflammability. The report was "accepted by the Commission and placed on file," and in several subsequent cases formal proceedings were instituted against concerns which failed to live up to the standards set.[74]

Less clear-cut in its results was the trade practice submittal in the silver plated hollow ware industry.[75] It seems that plated silver, originally made by welding silver plates on sheets or bars of copper, reached its highest development in Sheffield, England, and was therefore popularly known as Sheffield silver. With the invention of electrolytic processes, the old methods were discarded, but the name remained, and soon lost entirely its original significance. It was applied indiscriminately to all silver plated ware, regardless of quality or method of manufacture. Yet there was no doubt that the purchasing public attached some meaning to the term, and believed that it indicated in some way the better quality and durability which characterized the original Sheffield ware. Members of the trade asked the Commission to adopt a standard definition of Sheffield ware, but it was pointed out that this was beyond its power. "Suggestion was made, however, that the trade might establish its own definition, which if established in practice might be used as a test of improper marking so far as the trade is concerned." The conference therefore adopted, almost unanimously, the following definition:

RESOLVED, that the word "Sheffield" as a mark for silver

[74] F.T.C. v. Palais Royal, 4 F.T.C.D. 305 (1922); F.T.C. v. Louis K. Liggett Co., 4 F.T.C.D. 423 (1922); F.T.C. v. Peoples Drug Stores, 4 F.T.C.D. 446 (1922).

[75] Trade Practice Submittals, p. 40.

plated hollow-ware means quality, and that furthermore quality
is defined as meaning an article well plated on a base metal of
nickel silver of not less than ten per cent nickel content; and
that the same may have Britannia metal trimmings or mount-
ings.[76]

The Commission, however, refused to accept the definition as "dispositive of the issue." The Commission
pointed out that the name as used in the trade was without significance, but that the purchasing public did attribute to the silver ware to which it was applied a quality
"not accurately measured but corresponding generally
to the quality represented in the silver plated line by
original Sheffield plate." "This absence of meaning in
the trade," said the report, "in conjunction with what
seems to be an accepted meaning on the part of the purchasing public, known in the trade and relied upon
therein, seems to the Commission to constitute the use
of the word 'Sheffield' in connection with the sale of
silver plated hollow-ware an unfair method of competition because it tends to deceive and mislead the purchasing public."[77] The issue does not appear to have been
settled, as yet, in any test case.

Similarly inconclusive, but containing much valuable
technical information, is the trade practice submittal as
to the marking of knives mounted in gold.[78] The meeting
adopted resolutions defining the conditions under which
the term "gold mounted knife" could be used, and the
knife stamped with a mark indicating the karat fineness.
It condemned, for instance, the insertion, between the
knife skeleton and the gold sheet, of a stiffening of base
metal, as well as other devices by which the knife was
made to appear to contain more gold than was in fact
present. The Commission in its report referred to the

[76] *Ibid.*, p. 43.
[77] *Ibid.*, p. 43.
[78] *Ibid.*, p. 44.

resolutions as valuable and informative, but refused to accept them as conclusive. The Commission pointed out that the National Stamping Act[79] sets forth under what conditions the karat mark could be used, prescribes the permissible tolerances, and requires special markings where gold and a base metal are combined. Other technical complications were described, and the report concluded that judgment should be reserved until specific complaints were made and concrete cases arose.

In the trade practice submittal of the gold filled watch industry similar issues were involved,[80] although in this case the Commission expressed affirmatively its opinion that watches should not be labeled "gold filled" unless the backs and caps are made of two sheets of gold or gold alloy, and the centre, bezel, pendant, crown, and bow of one sheet, and the watch marked with words indicating the fineness of the gold, with not exceeding three one-thousandths tolerance. Commissioner Nugent dissented, believing that not only the fineness but the weight of the gold should be indicated.

SECONDHAND OR "REBUILT" ARTICLES

In another group of cases the misrepresentation was found to consist in passing off secondhand or "rebuilt" products as new. The business of salvaging used materials and converting them into products which, though inferior, are usable, has a legitimate economic function. Every housewife who has "reconstructed" new clothing out of worn materials will agree that there is nothing improper in the practice. The danger lies in the fact that modern technical arts have been brought to the point where it is possible in many cases to "dress up" the old

[79] 34 Stat. at L. 260.
[80] Trade Practice Submittals, p. 34.

material so that the finished article is superficially indistinguishable from one made of new ingredients. It is only when it has been used for some time that the inferior quality becomes apparent. In such cases the temptation to sell the product as a new one is obvious, and the legal and practical difficulty of preventing deception not easy of solution. Where there is a direct representation that the "rebuilt" product is new, an unfair method of competition is clearly involved. The difficult problem is whether it is unlawful to offer for sale a "rebuilt" product, so made as to seem in all respects new, without specifically stating that it is "rebuilt." It will doubtless occur to the reader that much may depend in a specific case upon the oral representations or "seller's talk" by which the sale is effected. The Commission, however, deals with trade practices, and it can hardly afford to investigate every salesman's conversation. Generally its complaint will be based upon a published advertisement and upon samples of the goods sold, and most of the cases present squarely the question whether a mere sale of the "rebuilt" product, without explanation, and without regard to any oral representations, is deceptive.

The "rebuilt" tire industry presents the problem in a typical way. The process consists in selecting, from partially worn tires, such of the cotton fabric as is still serviceable, replacing the worn parts with fabric in good condition taken from other tires. Several coats of vulcanized cement are applied, a breaker strip is added, and the tread stocks put on. A final coat of sheet rubber is applied, and the tire is vulcanized in a hydraulic mold. The finished product is sold, under a new brand, of course for less than the standard makes of new tires, and without any comment as to the source or previous history of the raw material. In two cases the Commission has held that sales made under these circumstances are deceptive, and has required that such tires be plainly marked in such a way as to show they are "rebuilt" or "reconstructed."[81] Of course no reasons are given, and the findings are not very satisfactory. The complaints in the two cases are so drafted as to convey the implication that there was something in respondent's advertising to create, affirmatively, the impression that the tires were made of new materials. The findings, however, do not give the text of the advertisements, and suggest that the Commission's only ground for criticising them was the failure to mention that the tires were "rebuilt." The orders prohibit selling or advertising "rebuilt" tires unless it is clearly indicated on the tires or in the advertising that they are not made of new materials.

The "rebuilt" typewriter industry has presented the problem in a somewhat different aspect. A firm engaged in "rebuilding" typewriters, purchases at secondhand standard makes of machines, overhauls and repairs them, replaces defective parts, and offers the product for sale, not under its own brand, but under the name or mark of the original maker. The Commission has held this practice to be unlawful unless it is clearly stated in the advertisements, circulars, letters, or other sales devices employed, that the machines are used, secondhand, repaired, or rebuilt machines.[82] These cases are of interest because they are on the border line between the "passing off" and the "misbranding" cases. A customer is misled

[81] F.T.C. v. Akron Tire Co., Inc., 2 F.T.C.D. 119 (1919); F.T.C. v. E. P. Janes et al., 1 F.T.C.D. 380 (1919).

[82] F.T.C. v. Typewriter Emporium, 1 F.T.C.D. 105 (1918) and three cases cited in footnote, 1 F.T.C.D. 109. Cf. F.T.C. v. The Check Writer Manufacturers, Inc., et al., 4 F.T.C.D. 87 (1921), and see the case of the "rebuilt" adding machines, discussed supra, p. 143.

The practice of "selling or offering for sale of rebuilt typewriters as new machines" was condemned in a trade practice submittal of the rebuilt typewriter industry, in 1920, but the submittal does not say whether a sale without further comment or characterization is a representation that the machine is new. See Trade Practice Submittals, p. 8.

as to the newness or previous use of the machine, and he is also misled into thinking that he is buying a machine in the condition in which it leaves the factory of a well-known manufacturer, and hence guaranteed by his reputation.

An analogous practice has apparently existed in the moving picture industry. It consists in purchasing (quite legitimately and for value) an old film, changing the title and the captions, adding, perhaps, a small amount of new film, and exhibiting the product as if it were a new film not previously published. Here the fraud seems clear, for the adoption of a new name is itself a representation that the film is new, and orders prohibiting the practice have been issued in several cases.[83]

Merely to illustrate the infinite variety of the frauds which human ingenuity can devise, mention may be made of Federal Trade Commission v. Waverly Brown et al.,[84] where the charge was in effect that respondent was endeavoring to pass off new phonographs for old ones. It seems that he manufactured very cheap machines, and sold them as secondhand instruments of more expensive standard makes. He was ordered to cease and desist from advertising as slightly worn standard makes, new phonographs of his own manufacture.

"PRICE-UP" CASES

I pass now to an interesting group of cases in which the deception is of a somewhat more intangible character. In certain lines of trade, especially in the sale of razors, razor hones, cheap fountain pens, and pocket knives, it appears to have been a widespread practice to mark on

---

[83] F.T.C. v. The Royal Cinema Corp. et al., 2 F.T.C.D. 88 (1919); F.T.C. v. Joseph Simmonds, 2 F.T.C.D. 11 (1919); F.T.C. v. The Lasso Pictures Co., 1 F.T.C.D. 374 (1919); F.T.C. v. Eskay Harris Feature Film Co., 5 F.T.C.D. 219 (1922).

[84] 3 F.T.C.D. 156 (1920).

the article or its container a price two or three times the amount which the retailer expects to get for it. The retailer then crosses out the fictitious price, and writes under it in pencil or ink the real retail price. In one case the respondent admitted advertising a "Standard Self-Filling Fountain Pen, $1.50," when in fact he never got more that 25 cents for the pen.[85] In another case respondent bought razors at about 45 cents apiece, had them all marked "Price $3.50," and sold them for $1.95.[86] Again a manufacturer was found to have sold at from $4.25 to $4.75 a dozen, a knife marked "The Latest Bathing Girl Pocket Knife, Choice $1.50." In fact it was retailed for much less.[87] The practice is doubtless a silly one, and in isolated cases may be harmless enough. Yet it seems to have been so widespread and to have attained such a grip on the industry, that individual firms were afraid to drop it. The manufacturer claimed that the dealer demanded it, and the dealer claimed that the public demanded it. The practice is undoubtedly deceptive, though it is not so easy to put one's finger on the exact nature of the fraud. The mere fact that a manufacturer makes an "asking price" which he expects the dealer to shade if necessary, does not brand him as unfair. That is a recognized method of bargaining which the most honorable horse trader would not spurn. We are not dealing, however, with the sale of a horse, or a piece of land, or a secondhand automobile. The subject matter of the sale is a standard manufactured article, turned out in large quantities in uniform kinds and sizes. A price printed or engraved on such an article is more than a mere "asking price"; it will be understood to be the price which the manufacturer expects the dealer to charge, and will represent his estimate of what he can get for the article in

[85] F.T.C. *v.* Berk Bros., 2 F.T.C.D. 377 (1920).
[86] F.T.C. *v.* Solus Manufacturers Co., 4 F.T.C.D. 317 (1922).
[87] F.T.C. *v.* Singer, Stern & Co., 4 F.T.C.D. 338 (1922).

the long run. If this printed or engraved price is admittedly fictitious, and put on the article solely to give the buyer the impression that he is paying much less than the manufacturer expected to get, and where the practice is as widespread as it appears to have been, it would seem that a case was made out for the intervention of the Federal Trade Commission.[88]

A case against the Chicago Portrait Company is illuminating, both because the facts are exceptionally well presented, and because it is one of the few decided cases in which a dissent accompanies the formal report.[89] The respondent made a business of selling "portraits," copied partly by hand and partly by mechanical means from photographs supplied by the customer, its output ranging from 250,000 to 500,000 annually. The complaint was based entirely on the "selling talk" of the company's salesmen, but the findings show that the words were, in fact as well as in theory, the words of the head office. Indeed, it is found that "Respondent at one time offered prizes for the best sales talks, indicating the best description of the portrait, the best method of approach to the home, the best method of securing the confidence of the prospective customer, the best method of arousing the prospective customer's interest, the best method of creating a desire for the painting, and the best method of closing. Respondent found that its best salesmen had similar methods, and took steps to make the sales method as uniform as it could so that respondent could pass it along

[88] The following cases involve fictitious cut prices: F.T.C. v. Marx Finstone, 4 F.T.C.D. 163; F.T.C. v. Shatkun & Kahn, 4 F.T.C.D. 167; F.T.C. v. U.S. Novelty Co., 4 F.T.C.D. 171; F.T.C. v. Macfountain Pen & Novelty Co., 4 F.T.C.D. 172; F.T.C. v. N. Shure Co., 4 F.T.C.D. 177; F.T.C. v. Levin Bros., 4 F.T.C.D. 182; F.T.C. v. James Kelley, 4 F.T.C.D. 188; F.T.C. v. Standard Pen Co., 4 F.T.C.D. 193; F.T.C. v. Karl Guggenheim, Inc., 4 F.T.C.D. 199; F.T.C. v. Ed. Hahn, 4 F.T.C.D. 204, and F.T.C. v. Union Soap Co., 4 F.T.C.D. 397.

[89] F.T.C. v. Chicago Portrait Co., 5 F.T.C.D. 396 (1923).

to other salesmen. Out of that grew a uniform selling method.'"[90] The sales talk was designed to create the impression that the "portrait" usually sold for $20, but that as a special concession a price of $10 would be made for two portraits, provided the customer agrees to spread the news among her friends and neighbors.[91] Other exaggerations were dwelt upon. The Commission ordered respondent to cease and desist from "representing to customers or prospective customers that the usual prices which it receives, or has received for its portraits, are greater than the prices at which similar portraits are offered, to such customers or prospective customers, when such is not the fact.'"[92] Commissioner Van Fleet, however, filed a memorandum of dissent on the ground that the portraits sold were "well worth the money received," and that there was no evidence that a single customer had

[90] *Ibid.*, p. 406.

[91] Following are some samples of sales talk, embodied in the findings:

"Now here is what I am going to do for you. As I told you in the beginning, I did not come here to sell you anything, but I am sure you have decided this is an expensive painting. You are absolutely right and when we sell this work we get $20 for each painting, but here is what I am going to do for you. I am going to make this one of your mother in our $20 'Tritone' painting, and I am going to give you a $10 trade check which pays $10, or one-half, on Mother's painting, which is a wonderful present in itself, but here is the real big present. I am going to make this one of your father in our $20 'Tritone' painting absolutely free, that is, on condition that you tell your friends and neighbors who made the work, and you will do that. . . .

"There are many things which make this painting beautiful. You will notice that it is oval with a raise in the center showing a natural rounded forehead and chest. Notice how the artist has brought out the features. Notice how the hair is painted. You can see every stroke of the artist's brush, with just enough color in the face to give it life and warmth. The background is taken from our famous sepia paintings. It seems to set the person right out into space. This wonderful painting is our special hand-made 'Tritone.' " *Ibid.*, pp. 403-404, 405.

[92] *Ibid.*, p. 408.

been deceived. The Commissioner conceded that "a representation of value may be a representation of fact," where the article has a market value. "But the article in question had no market value. It was an article of respondent's sole manufacture and depended for its value on its artistic merit and was worth nothing to anyone except the purchaser."[93]

SALES OF "GOVERNMENT" SUPPLIES

IN another group of cases, the intervention of the Commission seems to have been warranted upon special grounds. As is well known, the United States Government has, since the war, found it necessary to liquidate an enormous accumulation of stores and supplies and equipment of every conceivable variety, and thrifty purchasers have found excellent bargains at the retail stores which make a specialty of these articles. The goods are cheap, yet there is a fair assurance that they are of good material and workmanship. To take advantage of the good will attaching to articles of this sort, unscrupulous traders began to offer for sale as former government property, inferior products which had never belonged to the Government. The Commission appears to have been especially active in stamping out this practice, which is obviously a fraud on consumers, and in addition does injury to the good name and reputation of the government service.[94] The Commission has forbidden the use of the term "government spar" to characterize a product

[93] *Ibid.*, p. 409.

[94] *Cf.* the Act of February 21, 1905, making it unlawful to stamp on gold or silver goods the words "United States Assay" or other words calculated to convey the impression that the United States Government has certified to the fineness or quality of the gold or silver. 33 Stat. at L. 732.

National Stamping Act (also known as the "Hallmark Act"), 34 Stat. at L. 260.

not (1) obtained from the United States Government; or (2) manufactured for and accepted by the Government; or (3) made according to government specifications, in which case such fact may be stated (as "made in accordance with Government W. D. Specification No. 97"). Where the product has been obtained from or made for a foreign government, or according to the specification of a foreign government, such fact must be stated; the word "government" alone is taken to refer to our own Government.[95] It was held improper to sell as "Navy Architectural Spar" a product which had been rejected by the Navy because not in accordance with specifications.[96] The "U. S. Salvage Company," also operating as "Army & Navy Paint Company," was ordered to cease and desist from selling "Army & Navy Paints," including camouflage green, submarine black, and battleship grey, which were not in fact resold government stocks.[97] Another retailer was ordered to cease using the name "Government Supply House," and the words "Government Supplies" or "War Supplies," where the goods were bought in ordinary course from dealers and not from the Government.[98]

Other cases involve a claim that a certain article has been officially "adopted" by a government department. In advertising a brand of salt blocks for cattle, it was said that it had been "adopted" by the United States Government for the use of the cavalry, whereas in fact only one such purchase had been made.[99] The maker of

[95] See F.T.C. v. Tousey Varnish Co., 4 F.T.C.D. 144 (1921); F.T.C. v. McCloskey Varnish Co., 3 F.T.C.D. 413 (1921); F.T.C. v. Wm. E. Hinch, 5 F.T.C.D. 112 (1922).

[96] F.T.C. v. C. H. Parker Co., 5 F.T.C.D. 253 (1922).

[97] F.T.C. v. U.S. Salvage Co., 3 F.T.C.D. 130 (1920)

[98] F.T.C. v. Lewis Pelstring, 3 F.T.C.D. 42 (1920).

[99] F.T.C. v. Guarantee Veterinary Co. et al., 3 F.T.C.D. 402 (1921). Affirmed, 285 Fed. 853.

an accounting machine advertised that it had been "adopted" by the United States Government and the city of New York, whereas in fact neither the Government nor the city uses it "exclusively," but only in connection with others.[100] A maker of motor fuel advertised that his product had been tested by the United States Bureau of Mines, when it had not been so tested.[101] A spark plug manufacturer represented that his spark plug was the first plug officially approved for the Liberty Motor. It had been approved for the Liberty Motor, but it was not the first.[102] These cases have in common an attempt to appropriate good will belonging to the Government, or to claim for a product the reputation properly borne by an article made according to government specifications or standards, or under government supervision.

"COMBINATION SALES" AND "LEADERS"

THE so-called "combination sales" cases, although originally based in part upon broader grounds, come properly within the scope of this chapter. During the war and immediately afterwards, it will be recalled, sugar was being rationed out for sale at fixed prices. In an endeavor

[100] F.T.C. v. Accounting Machine Co., Inc., 3 F.T.C.D. 361 (1921).

[101] F.T.C. v. Chemical Fuel Co. of America, Inc., 4 F.T.C.D. 387 (1922). Cf. F.T.C. v. The Silvex Co., 1 F.T.C.D. 301 (1918), where the claim was that a spark plug had been tested by the "United States Department of Mines," when in fact it had been tested by the Bureau of Standards.

[102] F.T.C. v. The Silvex Co. et al., 4 F.T.C.D. 41 (1921). Compare F.T.C. v. Plunkett Chemical Co., 3 F.T.C.D. 53 (1920), where it appeared that a physician had in a public address condemned "the fallacious drip machine, the so-called toilet disinfector," as useless for the purpose. The address was reprinted in a United States Health Bulletin. Respondent, a maker of disinfectants, reproduced the article in an advertisement, making it appear that the address was a "public health report" instead of merely a reprint of a private speech. The offense seems somewhat technical.

to profit indirectly from the scarcity value which the product commanded, some unscrupulous dealers devised the "combination order," by which a customer was allowed a certain amount of sugar at the fixed price on condition that he buy also a stated amount of other supplies upon which the margin of profit to the retailer was larger. The practice was vicious in that it tended to defeat the efforts of the Food Administration and the Sugar Equalization Board to ration sugar at a fair price. The Federal Trade Commission, however, had no special jurisdiction over the distribution of necessaries or the prevention of "profiteering." It had jurisdiction only if the practice was an unfair method of competition or a violation of the Clayton Act.

In the leading case attacking this practice, the Commission appears to have taken the position that it is unlawful for a dealer to sell "certain of its merchandise," in interstate commerce, at less than cost, on condition that the customer purchase at the same time other merchandise upon which the dealer makes a profit.[103] Such, at least, is the implication of the complaint, findings, and order, for of course no opinion or statement of reasons was rendered. One paragraph of the complaint charges the offense in substantially the words given above, with the formal allegation that the sales were made "with the purpose, intent and effect of harassing and embarrassing its competitors, and destroying their trade and suppressing and stifling competition." The findings confirm the charge and conclude that the method of competition is unfair. Nothing is said as to war time control of sugar; the conclusion apparently does not rest upon the evasion of the Food Administration's rationing system. Apparently the view was that the practice would be illegal at all times. The order was even broader; one paragraph

---

[103] F.T.C. *v.* Sears, Roebuck & Co., 1 F.T.C.D. 163 (1918).

prohibited "selling, or offering to sell, sugar below cost through catalogues circulated throughout the States and Territories of the United States, and the District of Columbia, among its customers, prospective customers, and customers of its competitors." The order says nothing of combination sales, although this was the essence of the complaint. In the Circuit Court of Appeals,[104] however, this theory of the case was rejected. "We find in the statute," said the court, "no intent on the part of Congress, even if it has the power, to restrain an owner of property from selling it at any price that is acceptable to him or from giving it away."

A combination sale may, however, involve an element of deception. The dealer (generally a mail order house) will advertise a series of "combination orders" made up in part of staple commodities, such as sugar or flour, and in part of miscellaneous groceries and condiments. To the customer, the market value of sugar or flour is of course well known, but he is probably unfamiliar with the price or value of the other groceries of nondescript brand and quality included in the combination. In the advertisement, the flour and sugar will be priced substantially below market value, but the other articles will be listed at such a price that the combination as a whole will bring the dealer a handsome profit. The advertising will stress the low price of the sugar and flour, and will convey the impression, by various forms of suggestion, that the other articles are as cheap as the staples. In a series of cases the Commission has condemned this practice, apparently because of its deceptive character,[105] in

[104] Sears, Roebuck & Co. v. F.T.C., 258 Fed. 307 (1919).

[105] F.T.C. v. The Cole-Conrad Co., 2 F.T.C.D. 188 (1919); F.T.C. v. Commonwealth Co., 3 F.T.C.D. 46 (1920); F.T.C. v. Errant-Knight Co. et al., 3 F.T.C.D. 95 (1920); F.T.C. v. Liberty Wholesale Grocers, 3 F.T.C.D. 103 (1920); F.T.C. v. Big Four Grocery Co., 3 F.T.C.D. 338 (1921); F.T.C. v. Alben-Harley, 4 F.T.C.D. 31 (1921).

that it misleads customers both as to the quality and value of the articles (other than the staples) included in the combination, and as to the price usually charged for such articles by competitors.

The complaint in the Sears, Roebuck case seems to have been framed in part upon this theory, since it alleges in one paragraph that respondent had offered sugar for sale at three to four cents a pound, and that "said advertisements are false and misleading, in that they cause customers and prospective customers to believe that respondent, because of large purchases of sugar and because of quick moving stock, is able to sell sugar at a price lower than others offering sugar for sale . . ." Paragraph 2 of the findings sustains this charge, and the order prohibits "(1) Circulating throughout the States and Territories of the United States and the District of Columbia, catalogues containing advertisements offering for sale sugar, wherein it is falsely represented to its customers or prospective customers of said respondent or to customers of competitors, or to the public generally, or leads them to believe, that because of large purchasing power and quick-moving stock, respondent is able to sell sugar at a price lower than its competitors."[106] Upon this theory the Circuit Court of Appeals sustained the Commission's order (modified, however, so as to cover only *deceptive* sales below cost). The court said:

Petitioner's sales of sugar during the second half of 1915 amounted to $780,000 on which it lost $196,000. Petitioner used sugar as a "leader" ("You save 2 to 4 cents on every pound"), offering a limited amount at the losing price in connection with a required purchase of other commodities at prices high enough to afford petitioner a satisfactory profit on the transaction as a whole, without letting the customer know that the sugar was being sold on any other basis than that of the other commodities.

[106] F.T.C. *v.* Sears, Roebuck & Co., 1 F.T.C.D. 163, 172. Sears, Roebuck & Co. *v.* F.T.C., 258 Fed. 307, 309-310 (1919).

Petitioner obtained its sugar in the open market from refiners and wholesalers. Competitors got their sugar from the same sources, of the same quality, and at the same price. Sugar is a staple in the market. Price concessions upon large purchases are unobtainable. From the facts respecting petitioner's methods of advertising and buying and selling sugar respondent found, and properly so, in our judgment, that petitioner intentionally injured and discredited its competitors by falsely leading the public to believe that the competitors were unfair dealers in sugar and the other commodities which petitioner was offering in connection with sugar.[106]

It will be noted that the order, and the reasoning of the court, are not confined to ostensible sales below cost in combination with other sales at a profit. They are applicable to any sale of a standard article below cost, as a "leader," where the accompanying advertisements give the false impression that other merchandise is sold at the same low price. The decision therefore strikes at a practice frequently indulged in by department stores and mail order houses, of purchasing either a staple commodity or a standard product customarily sold at a set price (such as a dollar watch) and offering it for sale as a "leader" at a price substantially below cost, in connection with display advertising suggesting a general price reduction or sacrifice sale.[107]

"DISPARAGEMENT" AND FAIR COMMENT

ONE of the deceptive elements in a "combination sale" has been found to be its tendency to mislead customers as to the fairness of prices charged by competitors for the article selected as a "leader." The advertising in the

[107] Cf. the converse case, where respondent advertised it was selling sugar below cost, when in fact it was making a profit. The case is based on a formal stipulation, which does not show the surrounding circumstances, and does not quote the advertisements, hence it is not very satisfactory as a precedent. F.T.C. v. E. J. Brach & Sons, 1 F.T.C.D. 186 (1918). See Docket No. 121.

Sears, Roebuck case gave the impression that the low list price of sugar was due to the superior purchasing efficiency of the respondent, implying that dealers who sold at the regular price were 'not so efficient or were profiteering. This element suggests a group of cases involving so-called "disparagement" of competitors or their products. Cases have already been considered which involved false statements concerning a specific competitor or product designated by name or brand.[108] Here common law principles, and it would seem common law and equity procedure, are fully adequate to deal with the situation. The disparagement may, however, be of a whole class of competing products or firms.

Cases of this sort present clearly what is perhaps the most difficult problem in cases involving a charge of deceptive advertising. Truthfulness in advertising is of the greatest importance; nothing is so degrading as the general lowering of commercial morality apparent in trades in which deceptive and tricky trade practices are prevalent. On the other hand, we must not underestimate the value of the right to express publicly, in advertising or otherwise, honest opinions concerning one's own wares and those of competitors, whether or not those opinions are believed to be correct by a jury or a board of public officials. An erroneous statement of fact concerning the ingredients, chemical qualities, or manner of preparation of a drug or an article of food, even if made in good faith, should of course be prevented. Indeed, the vendor can be indicted under the Pure Food and Drugs Act, despite his good faith, for the protection of the public is paramount. But the Supreme Court held (three Justices dissenting), that the Pure Food and Drugs Act, although in terms condemning any label containing a false or misleading statement "regarding such article or the ingredients or substances contained therein," did not cover

[108] *Supra*, p. 176.

a statement as to the alleged curative qualities of a drug, although believed by the jury to be false.[109] A similar issue arose under the Postal Laws. The Postal authorities issued a "fraud order" against the School of Magnetic Healing, charging that its advertisements, which offered to cure all human ills by mental treatment, were fraudulent. The Supreme Court, however, held that claims of this sort were not within the purview of the Postal Laws.[110] It is interesting to compare some cases in which the Commission has dealt with representations which seem close to the border line at which statements of fact become statements of opinion.

I have already described one such case, where the alleged misrepresentation was in reality a statement of one side of a long-standing scientific controversy.[111] In other cases the question is closer. Thus a company selling an electric belt advertised that the appliance was "prescribed and recommended by the leading doctors of the United States," would keep the feet at a moderate temperature and revitalize the blood, and that its electric battery was "Nature's Vitalizer" and would save doctors' bills. The order forbade advertising that "its products possess such curative qualities as set forth in the foregoing findings." The case was on an agreed statement, which shows that the practice had been abandoned, but there is no finding, except inferentially, that the claims were false.[112] It seems doubtful whether the decision can be supported. A statement as to the efficacy of a chemical may, however, be so extreme as to take it clearly beyond the realm of opinion. Perhaps this was

[109] U.S. v. Johnson, 211 U.S. 488 (1911). Subsequently, however, the effect of the decision was nullified by Act of Congress. See post, p. 229.

[110] American School of Magnetic Healing v. McAnnulty, 187 U.S. 94 (1902).

[111] Supra, p. 138.

[112] F.T.C. v. The Electric Appliance Co., 2 F.T.C.D. 335 (1920).

so in the Ginso Chemical Company case,[113] where the finding is that the respondent made "the false and misleading representation" that a disinfectant sold by them was "ten times stronger as a germicide than undiluted U. S. P. carbolic acid." The case is weakened, however, by the absence of positive findings as to the germicidal strength of respondent's product.

Where the statements concern competitors or competing products the problem is especially delicate. It is a rule of advertising ethics not to speak disparagingly of your competitors, but there are many rules of business or professional ethics which have by no means acquired the force of law. "Disparagement" is not a term of legal precision. It seems doubtful whether a statement concerning a competitor or his products can be considered to be an "unfair method of competition" within the meaning of the Federal Trade Commission Act unless it conveys a misrepresentation of fact injurious to his business. In two cases the respondents, who were mail order houses, had advertised that the "regular" lumber dealers were members of the "Lumber Trust." The Commission found that the statement was "in truth false," and deceived and misled the public, and prohibited the practice.[114] In another case the manufacturer of tires and rims was ordered not to apply the term "pirate" to a competitor who made spare parts to fit his rims, or to the spare parts themselves.[115] Since the stipulation in that case set forth that "parts made by other than the manufacturer of the rim are generally known and designated in the trade by various terms, the terms 'pirate' and 'gyp' parts being among those most extensively used," it seems doubtful

[113] F.T.C. v. Ginso Chemical Co., 4 F.T.C.D. 155 (1921).

[114] F.T.C. v. Chicago Mill Works Supply Co., 1 F.T.C.D. 488 (1919); F.T.C. v. Gordon-Van Tine Co., 1 F.T.C.D. 316 (1919).

[115] F.T.C v. Keaton Tire & Rubber Co., 5 F.T.C.D. 335 (1922). See the official Docket No. 882.

whether the use of the term exceeded the bounds of fair criticism or description. Indeed, the statement, in the sense in which the word "pirate" is understood in the trade, seems to have been true. In another case respondent was found to have circulated a reprint of a news article setting forth that a certain competitor had been found guilty of violating the Sherman Law, and had been enjoined by a federal district court.[116] There is no finding that the item was not accurately copied, or that it did not truthfully state the facts. The order prohibited "embarrassing, harassing or restraining" competitors by circulating the news item in question, "or by publishing or circulating in a similar manner, any printed clipping or circular similar in form, purport or effect, regarding any competitor of the respondent." Another company circulated a newspaper clipping telling of an application for appointment of a receiver of the assets of a competitor, whereas "such receiver has never been appointed." It was ordered to cease circulating "false and unfair matter concerning the business or standing of competitors."[117] In another case a mail order lumber house in an advertisement referred in exulting language to the Federal Trade Commission's proceedings against the "regular dealers."[118] The Commission filed a complaint against the lumber house, and found that the advertisement was

[116] F.T.C. *v.* Wayne Oil Tank & Pump Co., 1 F.T.C.D. 259 (1918).

[117] F.T.C. v. Sunlight Creameries, 4 F.T.C.D. 55 (1921). *Cf.,* however, F.T.C. *v.* Gartside Iron Rust Soap Co., 1 F.T.C.D. 310 (1919). Order forbids "falsely representing that certain of his competitors are financially irresponsible."

[118] F.T.C. *v.* Gordon-Van Tine Co., 1 F.T.C.D. 316 (1919). The advertisement read in part:

"A victory has been won for you and for us.

"Through coercion, threats, misrepresentation, and subterfuge, retail lumber dealers have for years attempted to prevent us from selling to you and to keep you from buying from us.

"Now, the Federal Trade Commission has stepped in, and said 'No "false, misleading, and a gross misrepresentation of the terms of the said order issued by the Commission," and ordered respondent to cease and desist from "Printing or causing to be printed, circulating or causing to be circulated, orders, findings, and other public records of the Federal Trade Commission unless the whole of the order, findings, or public record of said Commission be printed in full and in the exact wording of the Commission without any interpretation of, addition to, or subtraction from such order, findings, or public record, as made and entered by the Commission.'"[119] Such an arbitrary attempt to suppress free comment upon the Commission's own decisions is difficult to reconcile with the first amendment to the Federal Constitution.

In one aspect, the Sears, Roebuck case, although affirmed in this respect by the Circuit Court of Appeals, seems open to the same criticism. One of the advertisements contained the following:

For instance, every grocer carries granulated sugar in stock, but does he tell you which kind? There are two kinds—granulated cane sugar and granulated beet sugar—and they look exactly alike. Some people prefer the one and some the other. But beet sugar usually costs less than cane sugar, so if you are getting beet sugar you should pay less for it. Do you know which kind you are getting and which you are paying for?[120]

When the Commission's investigator called the advertisement to the attention of the company's officials, they admitted it was "unfair and unjust," and that it was "against the policy of the house" to send out such advertisements.[121] The Commission's findings do not

interference! A square deal for everybody.' From now on you can buy wherever you please without being bothered, boycotted, or bluffed."

[119] *Idem,* p. 324.

[120] Sears, Roebuck & Co. *v.* F.T.C., 258 Fed. 307, 309.

[121] *See* extract from stipulation, quoted in Judge Alschuler's dissenting opinion, Sears, Roebuck & Co. *v.* F.T.C., 258 Fed. 307, 313.

quote the advertisement, but describe it as representing "that respondent's competitors did not deal justly, fairly and honestly with their customers." There is no finding that the representation is untrue; indeed, common experience would seem to indicate that it was substantially correct. The Circuit Court of Appeals affirmed this part of the order, although without discussion. Upon this point, however, Judge Alschuler dissented, observing: "It seems to me that this does not amount to more than a statement or boast that petitioner, without being asked, describes the white sugars it proposes to sell, and the intimation is carried that competitors do not volunteer such description, but it is not suggested that they actually misrepresent the truth." The case suggests that perhaps the majority of the court did not fully appreciate that legitimate criticism of competitors may be of value in raising the standards of the trade, and that a rule of business ethics or "house policy" which forbids such criticism may not be entirely in the public interest.

A case which involves, not the right of fair comment, but the right of free competition, is Federal Trade Commission v. The Oakes Company.[122] Respondent was a manufacturer of radiator fans for automobiles, trucks, and tractors, the largest part of his output being of the "cup-and-cone" type. A competitor manufactured fans for the same purpose, but largely of the roller-bearing type, which was found by the Commission to cost about 48 cents more to manufacture than the cup-and-cone type. The respondent, however, offered to the trade a roller-bearing fan at a lower price than the competitor was charging, and the Commission found that "respondent does not offer its roller-bearing fan to the trade in good faith for the purpose of selling it, but solely for the purpose of depreciating the value of the roller-bear-

[122] 3 F.T.C.D. 36 (1920).

ing type of fan as manufactured by its competitor and inducing the public to believe that its competitor is selling its roller-bearing type of fan at more than a fair price.'' The complaint, it should be noted, charged that respondent was selling the roller-bearing fan ''below cost,'' but this charge was apparently disproved, for the finding is merely that the price was below that of the competitor. No grounds are stated for concluding that the offer was not in good faith. If this remarkable case is good law, every manufacturer who undersells a competitor in interstate commerce does so at the risk that the Federal Trade Commission may conclude that his purpose is to ''depreciate'' the goods of a competitor rather than to sell his own.

It is with some reservations that I express a judgment concerning these decisions. The form which the ''findings'' take, in these as in other cases, is such that one cannot be certain that all the relevant facts are there, and, since no reasons are given, one cannot be certain that cogent and persuasive grounds for supporting the decisions do not exist. The cases seem to me to show, however, a dangerous tendency to look at a controversy too much from the viewpoint of the complaining competitor, and to fail to balance impartially not only the interests of the respondent, but the public interest in free competition and fair comment. It is easy to understand the indignation of the maker of roller-bearing fans when his rival began to undersell him, or of the competitor who was publicly described by the crude but technically correct term ''pirate,'' or even of the Commission itself when the lumber house had the temerity to give a colloquial version of one of its official orders. Yet a more judicial attitude should, it seems, have recognized that these practices were not among those which the law could properly prevent.

SECRET COMMISSIONS TO DEALERS

ONE reason why the law is rightly more lenient toward erroneous statements of opinion is that they are as a rule less damaging than false statements of fact. When a salesman says that a piece of furniture is made of mahogany, the purchaser, unless sophisticated by experience, will take him at his word, but when the salesman says it is "as good as mahogany" few customers are misled.

The Commission appears to have taken the position, however, that under certain conditions the customer can insist that the expressions of opinion of the salesman be at least disinterested and made in good faith. Two cases involving retailers of vacuum cleaners illustrate the theory. A dealer published what purported to be an impartial "rating sheet" of vacuum cleaners, upon which were listed, in the order of supposed excellence, the various brands on the market. A relatively unknown brand headed the list. The list did not reveal the fact that this particular brand was the one in which the dealer was especially interested, and upon which it received the largest commission.[123] Another dealer stated in his advertising that he was an expert and impartial vacuum cleaner specialist, and was not specially interested in any company. He invariably recommended the purchase of two brands of cleaners, in which he was in fact especially interested.[124] The findings in both cases are not very explicit as to the nature of the "special interest" in question, but the conclusion that the method of competition was unfair seems to have been warranted.

In these cases the dealer appears expressly to have held himself out as an impartial judge of the various

[123] F.T.C. *v.* Vacuum Cleaner Specialty Co., Inc., 3 F.T.C.D. 377 (1921).

[124] F.T.C. *v.* Muenzen Specialty Co., 1 F.T.C.D. 30 (1917).

makes. To what extent is such a representation implied from the mere fact that a dealer handles different brands and expresses to the customer his belief that one or the other is the better one? In a great many cases a customer will ask for a particular commodity, say, flour, or talcum powder, or red pepper. The storekeeper will ask, "What kind do you want?" The customer will reply, "Whichever is best," and the storekeeper will select one of the brands. Is the customer entitled to assume that the storekeeper's judgment is unbiased, and is the manufacturer or jobber competing unfairly if he gives the storekeeper a pecuniary incentive to give a biased judgment in favor of his particular brand?

Such appears to be the view which the Commission has taken. A mail order lumber house was found to have offered to local contractors "a bonus or so-called commission without the knowledge of the purchaser or consumer, as an inducement to influence such contractors or builders to push or favor the sale of respondent's lumber and building materials over those of its competitors." The company was ordered to cease and desist from such practice.[125] The Aeolian Company inserted in its contract with retailers a clause that if the retailer handled any other makes of phonograph, it would "directly and indirectly" advertise and promote the Aeolian phonographs and records "as its best and unqualified leader of any and all goods of the phonograph type." The practice was found to be unfair.[126] A number of cases condemn a practice apparently common in some lines of retail distribution, of giving cash bonuses to the salesmen of the retail store. These bonuses or commissions are given by the manufacturer with the knowledge and approval of the salesman's employer. It is not a case of

[125] F.T.C. *v*. Gordon-Van Tine Co., 1 F.T.C.D. 316 (1919).
[126] F.T.C. *v*. The Aeolian Co., 3 F.T.C.D. 124 (1920).

commercial bribery.[127] The wrong, if there is any, is in giving the salesman a special incentive to make sales of the favored brand, while concealing the incentive from the purchaser.[128] In the Seventh Circuit, however, the Circuit Court of Appeals has annulled an order of the Commission forbidding this practice. The court pointed out that the premiums were given with the knowledge of the salesman's employer and by arrangement with him, and rejected the argument that consumers were misled by the failure to disclose the salesman's special interest. The court observed that "a salesman, with the master's consent, may discriminate all he pleases between the goods he has to sell."[129] Undoubtedly, the court was influenced by the startling consequences which the Commission's theory would lead to. The dealer's profit or commission on different brands varies. Must he post in his shop window a schedule of commissions, so that customers may learn by how much they should discount his "seller's talk" as to each brand? The dealer himself often employs his salesmen on commission, and the commission may vary according to the article sold. Must the salesman bear a placard setting forth circumstantially what he makes on each article? Such is the logic of the Commission's theory. Common sense suggests, however, that a customer is not entitled to regard a salesman as a judicial officer or even as an impartial professional adviser; that it is common knowledge that both dealers

---

[127] *See post*, p. 217.

[128] In the following cases it was held unlawful for a manufacturer to give cash bonuses, prizes, or commissions to salesmen of retail dealers, though apparently they were given with the knowledge and consent of the dealer: F.T.C. *v.* The Hoover Suction Sweeper Co., 1 F.T.C.D. 476 (1919); F.T.C. *v.* Royal Easy Chair Co., 2 F.T.C.D. 139 (1919); F.T.C. *v.* Carter Paint Co., 2 F.T.C.D. 181 (1919); F.T.C. *v.* The Utah Bedding & Mfg. Co., 2 F.T.C.D. 185 (1919); F.T.C. *v.* Shotwell Mfg. Co., 3 F.T.C.D. 25 (1920).

[129] Kinney-Rome Co. *v.* F.T.C., 275 Fed. 665 (1921).

and salesmen are in business for profit; and that opinions expressed in making a sale do not profess to be unbiased by self-interest.

COMMERCIAL BRIBERY

THE cases which show most clearly the importance of the Commission's work in stamping out dishonest trade practices, and the difficulties inherent in its procedure and in its jurisdictional limitations, are those which involve commercial bribery. This disgraceful practice appears to have become distressingly prevalent in certain lines of trade. In nearly a hundred cases the Commission has entered formal orders prohibiting the practice, and many others are still in process of litigation. They do not indicate mere sporadic instances of dishonesty, but settled commercial practices which often permeate the trade. It seems to have been universally expected that companies selling chemicals and dyes, or paints and varnishes, should give to the buyer or superintendent of their customer a secret "commission" on all purchases, and that the ship's steward and chief engineer, on American as well as foreign vessels, should get his 5 or 10 per cent from the chandler who supplied the ship's stores. In a special report to Congress in 1918 the Commission gave a vivid picture of the prevalence of the practice in certain lines:

The practice is one which has been condemned alike by business men, legislatures, and courts, including among the business men those who have finally resorted to it in self-defense in competing with less scrupulous rivals or in selling to concerns whose employees have extorted commissions under threats to destroy or disapprove goods submitted to them for test.

How prevalent the practice is and how great the need of legislation seems to be is illustrated by the statement of one man of prominence in an industry who welcomed the proceedings of the Commission destined to destroy the practice with this statement:

"From an experience of 30 years in the industry I don't believe that there is a single house in it that has not had to pay bribes to hold old business or to obtain new business. Bribery is inherently dishonest and tends to dishonesty and is unfair to competitors and customers, and I don't believe it ever will be stopped until made a crime by the United States Government."

How thoroughly insidious this practice has become may be illustrated by two experiences of representatives of the Commission. In one case an employee frankly stated that he was "entitled to 10 per cent, and anyone who demands more is a grafter." Another was so fully imbued with the justice of his claim that he desired the representative of the Commission to assist him in enforcing the collection of an unpaid so-called commission.

Corrupt employees having the power to spoil and disapprove materials have been able to bid one salesman against another, until in many cases they have extorted secret commissions, so-called, as large as 20 per cent of the value of the goods sold.[130]

The published findings of the Commission in the commercial bribery cases generally contain no more than a bare statement that the respondent firm is engaged in selling the article in question in interstate commerce; that it is in active competition with other firms; and that, in the course of its business, respondent "for several years last past has given cash gratuities to employees of its customers, without the knowledge or consent of their employers and without other consideration therefor, as an inducement to influence their employers to purchase respondent's products and to refrain from purchasing the product of its competitors."[131] Now and then, however,

[130] 1920 Annual Report, p. 53.

[131] *See,* for instance, F.T.C. *v.* Essex Varnish Co., 1 F.T.C.D. 138 (1918); F.T.C. *v.* Twin City Varnish Co., 1 F.T.C.D. 190 (1918); F.T.C. *v.* The Royal Varnish Co., 1 F.T.C.D. 194 (1918); F.T.C. *v.* The Printers' Roller Co., 1 F.T.C.D. 240 (1918); F.T.C. *v.* The American Printers' Roller Co., 1 F.T.C.D. 244 (1918); F.T.C. *v.* Blakely Printing

we get a more realistic glimpse of the nature and extent
of the practice. In the case of a ship chandler at Savannah
it is found (upon an agreed statement of facts) that cash
gratuities to ships' officers amounted to approximately 5
per cent of the total volume of sales of ships' supplies, in
addition to approximately 2½ per cent spent for entertainment.[132] A Galveston ship chandler paid 5 per cent
of all invoices to the ship's officers.[133] In Pensacola the
figure seems to have been from 3 to 5 per cent.[134] In a case
involving a New Orleans ship chandler[135] the practice is
described more in detail:

Most of the owners of vessels to which the respondent fur-
nishes supplies leave the purchasing or ordering of the supplies
for their ships to the captain, steward, or chief engineer, par-

Co. et al., 1 F.T.C.D. 277 (1918); F.T.C. v. Stewart, Dickson & Co.,
Inc., 1 F.T.C.D. 331 (1919); F.T.C. v. Wall Rope Works, Inc., 1
F.T.C.D. 468 (1919); F.T.C. v. Standard Soap Mfg. Co., 1 F.T.C.D.
480 (1919); F.T.C. v. The Engineering Supply Co., 2 F.T.C.D. 62
(1919); F.T.C. v. Federal Color & Chemical Co., 2 F.T.C.D. 71 (1919);
F.T.C. v. Woodley Soap Mfg. Co., 2 F.T.C.D. 78 (1919); F.T.C. v.
F. E. Atteaux & Co., Inc., 2 F.T.C.D. 82 (1919); F.T.C. v. Twin
City Printers' Roller Co., 2 F.T.C.D. 102 (1919); F.T.C. v. Ma-
rine Supply Co., 2 F.T.C.D. 107 (1919); F.T.C. v. Flood & Calvert,
3 F.T.C.D. 205 (1921); F.T.C. v. John R. Adams & Co., 3 F.T.C.D. 209
(1921); F.T.C. v. Geo. C. LeGendre & Son, 3 F.T.C.D. 213 (1921);
F.T.C. v. T. C. Hurst & Son, 3 F.T.C.D. 223 (1921); F.T.C. v. Marine
Equipment Co., 3 F.T.C.D. 227 (1921); F.T.C. v. Cowles Ship Supply
Co., Inc., 3 F.T.C.D. 235 (1921); F.T.C. v. W. A. Rhea, 3 F.T.C.D.
239 (1921); F.T.C. v. Richardson Bros., 3 F.T.C.D. 242 (1921); F.T.C.
v. U.S. Color & Chemical Co., Inc., 3 F.T.C.D. 313 (1921); F.T.C. v.
Runyan Co., 3 F.T.C.D. 353 (1921); F.T.C. v. Sealwood Co., 4 F.T.C.D.
65 (1921); F.T.C. v. Seymour Chemical Co. et al., 4 F.T.C.D. 69 (1921).

[132] F.T.C. v. Thomas Duggan & Son, 3 F.T.C.D. 316 (1921).

[133] F.T.C. v. John W. Focke, 3 F.T.C.D. 320 (1921).

[134] F.T.C. v. McKenzie Oerting & Co., 3 F.T.C.D. 323 (1921); F.T.C.
v. White Star Market, 4 F.T.C.D. 313 (1922).

[135] F.T.C. v. F. G. McFarlane, 4 F.T.C.D. 292 (1922). See also
F.T.C. v. D. A. Winslow & Co., 3 F.T.C.D. 217 (1921), where the practice is well described.

ticularly the captain, and the practice of giving gratuities to such officers by the respondent and his competitors is followed to such an extent that the captain or other purchasing officer of the vessel will patronize the ship chandler who will pay the gratuity. Many captains of these vessels get small salaries and this custom of receiving gratuities enables them to increase their compensation to the extent of the gratuity paid. The gratuity is not accounted for to the owners of the vessel. The amount of the gratuity differs among different chandlers—the minimum is 5 per cent and the maximum 10 per cent of the amount of the invoice.[136]

More particularly, it was found that:

The method of doing business was for the respondent to visit vessels in the harbor at New Orleans and if the vessel was under contract to do business with the respondent, the captain would be so advised. If the vessel was one known as a free ship, the captain's business would be solicited by the respondent. Upon securing the captain's business, the respondent would convey him ashore in a launch which was part of the equipment of the ship chandlery owned by respondent. The captain would be taken to respondent's place of business where headquarters would be provided for him. A room being furnished, known as the captain's room, for the captain's convenience, was used. Many times lavish entertainment was provided, consisting of automobile parties, joy rides, theater and dinner parties, tickets for a prize fight, meals, lodging accommodations, and other forms of entertainment and amusement as well as cash gratuities.[137]

In a case involving a ship chandler at Sparrows Point[138] the names of the ships are given. In the complaint about half of the ships named are said to be "private-owned," and the remainder "operated for" the United States Shipping Board Emergency Fleet Corporation. The findings merely give the names of the vessels.

The expenditures of a Norfolk chandler, for entertain-

[136] 4 F.T.C.D. 295.
[137] *Ibid.*
[138] F.T.C. *v.* Sparrows Point Store Co., 3 F.T.C.D. 20 (1920).

ment of ships' officers, was found to be approximately $850 per month.[139] A ship repair company made an agreement to pay the port engineer of a line of vessels (not named) 10 per cent of all repair work, the amount being added to the bill for the work.[140] A Rhode Island dye manufacturer was found to have given, since the date of its incorporation in 1919, bribes ranging from $30 to $150 per month to the dyers and finishers in about 20 per cent of the textile mills with which it did business.[141] A British dye company did an annual business in the United States of approximately $700,000, and its expenditures for entertainment and gratuities to employees of customers were found to have averaged during three years from $40,000 to $50,000 a year.[142] A paint manufacturer was found to have instructed his salesmen to offer secret gratuities to foremen of automobile and carriage establishments and other customers, and to have appropriated funds for the purpose. The names of the salesmen are given, and the amount which each spent in this way in the space of four months, the amounts ranging from $90 to $1960.[143] In a case in which the findings are more detailed and specific than is usual, it is found that a maker of glue had paid secret commissions to an employee of the Victor Talking Machine Company, which in twenty-three months amounted to $34,000. To the credit of the company be it said that upon discovery of the facts the employee was dismissed.[144] Secret commissions paid by a chemical company were found to have amounted to from $30,000 to $40,000 in a single year.[145] In two

[139] F.T.C. v. Everett Supply Co., Inc., 3 F.T.C.D. 231 (1921).

[140] F.T.C. v. Southern Machine Works, 4 F.T.C.D. 97 (1921).

[141] F.T.C. v. Ricco Co., 3 F.T.C.D. 418 (1921).

[142] F.T.C. v. United Indigo & Chemical Co., Ltd., 3 F.T.C.D. 425 (1921).

[143] F.T.C. v. Beckwith-Chandler Co. et al., 4 F.T.C.D. 108 (1921).

[144] F.T.C. v. Baeder, Adamson Co., 4 F.T.C.D. 129 (1921).

[145] F.T.C. v. United Chemical Products Corp., 4 F.T.C.D. 220 (1922).

cases[146] there are long lists of ships, with the amount paid
as bribes to captains and stewards on each ship.[147]

A serious difficulty in these commercial bribery cases,
is of course the jurisdictional necessity of proving that
the acts were done in the course of interstate or foreign
commerce. The difficulty does not appear in the Commission's published findings, since the jurisdictional fact is
almost invariably embodied in a conclusion that respondent is engaged in the business of selling certain commodities in interstate commerce, and that in the course of
such commerce the acts complained of were committed.
In two cases against ship chandlers in Norfolk, however,
the Circuit Court of Appeals, upon petition to review,
vacated orders of the Commission on the ground that the
transactions were purely intrastate.[148] From the court's
opinion it appears that two features were relied upon by
the Commission in support of its jurisdiction: first, that
the materials were purchased from other states, and
second, that they were sold to foreign flagships engaged
in interstate commerce. Since the bribery took place in
the course of sales, and not of purchases, the first feature
was considered irrelevant, and as to the second, the court
held that a sale of supplies to a foreign flagship, even
pursuant to orders placed from the home office abroad,
was not a transaction in foreign commerce. In these cases
the Supreme Court denied *certiorari*.[149] The decision casts

[146] F.T.C. *v.* Haas Bros. Packing Co., Inc., 4 F.T.C.D. 248 (1922);
F.T.C. *v.* Cowley Packing Co., Inc., 4 F.T.C.D. 253 (1922).

[147] Mention may be made at this point of the closely allied though
apparently less prevalent practice of commercial espionage. Orders
against this practice were entered in the Botsford Lumber Co. case, 1
F.T.C.D. 60, the C. W. Baker & Sons case, 1 F.T.C.D. 452, the case
against the Oakes Co., 3 F.T.C.D. 36, and in F.T.C. *v.* Warewell Co.,
5 F.T.C.D. 294.

[148] Winslow *v.* F.T.C. and Norden Ship Supply Co., Inc., *v.* F.T.C.,
277 Fed. 206 (1921).

[149] 258 U.S. 618 (1922).

doubt upon all the cases against ship chandlers above referred to.

The cases which I have described involved commercial bribery in its grossest form—the secret payment of money to influence an employee in the performance of his duties. As a matter of legal analysis it should make no difference whether the bribe was paid in cash or in kind, and a number of cases, accordingly, condemn the practice of giving "gratuities" of any description, including liquor, cigars, meals, theatre tickets, entertainment, and "other valuable property." Common conceptions of honesty, however, suggest a difference between bribery and mere "treating," and it seems probable that some of the orders of the Commission in these cases go too far. In the first place, an offer of a cigar or a meal to a buyer is not generally made furtively. It would probably be made in the presence of the buyer's employer as freely as in his absence. The element of secrecy seems to be an essential characteristic of a true commercial bribe. In the second place, the fact that a buyer has accepted the hospitality of a salesman, even to the extent of going to lunch with him and smoking his cigars, does not as a matter of current commercial morality impose any obligation on the buyer to exercise a corrupt judgment in placing his orders. It does not necessarily imply an improper bargain, as does an agreement to pay 5 per cent on all purchases. I suggest these distinctions, again, with some hesitation, for the "findings" in the commercial treating cases are so generally inadequate that it is impossible to ascertain the form or extent of the practice in the great majority of cases. The finding, made in substance in almost all these cases, that respondent has given to employees of customers to influence them to buy from respondent or to refrain from dealing with respondent's competitors, "without other consideration therefor," liquor, cigars, meals, theatre tickets, "and other personal property," is purely formal, and was rightly described by the Circuit Court of Appeals in the Second Circuit as a mere conclusion.[150] Often the findings do not indicate whether the "treating" was secret or open; the reasonable assumption is that there was no secrecy involved. I have reviewed elsewhere the testimony in one of these cases to show how inadequately the formal findings reveal the real issues involved.[151] In the absence of special facts, however, it is difficult to avoid the conclusion reached by the Circuit Court of Appeals in the Second Circuit, that the mere entertainment of buyers, even to the extent of wining and dining them, is not necessarily an unfair method of competition.[152]

It is difficult, however, to follow a dictum of the court in the same case, that even a true case of commercial bribery is beyond the jurisdiction of the Commission, because it is "a matter between individuals" and does not affect the public. In a sense every act of unfair competition is a matter between individuals. If the court had been fully familiar with the extent and scope of the practice, as revealed by the decisions of the Commission, and with its insidious effect upon fair and honorable competition, it could not, it seems to me, have reached the conclusion that proceedings by the Commission in such cases were not in the public interest.

The value of the Commission's work in these commercial bribery cases is difficult to overestimate. It has brought the evil into the light of public discussion, and

[150] New Jersey Asbestos Co. v. F.T.C., 264 Fed. 509 (1920). *See,* among other cases, the following, which illustrate the point: F.T.C. v. The Printers' Roller Co., 1 F.T.C.D. 240 (1918); F.T.C. v. The American Printers' Roller Co., 1 F.T.C.D. 244 (1918); F.T.C. v. Rome Soap Mfg. Co., 1 F.T.C.D. 484 (1919); F.T.C. v. Woodley Soap Mfg. Co., 2 F.T.C.D. 78 (1919).

[151] *See supra,* p. 135.

[152] New Jersey Asbestos Co. v. F.T.C., 264 Fed. 509.

has undoubtedly led many a business man, who had bowed to the practice before, to make the necessary effort to stamp it out in his own establishment, and to insist that it be discontinued by the firms with which he does business. As long as no other federal agency exists to deal with the evil, it is clearly in the public interest that the Commission's work in such cases be pressed with unremitting vigor. The Commission itself, however, has frankly recognized the inadequacy of its powers so far as commercial bribery is described.[153] The Commission has no criminal jurisdiction, whereas commercial bribery is (or more accurately, should be) a criminal act. The Commission, moreover, can only deal with the bribe giver, whereas the bribe taker is equally guilty. The special report recommends a drastic criminal statute, applicable to any person who participates in the dishonest transaction and of sufficient scope to cover every case in which commercial bribery is used in the course of interstate commerce, or as a means of competition injurious to interstate commerce.

MISCELLANEOUS CASES

A FEW miscellaneous cases may be mentioned briefly. I have already discussed two cases in which a "guarantee" that rebuilt tires would give 4000 miles of service was held to contain a false and misleading representation that they were expected to run 4000 miles.[154] It seems doubtful whether the orders in these cases can be supported. There is a curious case in which a District of Columbia tailor was found to have advertised suits for sale on the installment plan, at 50 cents a week for 60 weeks, with a provision that each week one customer, selected by lot, would get a remission of all unpaid in-

---

[153] *See* the special report above referred to, *supra,* p. 217.

[154] F.T.C. *v.* E. P. Janes et al., 1 F.T.C.D. 380 (1919); F.T.C. *v.* Akron Tire Co., Inc., 2 F.T.C.D. 119 (1919). *Supra,* p. 146.

stallments.[155] In fact, the lottery was not conducted as advertised, and the order in effect forbids the respondent to represent falsely that he conducts a lottery. Another dealer was ordered to refrain from advertising that he made "no extra charge for credit" when in fact he gave a discount for cash.[156] In another case a fictitious forced sale by mercantile adjusters took place, and the respondent was ordered not to do it again.[157]

A few cases involve a practice of which much was said in the discussion leading up to the passage of the Trade Commission Act, namely, the employment of so-called "bogus independent" subsidiaries. For one reason or another some large business concerns have seen fit to segregate part of their business in a separate corporation, and to permit the subsidiary to operate without revealing its affiliation with the parent concern. The motive may be to create a false semblance of competition, or to reach customers who are considered hostile to the parent concern, or perhaps to facilitate price concessions in special cases without imperiling the price level of a regular brand. The practice has a deceptive element, and has been condemned in several cases by the Commission,[158] although none of the orders have yet been tested in the courts. Another group of cases involves a form of deception common in some lines of retail trade. To lead customers to believe that they are getting cheaper service because the middleman's profits are eliminated, a retailer will adopt a trade name, or style of advertising, designed to create the impression that he is a manufacturer operating a branch retail store, although in fact he buys

---

[155] F.T.C. *v.* Budd Tailoring Co., 5 F.T.C.D. 207 (1922).

[156] F.T.C. *v.* National Furniture Co., 4 F.T.C.D. 330 (1922).

[157] F.T.C. *v.* Stinemetz & Son Co., 5 F.T.C.D. 424 (1923).

[158] F.T.C. *v.* Armour & Co., 1 F.T.C.D. 430; F.T.C. *v.* A. A. Berry Seed Co., 2 F.T.C.D. 427 (1920); F.T.C. *v.* St. Louis Lightning Rod Co., 3 F.T.C.D. 327 (1921).

his stock from manufacturers or even wholesalers or jobbers in the usual manner. Thus a retailer will call himself "National Tailoring Company," or "The Old Woolen Mills Company,"[159] or "Pure Silk Hosiery Mills,"[160] or in some other manner will imply in his advertising that the goods he is offering are of his own manufacture.[161] Or a coal dealer will call himself "Bernice Coal Company," and advertise that he is ready to ship coal direct from his "Bernice mines," when in fact he buys his coal from operators and dealers.[162] Often the misrepresentation will be pictorial, e.g., by putting on the letterhead a print of a factory.[163] Analogous also is the practice of exaggerating one's importance in the commercial world by falsely claiming to have offices in a number of leading cities.[164]

LIMITED EFFECTIVENESS OF THE COMMISSION'S PROCEDURE

THE summary which I have made of these cases presents only an inadequate picture of the work of the Commission in combating misbranding and other untruthful trade practices in the course of interstate commerce. It covers only the cases in which formal proceedings have been conducted. Doubtless the indirect influence in educating

[159] F.T.C. v. Briede & Rogovsky, 4 F.T.C.D. 215 (1922).

[160] F.T.C. v. Pure Silk Hosiery Mills, 5 F.T.C.D. 245 (1922).

[161] See F.T.C. v. C. L. Chase, 1 F.T.C.D. 495 (1919); F.T.C. v. St. Louis Lightning Rod Co. et al., 3 F.T.C.D. 327 (1921); F.T.C. v. The Check Writer Mfrs., Inc., et al., 4 F.T.C.D. 87 (1921); F.T.C. v. Solus Mfrs. Co., 4 F.T.C.D. 317 (1922); F.T.C. v. American Turpentine Co., 5 F.T.C.D. 410 (1923).

[162] F.T.C. v. Bernice Coal Co., 4 F.T.C.D. 209 (1922).

[163] See F.T.C. v. Consolidated Oil Co. et al., 1 F.T.C.D. 285 (1918); F.T.C. v. Midwest Linseed & Paint Oil Co., 2 F.T.C.D. 295 (1920); F.T.C. v. Boston Piano & Music Co., 3 F.T.C.D. 168 (1920).

[164] See F.T.C. v. Federal Press, Inc., 3 F.T.C.D. 345 (1921); F.T.C. v. Union Soap Co., 4 F.T.C.D. 397 (1922).

the business world to a higher conception of trade ethics has been fully as great as the direct effect of the Commission's orders. In lending assistance and encouragement to trade associations in stamping out vicious trade practices the Commission has contributed much toward the success which these associations have achieved.

Looking at the matter from a more critical viewpoint, however, it becomes apparent that there are certain limitations in the powers of the Commission and certain obstacles in its procedure which impair its usefulness in some of the cases involved.

One such limitation I have already mentioned. Where the deceptive brand or name, or the misleading advertisement, is designed to lead customers to confuse respondent's product with the product of a specific competitor, there is a remedy in the courts of law and equity which is more prompt and more efficacious than the cumbersome procedure of the Commission. The same is true where the offense consists of a false statement concerning a named competitor or his merchandise. In such cases it would seem that the person injured should be made to pursue his remedy in a private litigation, and that public funds should not be expended by a governmental agency to relieve him of that burden. Unless there are countervailing facts which do not appear in the formal findings, it would seem that in most of the cases involving unfair methods of competition directed primarily against a named competitor, the Commission should not, in the public interest, have issued a complaint.[165] Of course this

[165] This criticism applies not only to the "passing off" cases referred to on pages 167 ff., *supra,* but to the following also, in which, in so far as there is any merit to the case, the person primarily injured would seem to have an adequate remedy at law or in equity: F.T.C. *v.* John Bene & Sons., Inc., 5 F.T.C.D. 314 (1922), (circulating chemical analysis of a competitor's product with inaccurate comments); F.T.C. *v.* Geographical Pub. Co., 1 F.T.C.D. 235 (1918), (appropriating, for advertising

should be no more than a rule of discretion. There may be special factors which render the legal or equitable remedy inadequate, as where the wrongdoer is so strong that the competitor does not dare to oppose him openly; or where a practice, although directed against specific individuals, is so prevalent that only drastic action by a government agency can put an end to it;[166] or where the injury to the competitor is too slight to move him to action but the public injury is great. Yet it seems reasonable that where such special circumstances exist, the Commission should state in its complaint and its "report in writing" the facts upon which it bases its finding that the public interest warrants the issuance of a complaint. The formal assertion, included as a matter of routine in each complaint, that it appears "that a proceeding by it in respect thereof would be to the interest of the public," does not carry conviction.

The second limitation which suggests itself, is that the Commission should not, except in special cases, institute proceedings where the practice in question falls within the scope of the Pure Food and Drugs Act, or of similar federal legislation. The reason is that in such cases the

purposes, the typographical arrangement, language, and appearance of a competitor's advertising); F.T.C. *v.* Warewell Co., 5 F.T.C.D. 294 (1922), (a competitor published the "Little Leather Library," a collection of classics on which the copyright had expired; respondent published under the name "Classic Publishing Co." a similar set in which precisely the same selections were presented); F.T.C. *v.* Keaton Tire & Rubber Co., 5 F.T.C.D. 335 (1922), (referring to a competitor as a "pirate." *See supra,* p. 209); F.T.C. *v.* Orient Music Roll Co., 2 F.T.C.D. 176 (1919), (buying music rolls made by competitors, making copies, and selling the copies to the public).

[166] As, perhaps, in F.T.C. *v.* Sunlight Creameries, 4 F.T.C.D. 55 (1921), where it appears that it was necessary to have a "Trade Practice Submittal" to cope with the practice among dairy companies of soliciting farmers to break their contracts with competing dairy concerns.

law confers on the Department of Agriculture powers in many ways more effective than those of the Federal Trade Commission, and that the Department has a scientific personnel more competent to deal with the technical questions involved. The Food and Drugs Act of June 30, 1906,[167] makes it unlawful to manufacture in any territory or in the District of Columbia, or to ship in interstate or foreign commerce, any article of food or any drug which is "adulterated or misbranded." The words "adulterated" and "misbranded" are comprehensively defined, and it is obvious that the definitions are framed with an eye to practical administration as well as scientific accuracy.[168] They cover every conceivable case of misrepresentation as to the ingredients, strength, quality, or purity of a drug or food product, or (by an amendment added in 1912) as to its curative or therapeutic effect; and all cases of misbranding, including imitation of the distinctive name of another article, misstatement as to weight, measure, or numerical count, and misrepresentation as to the state, territory, or county in which the article is produced. In its enforcement the act has great advantages over the cumbersome procedure of the Federal Trade Commission. One who violates the act may be criminally prosecuted,[169] whereas the Federal Trade Commission can only order him to cease and desist, without even forfeiting the unlawful gains derived from the violation. An adulterated or misbranded article, if transported in violation of the law, may be libeled and forfeited in proper proceedings,[170] whereas there is nothing in the Federal Trade Commission Act to prevent a dealer who has been ordered to cease from shipping certain misbranded articles in interstate commerce, from selling

[167] 34 Stat. at L. 768.
[168] Secs. 7 and 8 of the Food and Drugs Act.
[169] Secs. 1 and 2 of the Food and Drugs Act.
[170] Sec. 10 of the Food and Drugs Act.

them to another dealer in the same state. The latter can ship them with immunity, so far as the Federal Trade Commission Act is concerned, until the Commission's procedure has again been set in motion and a new order issued and confirmed by the court. As a police measure the Food and Drugs Act is therefore vastly superior to the Trade Commission law.

Aside from the Food and Drugs Act, there are several other statutes which confer on the Department of Agriculture authority to prevent misbranding or adulteration. The Act of April 26, 1910,[171] contains criminal and administrative provisions, modeled on the Food and Drugs Act, specially applicable to the misbranding or adulteration of insecticides and fungicides.[172] The Act of August 24, 1912,[173] prohibits importation of adulterated or misbranded seeds of certain kinds. The Act of July 1, 1902,[174] prohibits false labels on any virus, serum, toxin, antitoxin, or analogous product sold in interstate or foreign commerce. The Meat Inspection Acts of June 30, 1906, and March 4, 1907,[175] prohibit the sale of meat food products under a false or deceptive name. Another statute prohibits interstate or foreign commerce in gold or silver goods erroneously stamped as to fineness.[176] The superior methods of enforcement provided in these statutes, no less than the importance of preventing conflicts of jurisdiction or policy in such cases, suggest that the Federal Trade Commission should refrain from taking action in all cases for which statutes of this sort make special provision. As indicative of Congressional policy

[171] 36 Stat. at L. 331.
[172] *See* U.S. *v.* Thirty Dozen Packages of Roach Food, 202 Fed. 271 (1913).
[173] 37 Stat. at L. 506.
[174] 32 Stat. at L. 728.
[175] 34 Stat. at L. 669, 1260.
[176] 34 Stat. at L. 260.

as to such cases is the provision of the Packers and Stockyards Act of August 15, 1921,[177] which confers on the
Secretary of Agriculture power to prevent, among other
things, "any unfair, unjustly discriminatory or deceptive
practice" on the part of any packer, and provides that
"the Federal Trade Commission shall have no power or
jurisdiction so far as relating to any matter which by
this act is made subject to the jurisdiction of the Secretary," except as to complaints served prior to enactment
of the law, and except that it may at the request of the
Secretary of Agriculture "make investigations and report in any case."

The jurisdiction of the Department of Agriculture in
misbranding cases is limited to misstatements in the name
or label of the article in question, including, in cases under
the Sherley amendment, misrepresentations in circulars
contained in the package.[178] Where the misrepresentation
is in advertising not physically connected with the article,
the intervention of the Federal Trade Commission is
clearly warranted,[179] and has, indeed, on several occasions been solicited by the Department of Agriculture.[180]

A third limitation must be recognized. Where the issue
is not as to the fairness or unfairness of a general trade
practice, but involves merely the suppression of a sporadic or individual act of dishonesty, the Commission's
powers are so defective that they should be invoked only
where no other remedy exists. A series of cases involving
the sale of fraudulent securities illustrates the point. If

[177] 42 Stat. at L. 159.

[178] *See* U.S. *v.* America Druggists' Syndicate, 186 Fed. 387 (1911).
Seven Cases of Eckman's Alterative *v.* U.S., 239 U.S. 510 (1916).

[179] As in the "Sal Tonik" case, F.T.C. *v.* Guarantee Veterinary Co.,
3 F.T.C.D. 402, 4 F.T.C.D. 149, 285 Fed. 853; the "Creme Angelus"
case, F.T.C. *v.* Louis Phillipe, Inc., et al., 5 F.T.C.D. 136 (1922); and
the case of the sterilizer said to be "ten times stronger than undiluted
carbolic acid," F.T.C. *v.* Ginso Chemical Co., 4 F.T.C.D. 155 (1921).

[180] As in the Royal Baking Powder case, *supra,* p. 187.

the respondent is really selling securities by means of dishonest advertising, the remedy must be immediate to be effective. Yet in one of the "blue sky" cases, the chronology was as follows:

Complaint issued,	September 25, 1919.
Answer filed,	November 1, 1919.
Examiner appointed,	January 25, 1921.
Case set for hearing at Houston, Texas,	February 23, 1921.
Amended answer filed,	February 24, 1921.
Commission's brief filed,	November 8, 1921.
Case set for argument,	November 16, 1921.
Argument postponed to,	November 28, 1921.
Argument again postponed to,	December 19, 1921.
Respondent's brief filed,	January 3, 1922.
Final order issued,	January 24, 1922.
Application by Commission to C. C. A., 5th Circuit, for confirming order,	May 7, 1923.
Preliminary injunction granted by court,	June 20, 1923.

The case was against a vendor of securities in certain doubtful oil promotions in Texas,[181] and does not appear to have involved any unusual features, yet even after a formal complaint had been filed (disregarding the previous period of investigation) only five days less than three years and nine months elapsed before there was a legally binding order to discontinue the practice. If the facts found by the Commission are true, one is tempted to ask how many gullible citizens were separated from their savings while the case was in progress! In another case the evidence shows that the sales of stock took place in 1918 and early 1919. The complaint was issued July 15, 1921. During 1922, testimony was taken in Houston, Oklahoma City, Fort Worth, and New York, and on May 16, 1923, more than four years after the stock had been sold,

[181] F.T.C. *v.* S. E. J. Cox et al., 5 F.T.C.D. 38 (1922). *See* Docket No. 402.

the Commission issued its order to cease and desist.[182] The inadequacy of the Commission's procedure in such cases is admitted in its 1919 annual report.[183] By way of contrast, it is only necessary to refer to the procedure of the postal authorities, in such cases, under the Act of March 2, 1889.[184] Anyone who uses the mails in furtherance of a fraudulent stock promotion scheme can be indicted. Moreover, by the simple expedient of issuing a "fraud order" the postal authorities can at once exclude from the mails all matter addressed to or by the fraudulent promoter. Of course the remedy is not complete; it is still possible to use some other means of distribution than the mails. Yet even in such cases the Commission's procedure is so inadequate that it would seem better to leave the matter to the state authorities.

[182] F.T.C. *v.* Big Diamond Oil & Refining Co., 6 F.T.C.D. 51 (1923) (Docket No. 795). *See* also F.T.C. *v.* Lone Star Oil Co. et al., 6 F.T.C.D. 60 (1923) (Docket No. 796), where a year and eight months elapsed between complaint and order.

[183] The report refers to these "blue sky" cases as follows: "The Commission finds in the 'blue-sky' cases that frequently its order to cease and desist does not issue until some overt practice has occurred. Those desiring to evade the order put on a campaign under high pressure, which results in complete sale of the stocks or securities floated before the Commission can act. Legislative action in respect to the control of the advertisements or representations of the promoters of the stock will be the most effectual way of keeping the situation *in statu quo* until the Commission's processes can function. The law should provide that the advertising be in a form requiring every individual, corporation, or association offering for sale to the public in interstate commerce, bonds, stocks, or other evidences of ownership in any corporation to print on the front page of any and all circulars, prospectuses, letters, literature, and in the body of any advertisements describing or mentioning the securities for sale, in type larger than the type otherwise used, the rate of commission or commissions, the profits received by those promoting, consolidating, underwriting, or selling said securities, and the net amount to be received from said sale by the issuing entity, corporation, or association." (Pp. 47-48.)

[184] U.S. Rev. Stat. 5480.

The cases which the Commission is in my opinion peculiarly fitted to handle are those involving a trade practice common in an industry, such as the current use of misleading terminology in describing goods, or trade "tricks" of a deceptive character, where the practice does not come within the scope of such special legislation as the Food and Drugs Act. The cases considered in this chapter, involving misbranding and adulteration of wool, silk, and cotton, or the cases involving sale of "rebuilt" or secondhand articles in the guise of new ones, are typical examples. The misbranding cases frequently involve in substance a "trade name" controversy between whole industries. Whether or not a particular trade name is properly used to designate a mercerized cotton, or whether it contains a false implication that the product contains silk, is an issue upon which the silk industry may be ranged on one side and the makers of mercerized cotton on the other. Courts of law cannot do complete justice in such a controversy. The Commission is in a position to study the problem as a whole, with the help of the respective trade associations, to institute test cases where advisable, and where the practice is demonstrably unfair to file complaints in sufficient number to compel adherence to the prescribed standard of truthfulness. The slow procedure of the Commission, and the absence of any punitive power, is a handicap so far as enforcement is concerned, but it is or should be an advantage where the problem is to make a just decision as between the competing claims of rival industries. Even where no issue between competing trades is involved, as in the cases involving fictitious cut prices on fountain pens and razors, the Commission seems to have a legitimate function. The only alternative is the time-honored method of criminal prosecution under state law, or in proper cases under the law relating to fraudulent use of the mails, but in cases of this kind criminal indictment is generally out of the question. Every prosecuting attorney knows how reluctant a jury is to brand a man as a criminal for doing what everyone else in the trade has been doing with impunity for years. On the other hand, the mere fact that the Federal Trade Commission is investigating such a practice, and has instituted a few test cases, may be sufficient to call attention to it, and to lead the great majority of the firms in the trade to abandon it.

Even in these cases, however, it is not clear that the Commission has yet succeeded in evolving a satisfactory procedure or technique. It is necessary to return for a moment to the discussion, in an earlier chapter, of the difference between an administrative and a judicial procedure. Administrative action of the kind provided in the Federal Trade Commission Act was valuable, it will be recalled, for two reasons: because it offered facilities for expert decision in specialized fields, and because it ensured uniformity of decision as to matters of importance in the business world. Questions of misbranding and deceptive advertising frequently involve technical problems of the most difficult kind. To appreciate this fully it is only necessary to read the illuminating testimony of Dr. Carl L. Alsberg, then Chief of the Bureau of Chemistry, and of Dr. S. W. Stratton, then Chief of the Bureau of Standards, before the Committee of Congress which was considering merchandise misbranding bills.[185] Take the simple question, much discussed at those hearings, whether cloth made of reworked wool could properly be labeled "pure wool." Representatives of the wool growers' associations insisted that it should be called "shoddy." Manufacturers of reworked wool pointed out that the term "shoddy," although technically designating a reworked textile material, had in the popular mind an opprobrious connotation. The testimony developed

[185] Merchandise Misbranding Bills. Hearings, House Committee on Interstate and Foreign Commerce, 66th Cong., 2d Sess., 1920.

that wool was of different grades, and that virgin wool of the coarsest grade might be greatly inferior in strength and wearing quality to reworked wool of finer grade. In other words, the system of branding advocated by the wool growers might make it necessary to brand as "shoddy" a product which was strong and durable, and as "virgin wool" a product which was in every respect inferior. Dr. Alsberg suggested that it might be possible to devise a system of optional grades, designated by letter or number, and to establish, by scientific tests of strength and wearing quality, standards for goods of each grade. These standards would not concern themselves primarily with the origin or method of manufacture of the material, but with those qualities which affected the serviceableness of the product to the consumer. I mention the controversy merely by way of illustration. The annual reports of the Bureau of Chemistry, which performs the technical work in the enforcement of misbranding laws relating to foods and drugs, show the importance and difficulty of these problems, and the opportunity which they offer for constructive scientific work.

The weakness of the Federal Trade Commission Act as a police measure I have already referred to.[186] As a means of determining the controverted questions of a technical nature involved in the branding of merchandise, it seems to me that the Commission's procedure could be strengthened and its usefulness increased by the adoption of a more scientific attitude toward the problem. Despite the size of its economic staff, the Commission does not seem to have regularly in its employ any recognized experts upon questions of trade terminology. Sometimes it avails itself of the facilities of the Bureau of Chemistry or of the Bureau of Standards, but such in-

[186] *Supra,* p. 232.

stances seem to be sporadic. There is no scientific bureau charged with the constructive work of formulating and developing policies, as there is in the enforcement of the Food and Drugs Act. Perhaps the fault is with the form of the Commission's findings, rather than with the nature of the intellectual process by which they are made, but they give the impression that misbranding cases are handled as matters of litigation and formal proof, rather than as matters for scientific inquiry. The cases are generally investigated by lawyers, tried by lawyers, and heard and determined by lawyers.

The point can be best illustrated by two examples from the Commission's dockets.

A complaint was made against a retail drygoods store in the District of Columbia, charging that it was offering for sale "Silkoline Covered Comforts" and "Superior Wool Finish" blankets, although both products were made entirely of cotton.[187] At the hearing, the Commission proved the advertisements and the composition of the products, and then put on the stand a number of women stenographers and clerks employed in the various offices of the Trade Commission. They were qualified as "ultimate consumers," and testified that to them the word "Silkoline" implied the presence of silk. There the Commission rested. Counsel for respondent presented a number of trade witnesses, such as buyers for department stores, who testified that "Silkoline" was a trade word which had been generally known for thirty years to designate a cheap mercerized cotton material used for interior room draperies. Apparently because counsel for respondent had suggested that the lady witnesses of the Commission might not have been entirely unbiased, counsel then selected at random, from the telephone directory, the names of a number of women, to whom subpœnas

---

[187] F.T.C. *v.* Behrend's, 5 F.T.C.D. 303 (1922).

were issued to appear and testify at an adjourned meeting. Fourteen of these "consumers" appeared, and were examined and cross-examined as to the word "Silkoline." Four of the witnesses said the word "Silkoline" designated mercerized cotton without any silk. Two more thought it contained "not much silk," or "little, if any" silk. Six testified that they did not know, but that the name suggested a mixture of cotton and silk. One thought it was "an inferior silk," and another that it was a mixture of silk and cotton.

On this record, the Federal Trade Commission made findings which properly describe the trade usage testified to by respondent's witnesses. But it also found that "the word 'Silkoline' as applied to the mercerized cotton fabric for which it has become the name is literally and palpably false."[188] Respondents were ordered to cease and desist from advertising for sale "Silkoline Covered Comforts" without clearly and distinctly bringing to the attention of the purchasing public that the fabric termed "Silkoline" contains no silk. As to the advertisement of "wool finished blankets," the record indicates that the charge was virtually, though not formally, abandoned by the trial counsel of the Commission. The findings set forth the text of the advertisement, and state that "The words 'wool finish' as used in the advertisement are synonymous with wool nap and do not mean and are not understood to mean that the blankets contain any wool but are used to indicate simply the finish of the blankets, namely, that the short fibres on the surface resemble a surface of a wool blanket, . . ." and that each blanket contained a label bearing the registered trade mark "Nashua Woolnap," and in prominent type the words "Pure Cotton." For this reason the adver-

---

[188] The phrase is obviously taken from the opinion of the Supreme Court in the Winsted Hosiery case, 258 U.S. 483 (1922).

tisement was found not to be an unfair method of competition.

In the second case the complaint was likewise against a District of Columbia retailer[189] and charged that respondent had offered for sale "Wool Sport Socks" composed partly of wool and partly of cotton; "Mercerized Satin Damask" tablecloths composed entirely of mercerized cotton; and "Wool-Finish Blankets" composed entirely of cotton. At the trial,[190] the Commission proved the advertisements and the materials out of which the goods were made, and rested. For respondent, several trade witnesses testified that the words "wool finish" described cotton blankets finished to look like wool; that the word "satin," in its technical meaning, described a finish rather than a material, and that the word "damask," although often used in conjunction with linen, properly described a design, regardless of the material. As to wool socks, the trade testimony was weak. By agreement of counsel, fifty names of women were then selected from the telephone directory, and a questionnaire sent to them, asking what they understood to be meant by the words "wool finish," the words "mercerized satin damask," and the words "men's wool sport socks." The results were substantially as follows:

1. Twenty-three answers stated that "wool finish" blankets were made entirely of cotton, some of them adding that they had a finish to make them look like wool. Eight answered that the term designated a cotton blanket with wool fibres, or a wool surface or finish. Eight thought they contained "a small quantity" of wool, or "some wool," or were "largely cotton." One gave the percentages: 80 per cent wool and 20 per cent cotton. Five described it as "cotton and wool mixed," or "part wool,"

---

[189] F.T.C. v. King's Palace, 5 F.T.C.D. 345 (1923).
[190] See Transcript of Testimony, Docket No. 799.

and one reported that "as the word 'wool' is used," one is led to expect wool in the blankets.

2. Thirty-eight answered that the term "mercerized satin damask" described cotton, some adding that it had a mercerized finish to look like either silk or linen or some other material. Two called it an "imitation" of satin or linen, and one as a "linen damask." One answer merely stated that the word "satin" described "the surface only."

3. As to the wool socks, the answers were virtually unanimous that they were made of wool.

Upon this record, the Commission entered findings and an appropriate order condemning the use of the word "wool socks." It ignored completely the charges as to "mercerized satin damask" tablecloths. As to the "Wool-Finish Blankets," it found that the term "signified to and was understood by a substantial portion of the purchasing public to mean that the blankets so described and offered for sale were composed of materials of which at least a part was wool." Respondents were ordered to cease and desist from "representing to the purchasing public in advertisements or by other means that blankets offered for sale and sold by them and made wholly of cotton are 'Wool Finished Blankets.' "[191]

As to the "wool socks," the findings and order were obviously right. As to "Silkoline," it should be noted that the article was apparently manufactured and distributed under that name throughout the United States. If the small retailer in the District of Columbia was violating the law, so, it would seem, was every manufacturer or jobber who shipped the goods in interstate commerce. The case in the District of Columbia seems to have been, however, the only one undertaken by the Commission with respect to "Silkoline." It seems to me that an order,

[191] 5 F.T.C.D. 348.

involving the propriety of a name which has been cur-
rently used in the trade for thirty years, should not have
been entered in a proceeding against this single retailer.
If the subject was worth taking up at all, it was worth
taking up with the leading factors in the trade, as a question affecting the trade as a whole. If an agreement could
not be reached with the manufacturers, the question
should have been raised in a test case brought against
them, rather than against an isolated retailer. Despite
the unanimous testimony of its stenographers, and the
by no means unanimous testimony of a few ladies selected
from the telephone book, it does not seem to me that the
record warranted an order upon so important a question
of trade terminology.

As to the "wool-finish blankets," the two cases seem
to be in direct conflict, although decided within less than
three weeks of each other. Perhaps the finding as to the
label on the blankets distinguishes them, but it should be
noted that the words "pure cotton" appeared only on
the label, and not in the advertisement. In the King's
Palace case, the findings do not show whether or not the
blankets were properly labeled. However, in one case
the words "wool-finish" were expressly found to signify
that the blankets contained wool, while in the other they
were found not to imply that the blankets contained wool.
It may be said that these were separate litigations, and
that the proofs differed, but the very purpose of the administrative procedure provided in the Federal Trade
Commission Act was to ensure uniformity of decision and
a consistent administrative policy.

The method of proof by the random selection of "consumers" from the telephone book can hardly be taken
seriously. It is too haphazard to be helpful, for the results may differ from day to day, according to the selections made. Moreover, many of the witnesses selected may
be ignorant of the proper terminology. Correct branding

of merchandise does not imply conformity to the mis-
conception or prejudice of every consumer. Some recognition must be given to the right to speak the truth about
one's goods, even if, on account of popular ignorance, the
truth may be misunderstood by a few.[192] Of course, I am
not suggesting that the "Silkoline" case or the second
"wool-finish" case were wrongly decided. Perhaps the
decisions were right, but the technique employed in making the findings seems to me to have been utterly wrong.

This criticism applies mainly to the formal proceedings
of the Commission, by complaint, hearing, and order. It
is interesting to note that the reports of the extra-legal
proceedings known as "trade practice submittals" are
invariably more illuminating, more judicial in tone, and
more imbued with the scientific spirit, than are the findings entered in formal proceedings. Distinctions are more
carefully stated, and arguments reviewed and disposed
of. Again it may be due to the form of the report rather
than to any flaw in the justice of the decision, but the

[192] Compare an interesting experiment conducted by the Associated
Knit Underwear Manufacturers of America. To find out to what extent
current trade terms were understood by consumers, the association's
representatives showed to a large number of people, samples of a few
of the better-known underwear materials, such as flat wool, balbriggan,
nainsook, and fleece-lined underwear. The results are given in the New
York *Times* of November 11, 1923. Flat wool was properly identified
by none, the answers ranging from "flannel" and "wool mixture" to
"something to put around a sore throat." Only 15 per cent of the
women and 25 per cent of the men identified balbriggan, some of the
other guesses being "lisle," "stockinette," "jersey," and "gauze." Twenty
per cent of the women and 30 per cent of the men recognized nainsook,
while others called it muslin, silk, longcloth, linen, and cheesecloth, or
applied to it the three letters which make up the registered trade name
of a well-known undergarment. Fleece-lined underwear was recognized
variously as flannel, plush, balbriggan, and eiderdown, only 25 per cent
of the men and 36 per cent of the women giving it the correct name.
The experiment suggests that it is hardly safe to let consumers set their
own standards of trade terminology.

usual impression is that the man who drafts the report of the trade practice submittal is honestly searching for the truth, while the examiner or attorney who prepares the formal findings seems often to be trying to merely win the case for the Commission. The business men who attend these meetings seem to have accepted them in the same spirit, and I have no doubt that the educational influence of a single trade practice submittal is as valuable as the coercion of a host of formal complaints and orders. Experience has shown, however, that these informal proceedings cannot be relied upon exclusively. Ultimately, the Commission is responsible for its decisions, subject only to court review, and its decisions must be reached in the manner prescribed by statute. It should be possible to instill into the formal statutory proceedings the same spirit of scientific inquiry, the same impartial tone, and the same scrupulous fairness, as have characterized the best of the Commission's reports upon trade practice submittals.

CHAPTER V

PRACTICES WHICH RESTRAIN TRADE

THE practices to be considered in the present chapter do not lend themselves readily to orderly analysis or logical formulation. The traditional phraseology of the common law of restraint of trade and monopoly is, as I have previously shown, sorely lacking in precision, and the language of the Clayton Act and Trade Commission Act did not greatly improve matters. As applied to an act which is not dishonest or deceptive, the term "unfair method of competition" indicates no more than a state of mind toward the conduct in question, and the state of mind may obviously vary according to the point of view. To a loyal trade unionist, all non-union competition is of itself "unfair"; materials made by "scab" labor are technically known as "unfair" materials. To the "legitimate" dealer who sells standard products at fixed prices, the competitor who sells below the set price is "unfair." In business terminology, the phrase often indicates no more than a violation of a rule of trade ethics or of a traditional trade practice. Yet it hardly seems necessary to point out that Congress did not intend, in Section 5 of the Trade Commission Act, to give the sanction of law to all existing trade practices and to brand as illegal any violation of such a practice in the course of interstate or foreign commerce. The uncertainties presented by the unfortunate language of the Clayton Act I have already referred to. Without accurate phraseology any attempt at legal analysis is obviously difficult.

There is, nevertheless, both in common law and civil law countries, a body of law which governs the permissible limits of competition and cooperation among

business men, and which lies outside the scope of the law
of fraud, and outside the scope of the usual tort categories, such as assault and battery, libel and deceit,
trespass and conversion. Upon what legal principles this
body of law rests and what are its precise limits and out-
lines, it is not easy to tell. The poverty of language in
which the discussion is couched of itself renders analysis
almost hopeless. A manufacturer is the sole judge of the
price he shall set on his products, but he must not fix a
low price with the improper purpose of driving a competitor out of business. Two manufacturers may combine
if the object is efficiency, but not if the object is control
of the market. A manufacturer may refuse to sell to a
dealer for any reason that seems to him sufficient; but
he must not use this right of selection, coupled with adequate lists and records, to induce dealers to maintain set
prices in reselling his product. A person engaged in
commerce may discriminate in price, so long as the effect
may not be to substantially lessen competition or tend to
create a monopoly. Such is the jumble of words in which
current legal discussion is couched. The reader will for-
give me, therefore, if I forego any attempt to define the
scope of the present chapter, or to give logical expression
to the principles of substantive law with which the Commission must deal in the cases considered therein. This
study is not intended to be a contribution to analytical
jurisprudence, but is primarily concerned with procedure
and administrative methods, and with the practical and
juristic results achieved thereby.

UNFAIR PRICE TACTICS

In examining the work of the Commission within the
scope of this chapter, it will be convenient to begin by
segregating a group of cases in which the charge is that
a concern, engaged in commerce, has injured one or more
competitors by what may be called unfair price tactics.

Putting aside for the moment a definition of the word "unfair," it is obvious that a case involving such practices may be dealt with, according to the circumstances, under Section 5 of the Federal Trade Commission Act, or under Section 2 of the Clayton Act, or under both sections. If the price tactics involve discrimination, a question arises under Section 2 of the Clayton Act, which prohibits discrimination in price where the effect may be to substantially lessen competition or tend to create a monopoly. If the discriminatory price tactics are aimed against one or more competitors, the same state of facts may also give rise to a proceeding under Section 5 of the Federal Trade Commission Act. If no discrimination is involved, but merely an "unfair" manipulation of the general price level, the case can be dealt with, if at all, only under Section 5 of the Federal Trade Commission Act. The typical case, however, could be dealt with under either section, and it is the usual practice of the Commission, unless there are special reasons to the contrary, to include in the same complaint a count charging discrimination under the Clayton Act, and a count charging an unfair method of competition.

In the political discussion which ushered in the anti-trust legislation of 1914, the practice of local price cutting received much attention. The situation which seems to have been assumed was about as follows: A large and financially powerful corporation or "trust" sells its output, say, of petroleum products, throughout the country, and at a substantial profit. In a certain locality, however, a small competitor finds himself able, by dint of superior efficiency or because of advantages of location, to undersell the "trust" and yet make a profit. The board of strategy of the "trust" determines that the competitor must go out of business. A war fund is appropriated, and orders are sent to the local agent to under-cut any price the competitor may make. A price war ensues, and for a while both the trust and the local competitor lose money on each gallon sold. In time, of course, superior financial resources tell, and the competitor either goes out of business, a ruined man, or is absorbed by the trust on its own terms, or at best is allowed to continue in business on good behavior. Thereupon prices resume their former level, and the costs of the war are recouped at the expense of the consumer.

This is a dramatized version, but it serves to bring out the legal principle, and is probably not an inaccurate description of the methods used by some of the large industrial combinations in the heyday of their power.[1] It is obviously desirable that such tactics be forbidden. It is not in the public interest that brute force and financial power alone should determine the outcome of the economic struggle.

I have found one case among the decisions of the Federal Trade Commission in which the findings clearly show that buccaneering methods of this sort were involved.[2] It seems that a number of concerns, engaged in rendering and refining animal fats in the city of Philadelphia, had for some years held meetings at which prices were agreed upon which were to be paid to butchers for bones, fats, and similar waste material, and agreements made as to division of territory in making such purchases. Competition seems to have been virtually eliminated. In 1915, a small concern in Trenton, New Jersey, determined to invade the Philadelphia market, and sent a wagon each day to collect materials in that city. A meeting was held by the Philadelphia renderers, ways and means were discussed by which the intruder could be shut out, and finally an ultimatum was served on the Trenton company that if it did not cease buying in Philadelphia, the Philadelphia

---

[1] *See* the illustrations given by Stevens in Chap. 1 of his *Unfair Competition.*

[2] F.T.C. *v.* United Rendering Co. et al., 3 F.T.C.D. 284 (1921).

companies would retaliate by entering the Trenton field. A corporation was then formed, with $10,000 capital, to which all but one of the Philadelphia companies contributed *pro rata,* the other agreeing to share the losses of the company on an agreed basis. Under the management of a former employee of the Trenton company this corporation set out to buy raw materials from Trenton butchers. It had no rendering plant, but shipped the materials by rail and water to Philadelphia, where they were disposed of by competitive bidding to the stockholding companies and the guarantor. In due course the Trenton company sustained financial losses and was forced to sell out. The new owner, however, continued his purchases in Philadelphia, refusing an offer of $35,000 if he would get out. Thereupon the Philadelphia renderers raised the prices they were paying to Philadelphia butchers; the new Trenton company sustained a loss of $30,000 in a period of four months, and then sold out to the American Agricultural Chemical Company. Whether or not the new purchaser discontinued the Philadelphia business does not appear.

The use of a "fighting" company of this sort, with the sole purpose of forcing a competitor out of the field, seems to be clearly unlawful. The use of "fighting ships" was condemned by the Supreme Court in the steamship combination case,[3] and is specifically prohibited in the Shipping Act of 1916.[4] "Fighting" brands used twenty-five years ago by the old American Tobacco Company, and "knocker" machines at one time used by the National Cash Register Company to punish competitors, illustrate different aspects of the same practice.[5] The separate corporation formed by the Philadelphia renderers was

[3] Thomsen *v.* Cayser, 243 U.S. 66 (1917).

[4] 39 Stat. at L. 733.

[5] *See* Chap. 3, entitled "Fighting Instruments," in Stevens, *Unfair Competition.*

not organized with a view to conducting a legitimate business, but solely for punitive purposes. It was merely a vehicle by which the costs of the war could be conveniently distributed. Even apart from the fact that it was an instrument in the preservation of what may have been an illegal monopoly, the decision of the Federal Trade Commission that an unfair method of competition had been used was clearly warranted.

It is rare, however, that motives are as clearly evident as they were in the United Rendering case, and it is necessary to inquire more particularly what elements must be present in such a case to sustain a charge of unfair competition. Every business man tries to fix prices at a point where he will get business away from a competitor. If the competitor cannot meet the prices, he must in the long run go out of business, and it is certainly not improper for the business man to hope and wish for such an outcome. Survival of the fittest is the essence of legitimate competition. To say that a business man may not cut prices with a view to driving a competitor out of business does not, therefore, meet the situation, nor does it help matters to inquire whether his motive was "malicious." Is the test, then, whether or not the sales were made below cost? If a company undersells a competitor and yet makes a profit it is a sign of superior efficiency, but if it sells at a loss it is apparent that it is relying upon superior financial resources in bringing the competitor to terms. Obviously, however, any such distinction must be qualified in several respects. In a period of rapidly falling prices, as in the latter part of 1920, any company with a large stock of raw materials or finished goods may find it necessary to sell its output for some time at a loss in order to meet the competitive market and liquidate its inventory. Any other course might lead to financial disaster. In such a case the fact that sales are made below cost, to the embarrassment of competitors who may be pursuing a different policy, does not indicate any improper motive. Moreover, in any case it would seem to be necessary to distinguish between out-of-pocket operating costs and fixed or other continuing charges. When business is slack and a company is operating at only a fraction of capacity, it may find that by cutting its price on some or all of its products, it can take away business from certain competitors. To do so, it may be necessary to fix a price which, taking into account overhead and fixed charges, is unremunerative, but which will probably bring in enough to meet the extra out-of-pocket costs and perhaps contribute a little toward continuing charges. As a matter of sound cost accounting the sales may be below cost, but it does not seem that they are for that reason improper, even if they contribute to the troubles of weaker competitors. That the price concession is made only in one locality, or on one product, does not seem to change the situation. It is a familiar fact that certain points may be more highly competitive than others, and there is certainly no rule of law which requires a manufacturer to keep away from competitive territory unless he can make the same margin over costs as he can in less competitive areas. Section 2 of the Clayton Act specifically permits discrimination "in the same or different communities in good faith to meet competition."

It is sometimes suggested that the right to meet competition in a locality by cutting prices merely permits the newcomer to put his prices down to the level prevailing in the locality, but does not permit him to cut below the level. Such a distinction is clearly unsound. Often the only way to get business away from an established concern is to offer the product at a more attractive price. If the manufacturer has a right to invade the territory at all, and to make a lower price than he is making in other parts of the country, his right cannot be made to depend upon the price level set by local competitors. He must be allowed to compete in price as well as in quality and service.

What, then, is the distinction between the case put near the beginning of this chapter, or the case of the Philadelphia renderers, and the cases of justified local price cutting which I have described? It is difficult to distinguish them except in terms of motive. In one case the motive is to liquidate an accumulated inventory, or to obtain for the company, on the best terms possible, enough business to ensure a full utilization of its plant. In the other case the new business is sought for not because it is desirable in itself, but because by taking it away from the competitor it may be possible to force him out of business. I realize that such a distinction is unsatisfactory, and often difficult to apply, especially in the case of a large corporation. A motive is a state of mind, but whose state of mind is significant? If the local agent recommends a price cut because he believes it will force out a troublesome competitor, and the general manager approves it because he thinks the business worth while even at the reduced price, whose motive shall the law consider? At best, motives are hard to ascertain, and even where they are fully confessed they may be mixed and not easy to disentangle. However, this is an inherent difficulty; where it cannot be solved, the law had better abandon any attempt to interfere. In other cases, as in the case of the Philadelphia renderers, the facts may be such as to show quite clearly whether the motives were proper or improper.

From the point of view of administration, therefore, the first and also the most difficult task in a case of this sort is to obtain an accurate comprehension of the business facts. Learning in the law and logical skill are not enough, and preconceived theories of cost accounting or economics are worse than useless, unless accompanied by an accurate understanding of the conditions of the market and of the problems of manufacture and sale. Here, then, is a typical field for an administrative tribunal composed of men selected for their experience and practical judgment, and aided by technical experts.

Perhaps the fault lies mainly with the formal and legalistic mold in which the Commission's "findings" are cast; whatever the cause, the cases dealing with unfair price tactics do not reveal, on the face of the record, any great progress toward clarification of issues, nor can it be said that they afford a convincing picture of the business facts involved.

One such case I have already described in the previous chapter. In the case against The Oakes Company[6] one paragraph of the complaint (apparently intended as a separate "count") charged that until recently respondent had manufactured exclusively an automobile fan of the cup-and-cone type; that "a certain competitor" manufactured exclusively fans of the roller-bearing type; that it costs less to manufacture the cup-and-cone type than the roller-bearing type; and that "with the purpose and effect of putting its competitor out of business" respondent thereupon began to manufacture a roller-bearing fan, and to sell it "for considerably less" than the cup-and-cone type, and "at less than cost." Another paragraph charged substantially the same facts, and in addition claimed that respondent's salesmen had falsely represented to the trade that the roller-bearing type cost less to manufacture than the cup-and-cone type, these representations being made "with the intent and purpose of depreciating the value of the roller bearing fan in the opinion of the trade." Respondent answered, formally denying "each and every material allegation." The testimony disproved the charge that respondent had manu-

[6] F.T.C. v. The Oakes Co., 3 F.T.C.D. 36 (1920). *See supra,* p. 212.

factured the "cup-and-cone" type exclusively; in fact, it manufactured a whole line of accessories, and had made fans of the roller-bearing type before the "certain competitor" came into existence.[7] The charge that sales were made below cost seems to have been abandoned. As to the relative cost of the two types of fans, the brief of the Commission's counsel admits that there was "a sharp conflict of testimony."[8] The Commission found, however, that the roller-bearing type "as made by the Automotive Parts Company" (the "certain competitor" in question) cost approximately 48 cents more to manufacture than the cup-and-cone type. In making this finding, apparently, the Commission relied upon the testimony of officers of the competitor, and disregarded the contrary testimony of respondent's officers.[9] The Commission found that respondent offered its roller-bearing type at a price less than the price charged by the competitor, and that "it does not offer its roller bearing fan to the trade in good faith for the purpose of selling it, but solely for the purpose of depreciating the value of the roller bearing type of fan as manufactured by its competitor and inducing the trade and the public to believe that its competitor is selling its roller bearing type of fan at more than a fair price." The conclusion is that "the several acts and conduct of the respondent as set forth in the foregoing findings as to the facts are, and each of them is," unfair methods of competition in interstate commerce. Curiously enough, despite this conclusion, the order issued at the same time does not refer to these findings at all, but confines itself to prohibiting the use of private detectives for purposes of commercial espionage, as charged in another part of the findings. The

[7] *See* transcript of record in Docket No. 344. The evidence upon this point is summarized in respondent's brief, p. 9.

[8] *See* brief of respondent, p. 17.

[9] *See* brief of Commission, p. 6.

weakness of the findings, moreover, is apparent. Upon
the Commission's own theory, the relative cost of the
two types of fans was the crucial issue in the case, and
upon this issue the Commission's brief admitted that
there was a sharp conflict in the testimony. Yet the findings upon this issue contain only the barest conclusion,
without supporting authority or analysis of the evidence,
and without a suggestion of the difficult questions of
cost accounting involved in any such comparison. Moreover, the finding is only as to the roller-bearing type "as
made by" the competitor. Perhaps it is intended to imply
that respondent's costs are or should be the same, for it
is difficult to see why respondent should be guided, in
making his prices, by the cost of production in a competitor's plant. More likely, however, the phrase con-
ceals a weakness of proof as to respondent's own costs.
The other important issue in the case, upon the Commission's own theory, is as to the motive of respondent
in offering its roller-bearing fan, and here again there is
the barest conclusion, without any statement of the
grounds upon which it is based. The only suggestion is
in the finding that respondent has represented to the
trade that the roller-bearing type "would not work satisfactorily," but there is no indication as to the form which
the alleged statement took or the circumstances under
which it was made, or as to the bearing, if any, upon
the Commission's conclusion that the sales were not made
"in good faith." It is not surprising that the Commission
shrank from the consequences of its own findings, and
ignored this feature of the case in its order.

Another case, in some of its facts similar to the case
of the Philadelphia renderers, exhibits the same weak-
nesses.[10] The complaint charged that the American Agri-

[10] F.T.C. *v.* American Agricultural Chemical Co., 1 F.T.C.D. 226
(1918).

cultural Chemical Company and its corporate subsidiary, the Brown Company,[11] "with the purpose, intent and effect of stifling and suppressing competition, in the manufacture and sale of their products in interstate commerce, for more than one year last past, while conducting their business generally at a profit, have, in certain local areas, purchased and offered to purchase raw materials necessary in the manufacture of their product at and for prices unwarranted by trade conditions and so high as to be prohibitive to small competitors in such areas; that such prices were calculated and designed to, and did, punish certain competitors in such areas who refused to become a party to a working arrangement offered by respondents to their competitors generally whereby competition in bidding for such raw materials was to be eliminated." The findings are in almost the identical words quoted from the complaint, except that it is revealed that the "certain local areas" were Philadelphia and Atlantic City, and that the prohibitive prices were said to be calculated and designed to destroy "certain competitors" in such areas. Aside from the formal averment as to the intent, purpose, and effect of the conduct and the design to destroy competitors, there is nothing here but an unsupported conclusion that the prices were "unwarranted by trade conditions." Is this fact alone sufficient to make the conduct illegal? Apparently the Commission believes so, for the order prohibits without qualification as to motive all purchases of products "at and for prices unwarranted by trade conditions and so high as to be prohibitive to small competitors."[12] Yet there is no finding, except by

[11] Curiously enough, the same Trenton company which was the victim of the "fighting company" organized by the Philadelphia renderers, before it was taken over by the American. *See supra,* p. 248.

[12] *Cf.* the Trade Practice Submittal of the butter manufacturers, which condemned "the purchasing or offering to purchase, dairy prod-

a vague innuendo, that the prices made the business unprofitable to respondent. The prices are not given, the
circumstances are not indicated which rendered them
unwarranted, and no hint is given of the evidence which
established an intent to drive the unnamed competitors
out of business. Yet if the Federal Trade Commission is
to be considered as a body of experts upon commercial
and industrial matters, it is surely upon these issues
precisely that we look to it for enlightenment.

In the United Rendering Company case,[13] as I have
said, the wrongful intent was clearly inferable from the
organization of the "fighting company" and the discussions and ultimata which went before.[14] Upon its economic
facts also, the case is somewhat stronger than the case
against the American Agricultural Chemical Company.
In addition to the conclusion that the prices paid were
"unwarranted by trade conditions and prohibitive to
competitors," it is made to appear that the business of
the "fighting company" was conducted at a "substantial
loss"; and that the prices paid by the company in Trenton were "in excess of the prices the respondents were
paying for similar materials" in Philadelphia. Even so
the case would have been strengthened, it would seem, if
some figures had been vouchsafed, and a more complete
picture given of costs, prices, and trade conditions in the
rendering business.

In another case the order was entered by consent, but
the case shows the interpretation which the Commission
has placed upon the section of the Clayton Act which
deals with discrimination.[15] The Commission filed a

ucts at prices not warranted by market or trade conditions . . ." Trade
Practice Submittals, 1, 4, par. IX.

[13] F.T.C. *v.* United Rendering Co. et al., 3 F.T.C.D. 284, 294 (1921).

[14] *Supra*, p. 250.

[15] F.T.C. *v.* Fleischmann Co., 1 F.T.C.D. 119.

complaint against the Fleischmann Company, charging among other things that respondent had discriminated in price between different purchasers of yeast, "and that the effect of such discrimination may be to substantially lessen competition or tend to create a monopoly in the yeast industry." The findings, entered by consent, dealt largely with other charges not at this moment relevant, but contained also the following paragraph:

That owing to competition in various localities it has deviated from such basic prices in order to retain the patronage of its customers by reducing its prices to them to meet the price of its competitors, and in the event that such reduction in price did not result in the retention of the business of said customers, it has, in a number of cases, reduced its prices to a price below that offered to such customers by such competitors; and in many cases where, as a result of such competition, its customers have abandoned their contracts with respondent, it has reduced its prices to such customers to meet the price of such competitors to obtain said customers' business.[16]

The conclusion upon this point was as follows:

That the discriminations in prices in so far as they are admitted by respondent to be below the prices offered by its competitors, as set forth in the foregoing findings as to the facts in Division III, paragraph 1, are not made on account of differences in the grade, quality or quantity of the commodity sold, nor do such discriminations make due allowance for difference in the cost of selling or transportation, and are not made in good faith to meet competition, and the effect of such discriminations may be to substantially lessen competition or tend to create a monopoly in the sale of compressed yeast; that such discriminations are made in violation of section 2 of an act of Congress approved October 15, 1914, entitled, "An act to supplement existing laws against unlawful restraints and monopolies, and for other purposes."[17]

[16] *Ibid.*, p. 134.
[17] *Ibid.*, pp. 134-135.

The order was that respondent cease and desist discriminating in price in competitive territory, "where such discriminations in prices, if made, would be below the price or prices of a competitor or competitors of the Fleischmann Co. in such competitive territory." At a subsequent hearing to inquire whether the order had been obeyed, the Commission's attorney took the position that the order prohibited "the practice of cutting below competitors to retain or obtain business."[18] The authority of the case is weakened by the fact that the order was entered by consent, but it seems to accept the principle that while the price may be cut in a certain locality, either to get business away from a competitor or to avoid losing it to him, it must under no circumstances be reduced below the competitor's prices. As I have previously pointed out, it seems doubtful whether such a principle of law can be sustained. The finding that the effect of the discrimination may be to substantially lessen competition is again a mere conclusion, and the facts upon which it is based are not given. In the absence of special facts, it would seem that competition would probably be increased rather than diminished by the price cutting. There is no finding that the sales were below cost, or that the business was not desired on its own account rather than on account of the injury which would be done to the competitor by depriving him of it. The business facts do not seem adequate to sustain a charge of price warfare.

These are the only cases which I have found in the reports of the Commission which involve a charge of improper price warfare. Despite the importance which was attached to local price cutting in the debates and current discussions of the time, it seems doubtful whether in cases of this character the Federal Trade Commission is in a position to render any very useful service. Price

[18] *See* record of hearing in the official docket (Docket No. 6).

warfare, to be successful, must generally be aggressive and acute, and it is not likely to be of long duration. Within a few months the attempt is likely to be a success or a failure. While it is in progress, prompt and effective governmental action may be helpful; after it has run its course, all that remains is to fix the blame and award reparation and punishment. In view of the limitations of its procedure, the Federal Trade Commission is not capable of prompt action, and it has no power to inflict punishment or award damages. The only value which a proceeding can have in such a case lies in the moral effect of the publicity incident to the filing of a complaint.

In The Oakes Company case, the complaint was issued September 2, 1919. It does not appear when the sales of roller-bearing fans at low prices began; the acts of commercial espionage complained of appear to have taken place more than a year earlier (April to September, 1918). The hearing was held May 6, 1920, and the findings made September 9, 1920, a year and a week after the filing of the complaint. The findings in the American Agricultural Chemical case were made on an agreed statement of facts, but even there seven and a half months elapsed between the issuance of the complaint and the entry of the order to cease and desist. In the Fleischmann case, also disposed of by consent, the complaint was issued April 13, 1917, and a supplemental complaint June 29, 1917. The final order was made on April 8, 1918. The case of the Philadelphia renderers is even more illuminating. The "fighting company" in question was incorporated October 8, 1915, and began operations in Trenton November 1, 1915. The Trenton company against which its operations were directed sold out in December, 1916. Operations against the new owner appear to have been carried on until April 1, 1917, when he was forced to sell out to the American Agricultural Chemical Company. On June 10, 1918, the Federal Trade Commission filed

its complaint. At the close of the fiscal year ending June
30, 1919, the proceeding was before the Commission,
awaiting decision.[19] At the close of the fiscal year ending
June 30, 1920, its status was still unchanged.[20] On February 5, 1921, two years seven months and twenty-six
days after the complaint was issued, the final order was
made. This was more than four and a half years after the
original competitor had been forced out, and three years
and nine months after his company had been absorbed by
the "trust." Of what possible value was the final order
to anyone? It could not restore to the competitor his
ruined business, nor award him damages for his losses.
It punished no one. All that it could do was to admonish
the respondents to refrain from similar conduct in the
future, and even this admonition they were under no
legal duty to obey until a decree had been entered in the
Circuit Court of Appeals.

These comments do not necessarily imply any criticism
of the Federal Trade Commission as an organization.
Perhaps there were special circumstances which rendered
the delay excusable. I merely record the facts, and suggest that a private suit for damages, or, if the facts
warrant, a criminal indictment, will more adequately
protect both private and public interests in cases of this
sort.

These four cases are the only ones in which the charge
was that improper price warfare of an aggressive sort
had been used. I pass now to a group of cases of a different sort, although in a sense they are related.

PRICE CUTTING FOR ADVERTISING PURPOSES

ENORMOUS expenditures in promoting and advertising a
new brand of merchandise, or in extending the market

[19] *See* 1919 Annual Report, p. 54, Complaint No. 159.
[20] *See* 1920 Annual Report, p. 113.

for one already established, are a familiar feature of modern commercial life. Such a "campaign" is often planned and executed on a nation-wide scale; the details are worked over and perfected for months in advance by professional experts; and amounts running into the millions may be expended. The campaign may be conducted by means of nation-wide advertising in periodicals or by posters, or solicitation by circulars and through special salesmen. Or it may take the form of intensive sales, for a brief period, at a very low price, or even of free distributions on a large scale, with a view to the rapid introduction of the new article. In either event the expenditures are made without any expectation of immediate return, but in the belief that increased sales in the next year or so will more than pay for the cost. To a competitor already in the field, such a "campaign" by a newcomer is of course highly distasteful. A high-pressure advertising campaign is bad enough, and when in addition he finds that the new brand is being offered, in his neighborhood, at one-half or a third of its cost of production, or is even being given away free of charge, his indignation can be imagined. The immediate economic effect of such a campaign, passing like a storm through the trade, is disturbing and harmful.

In a case against the Ward Baking Company, the Federal Trade Commission dealt with an intensive campaign of this character. The company, in the spring of 1917, instituted a so-called "free bread campaign" in certain cities and towns in New England. Each purchaser, during the period of the campaign, was given each day free of charge a quantity of bread equal to the amount which he bought and paid for on the same day. Putting it another way, the price of bread was temporarily cut in half. In November, 1917, the Commission filed a complaint, and on April 8, 1919, made its findings. The Commission found that respondent, "with the intent, purpose and

effect of stifling and suppressing competition in the manufacture and sale of bread, in interstate commerce,'' did,
in conducting a so-called free bread campaign, at certain
periods ''daily give to each purchaser of its bread, in
certain places of the United States, a quantity of bread
equal to the amount of bread daily bought and paid for
by such purchaser from the respondent during the period
bread was so distributed free of charge.'' Another paragraph repeated the charge, but with more details as to
time and place, showing that while most of the shipments
for sale were within the state of Massachusetts, some
bread was distributed by wagon and truck across the
state line into Rhode Island. A final paragraph finds that
competing bakeries were ''injuriously affected'' by the
free bread campaign; that during the campaign respondent sold its bakery products ''at less than the cost of
production, and lost large sums of money in the vicinity
where such campaigns were carried on''; and that during
the period in question respondent ''greatly increased''
its shipments while local bakeries ''sustained a decrease''
in the amount of their sales. The order directed respondent to cease and desist from giving or offering its bakery
products free of charge, whether for the purpose of advertising its products, or to induce dealers to purchase
them, ''or for any other purpose whatsoever.'' Another
paragraph forbade selling or offering bread or other
bakery products upon the condition, understanding, or
agreement that it will give bread or bakery products
free of charge. Some months later a modified order was
issued, directing respondent to cease and desist from
''initiating or carrying on, in the course of interstate
commerce, any so-called free bread campaign or any practice of supplying bread free of cost to retail dealers in
quantities equal to those purchased from respondent by
such dealers, or in any other quantities, where such prac-

tice is calculated to or does stifle or suppress competition in the manufacture and sale of bread."[21]

Aside from the scanty facts revealed in the findings, the difficulty with the case is that the order in its final form evades the real issue. The practice of giving free bread in quantities equal to the amount purchased is forbidden only "where such practice is calculated to or does stifle or suppress competition in the manufacture and sale of bread." But the question is whether it does. To stifle or suppress competition, literally, means to eliminate it altogether, and of course no one supposes that the free bread campaign had any such effect. The phrase must, then, have some unexpressed meaning indicating unlawful injury to one or more competitors, but the issue of the case is precisely whether or not a free bread campaign conducted for advertising purposes does unlawfully injure competitors.[22]

The Fleischmann case, already referred to,[23] also involved a charge of giving free yeast to customers, as a means of inducing them to purchase or contract to purchase yeast from respondent. This appears to have been a continuous practice rather than a part of an intensive campaign. The only ground suggested for holding the gifts unlawful is that the free yeast was given "in quantities larger than required under the particular circumstances for proper sample or demonstration purposes." In another paragraph it is found that respondent has delivered to bakers "quantities" of yeast, "without making any immediate charge therefor," the price being later distributed over subsequent deliveries under the contracts. Advances of money, likewise subsequently re-

[21] 1 F.T.C.D. 394.

[22] The order was subsequently reversed in the Circuit Court of Appeals, on the ground that interstate commerce was not involved, Ward Baking Co. *v.* F.T.C. (C.C.A. 2d), 264 Fed. 330 (1920).

[23] F.T.C. *v.* Fleischmann Co., 1 F.T.C.D. 119 (1918).

couped, were also made. Apparently, though the findings are not explicit on the point, the subsequent charges were made with the knowledge and consent of the purchaser. These practices were found to be unfair methods of competition, and prohibited without qualification. Here again there was no finding that the sales, taking the free yeast into account, were unprofitable, or made from any other motive than the desire to get the business, and it is difficult to imagine the ground for objecting to the cash advances, or to the granting of credit upon initial deliveries. Since the order was consented to, it is perhaps beside the point to suggest that it was not justified by the facts set forth in the findings. As a precedent, however, the case is not a strong one.

In another case against a large yeast manufacturer, the same practices were involved, and the findings and order are in substantially the same words as in the Fleischmann case.[24]

Both of these cases went further. In addition to free yeast and the extension of credit upon initial deliveries, it was found that both companies had systematically given to operative bakers and their employees, liquor, cigars, meals, money, theatre tickets, and automobile rides, to influence them to buy yeast, and had made systematic contributions to master bakers' associations to help defray expenses of periodic conventions, all with the purpose of obtaining or retaining patronage. As to the employees, there was no charge that the presents were made secretly, and as to the operative bakers themselves there could, of course, be no question of commercial bribery. If I sell a man a dozen bananas for 25 cents, and add a thirteenth one as a gift, I am in effect selling him thirteen bananas for a quarter. If instead of the thirteenth banana, I add a nickel as a gift, I am selling

[24] F.T.C. *v.* National Distilling Co., 1 F.T.C.D. 88 (1918).

a dozen for 20 cents. Surely neither transaction is illegal, even if my object is to "induce" him to purchase from me rather than from a competitor. If instead of a nickel I add a five cent cigar, the situation is not changed. Unless there were facts that do not appear in the published findings, nothing more seems to have been involved in this part of the Fleischmann and National Distilling cases.

These cases suggest the common practice among retailers of giving, with purchases of a given size, coupons or certificates, which are redeemable, if presented in sufficient number, in objects of various kinds, useful, ornamental, or otherwise. If the Fleischmann Company and National Distilling Company cases were rightly decided, all such "premium" certificates, used in interstate or foreign commerce or in the District of Columbia, are illegal. The practice as such does not appear to have been disturbed by the Federal Trade Commission. In a series of cases, however, it has held that where distribution of the certificates was "determined by chance or lot," an unfair method of competition was involved.[25] The decisions may be justified under the policy against lotteries indicated by federal criminal statutes.[26]

TRADE AND QUANTITY DISCOUNTS

I pass now to a subject which is both inherently difficult and of great importance to the business world, namely, that of trade and quantity discounts.

It is a familiar fact that the distribution of goods under modern conditions has become to a large extent stratified. The goods pass through customary channels,

---

[25] Federal Trade Commission v. Brumage-Loeb Co., 1 F.T.C.D. 159 (1918). A note on 1 F.T.C.D. 163 states that similar orders were entered upon substantially the same facts against seventeen named respondents. *See* also F.T.C. v. Everybody's Mercantile Co., 3 F.T.C.D. 60 (1920).

[26] U.S. Criminal Code, Sec. 213.

from manufacturer to jobber, from jobber, perhaps, to an intermediate wholesaler, from wholesaler to retailer, and thus to the consumer. The strata vary according to the custom of different businesses and the policy of various houses, but some stratification is almost universal where a national market is appealed to. Unless he is holding his business by mere force of custom or by superior trade strategy, it must be assumed that each factor in the line of distribution (perhaps for lack of a better substitute) plays his legitimate part in the process. The retailer not only gives service to the consumer and carries the necessary local stocks, but he assumes the financial burden of sales on credit and of collections. The jobber and wholesaler keeps larger stocks at strategic distributing points, and maintains a close contact with the needs of retailers in his district. Each intermediary, being a purchaser and seller of the commodity, acts as an absorber of losses in a falling market, thus relieving the manufacturer of the impossible financial burden which would be involved if he alone had to carry the stocks and finance the sales on credit for a national market. In form, each factor in the chain is merely a trader, buying and reselling at a profit, but in reality he is performing a standardized service for the manufacturer and has a permanent and clearly defined place in the mechanism of distribution.

To be selected as the distributor, either wholesale or retail, of a successful nationally advertised product, is of course a much desired and profitable honor. In return, and as long as the relationship continues, the manufacturer will generally require adequate service. Even at considerable risk and expense, the dealer must carry enough stocks to meet all reasonable demands. Perhaps he is required to do a minimum of advertising and soliciting. The manufacturer may insist on proper physical conditions and reasonable service to consumers. For all these services, however, which may require expenditures or efforts not immediately remunerative, the distributor will ask for a reasonable assurance of a continuous income. He will try if possible to secure the elimination of speculative and fluctuating price elements, thus assuring himself, to that extent, of a standardized return from the business.

The manufacturer may desire, or may be compelled by trade custom, to confine his sales to wholesalers, or even to national jobbers, leaving them to supply the retail trade. In such a case no question of trade discounts will arise. The attempt to standardize returns will generally take the form of a system of set prices at which wholesalers and retailers are expected to make sales, the prices being in each case at a margin of profit sufficient to compensate the dealer for his services and spur him to further mutually profitable endeavors.[27] Often, however, trade custom will permit or the necessities of the situation require that the manufacturer supply a part of the retail trade as well. At this point the trade discount becomes important. If the manufacturer makes to the retailer the same price that he is quoting to wholesalers, of course the retailer will gradually absorb all the business. No margin of profit will be left to the wholesaler, and he will be forced out of the field. The important services which the wholesaler normally performs must be taken over by the manufacturer.

The quantity discount may to a certain extent meet the situation. Generally, the wholesaler will buy in larger quantities than the retailer, and the discount on the larger quantity may be sufficient to make the business worth while. Where there are continuous shipments and a large turnover, however, the quantity discount presents difficulties. Shipments to wholesalers may be made from day to day, aggregating large amounts, although each in-

[27] See post, p. 287.

dividual shipment may not be very large. On the other hand, a large retail house may buy at less frequent intervals but in larger individual amounts. If each shipment is taken by itself, there will be no discount in favor of the wholesaler. If, on the other hand, the discount is made to depend upon the value of shipments over a month or a year, a "deferred rebate" is involved, which may be from the business and financial point of view undesirable.

To meet this situation, many manufacturers prefer to make a division of customers on functional lines, rather than according to the volume of business which they do. Certain firms are recognized to be in business as wholesalers, and to perform the usual services expected of wholesalers. All others, regardless of size, are classified as retailers. Sales to wholesalers, whatever the volume, are made at a lower price than sales to retailers, the difference being the amount supposed to be necessary to make the business attractive to the wholesaler and to compensate for the services expected of him.

That this is a fertile field for controversy will be readily apparent. What test shall be applied in determining who is or is not a wholesaler? The wholesalers' association may publish an "official" list of accredited members. Can the manufacturer safely "recognize" only firms included in this list? A chain store organizes an affiliated "wholesale" house, which handles a volume of business comparable to an average-sized wholesaler, but confines its sales to the stores in the chain. Is it proper for the manufacturer to give the trade discount to such a company, or can the "legitimate" wholesalers insist that he disregard the corporate fiction and treat the concern as the purchasing department of the retail stores? The same question arises as to a wholesale company organized on a cooperative basis by a number of independent retailers. If such a company is classed as a wholesaler, the "legitimate" trade may be up in arms.

If it is excluded, a profitable avenue of distribution may be closed to the manufacturer. These are problems with which every sales manager of a large manufacturing establishment must deal, and they frequently arouse controversies which have stirred the bitterest feelings in the trade.

It appears to have been the position of the Federal Trade Commission that all trade discounts, that is, all discounts based on a classification of purchasers on functional lines, are illegal.

A complaint was issued against the South Bend Bait Company,[28] a large manufacturer of fishing tackle and artificial bait, charging that respondent, in furtherance of "a plan for the allowance of trade discounts," classified its customers "according to a basis of selection adopted by it"; that customers in one group received a 33⅓ per cent trade discount, in another a 40 per cent discount, and in the third a 50 per cent discount. This was said to be a violation of Section 5 of the Trade Commission Act. Part II of the complaint set forth the same facts, adding a formal allegation that the plan "has a dangerous tendency unduly to hinder competition in the interstate sale of fishing tackle, artificial bait, etc., and has tended to create for respondent a monopoly in the line of commerce engaged in by it," and charged a violation of Section 2 of the Clayton Act. From the findings it appears that the company classified as "jobbers" firms which "travel salesmen, issue a catalogue, and conduct a jobbing business, that is, calling on and selling to the retail trade and not doing a retail business," and allowed to all within the classification a discount of 50 per cent off list prices, regardless of the amount purchased. A "wholesaler" was defined as a customer who "does a combination retail and jobbing business"—a definition

[28] F.T.C. v. South Bend Bait Co., 4 F.T.C.D. 355 (1922).

apparently peculiar to the trade. He received a 40 per cent discount. A "retailer," or "dealer," was a customer who "maintains a store, carries stock and sells fishing tackle to the consumer," and he receives a 33⅓ per cent discount, except that on single purchases of over $300 the discount was 40 per cent. The consumer, "the party who buys the tackle to fish with," was charged net prices. The findings contain figures showing in detail the average and range of size of shipments to members of the several groups, clearly showing that the discounts bore no direct relation to the quantity purchased.

In the description of the practice, the findings are full and concrete, but in the conclusions as to its effect they are less satisfactory. All that appears is a formal statement that the tendency and effect of the plan is "to make discriminating prices to purchasers who are distributors, and to compel purchasers who are consumers to pay a fixed or list price for said products of respondent from whatever source said consumers may purchase"; and that "the effect of such discrimination in price by respondent may be to substantially lessen competition in the sale of fishing tackle, artificial bait and like products in the sale of such products [sic] in interstate commerce." In addition there are findings negativing the defense that the discrimination was based on selling or transportation costs, or on differences in quantity or quality, or that it was made in good faith to meet competition, or constituted a selection of customers "in bona fide transactions and not in restraint of trade." The charge that the plan tended to create a monopoly seems to have been abandoned, presumably in view of the fact that the company's output was found to be only from 5 to 8 per cent of the total volume of fishing tackle, artificial bait, and similar products in the United States. The order forbids "discriminating in net selling prices by any method or device between purchasers of the same grade, quality and quantity of commodities upon the basis of a classification of its customers as 'jobbers', 'wholesalers', 'retailers' or 'consumers' or any similar classification which relates to the customers' business policy, business methods, or to the customers' manner of doing business, in any transaction in, or directly affecting interstate commerce, in the distribution of its products;'"[29] with a proviso covering the exceptions in Section 2 of the Clayton Act.

In the South Bend bait case the only issue was as to the lawfulness of the practice of giving trade discounts to anyone. It is interesting to compare a case against a group of salt manufacturers, when the real issue was who was entitled to the trade discount.[30] The manufacturers were members of the Salt Producers' Association, and it was charged that through this association they had conspired to discontinue giving the regular trade discount to anyone not listed in a published wholesale grocers' directory, which it was charged did not contain all the wholesale grocers in the localities in which respondents were selling their products. The findings suggest, however, that the real difficulty lay in the fact that wholesale *dealers* who were not strictly wholesale *grocers* had formerly handled salt, but were excluded by the custom or agreement in question. The charge that there were wholesale grocers not included in the directory appears to have been abandoned. It was found, however, that "at least since January 1, 1919," the members had not confined the jobbers' discount "in all instances" to the firms listed in the directory, but had allowed the discount to any firm entitled in the opinion of the individual member to be classified as a wholesale dealer. The practice was found to be an unfair method of competition, and a violation of Section 2 of the Clayton Act. The true

[29] 4 F.T.C.D. 362.

[30] F.T.C. *v.* The Salt Producers' Asso. et al., 5 F.T.C.D. 67 (1922).

scope of the finding, however, appears only in the order, which is directed only against concerted action looking toward the establishment of trade discounts. Respondents are forbidden to enter any "agreement or understanding together or with one another" to limit the number of firms to be recognized as jobbers or wholesalers, or to refuse so to recognize anyone not in the official directory, or to agree that any list shall determine who is entitled to jobbers' discounts. There is nothing in the order to prevent any individual manufacturer from establishing trade discounts or to use any method that occurs to him in determining to whom such discounts shall be allowed. It is impossible to ascertain from the findings whether the limited scope of the order indicated a recession from the position taken in the South Bend case, or whether there was some other reason for prohibiting only concerted action.

The most important of the trade discount cases I have left to the last, because it brings together conveniently the issues presented in cases of this character, and because it gives an authoritative answer to the questions raised by the cases previously reviewed. I refer to the case against the Mennen Company,[31] in which the order of the Commission was set aside by the Circuit Court of Appeals in the Second Circuit,[32] and a writ of *certiorari* to review the court's decision was denied by the Supreme Court.[33]

The findings in this case, although couched in formal phraseology, leave little to be desired in the way of completeness. They describe clearly the evolution of the sales policy of the company, in the distribution of the toilet articles which it manufactures. Prior to 1917 the company sold on a quantity discount basis solely. Any pur-

[31] F.T.C. *v.* Mennen Co., 4 F.T.C.D. 258 (1922).
[32] The Mennen Co. *v.* F.T.C. (C.C.A. 2d), 288 Fed. 774.
[33] 262 U.S. 759 (1923).

chaser, whatever his status, could get the discount if he bought in sufficient amount. This policy seems to have aroused opposition from the "legitimate" wholesalers, and was denounced at conventions of the National Whole-sale Druggists' Association. The trouble arose especially with regard to the large cooperative purchasing agencies which were being organized in many cities by retail druggists. These were corporations, nominally engaged in the wholesale business, but in fact formed by the retail druggists solely to obtain the benefit of the "quantity discounts" generally allowed by manufacturers in the trade. Having a fixed and permanent clientele, these co-operative agencies were able to dispense with personal solicitation, and to carry much smaller stocks, and since they customarily sold to their members on a cash or short term credit basis, they were able to reduce the cost of financing and of bad debts. In this way they were able to save a substantial part of the trade discount, the savings being distributed among their members on a patronage basis or in some similar way. The growth of these co-operative corporations has been very rapid; in 1920, according to the findings, twelve such corporations alone made aggregate gross sales of $22,890,282.31.

Pursuant to the protests of the wholesalers, the Mennen Company in 1917 changed its sales policy. It divided its customers into wholesalers and retailers, and classi-fied the cooperative corporations as retailers. Those in the retail list were given a discount from list price of from 10 to 15 per cent, according to the price of the article, while those on the wholesale list received a dis-count of 15 to 17 per cent, according to price. The com-pany announced that it would sell to retailers in amount of $30 or more, smaller purchases being obtainable only through wholesalers. The discount to wholesalers was obtainable only on orders in excess of $150 net. For a time additional discounts were given to wholesalers on larger shipments, but later the company adopted a fixed discount to wholesalers of 15 per cent plus 3 per cent for cash, regardless of amount, provided the shipment exceeded ten gross, and of 10 per cent plus 5 per cent for cash to retailers, provided the shipment exceeded one and one-half gross. The result was that on shipments within a certain range, retailers and cooperative buying agencies had to pay more for shipments identical in size than regular wholesalers. The Commission found that this policy tended to drive from the field the cooperative corporations which I have described, and thus to substantially lessen competition. It concluded that both the Federal Trade Commission Act and the Clayton Act were violated, and ordered the company to cease and desist "from discriminating in net selling prices, by any method or device, between purchasers of the same grade, quality and quantity of commodities, upon the basis of a classification of its customers as 'jobbers', 'wholesalers', or 'retailers', or any similar classification which relates to the customers' form of organization, business policy, business methods, or to the business of the customers' membership or shareholders, in any transaction in, or directly affecting interstate commerce, in the distribution of its products:"[34] again with a proviso covering the exceptions in the statute.

The Mennen Company filed a petition in the Circuit Court of Appeals to review the order. The litigation by this time had aroused great interest in trade circles, and briefs were filed as *amicus* on behalf of a number of trade associations. On March 13, 1923, the court unanimously reversed the order of the Commission.[35] The court referred to the opinion of the Supreme Court in the Gratz case,[36] and pointed out that there was no suggestion that

[34] 4 F.T.C.D. 283.
[35] Mennen Co. *v.* F.T.C. (C.C.A. 2d), 288 Fed. 774.
[36] F.T.C. *v.* Gratz et al., 253 U.S. 421 (1920).

the Mennen Company had a monopoly of the business of
selling toilet articles, or that there was any deception,
misrepresentation, or oppression. Nothing was alleged
in the complaint to justify the conclusion that the public
suffered injury or that competitors had any ground
for complaint. The allegation that competition between
distributors was hindered, the court dismissed as a
"pleaders' conclusion."

The opinion then pursues a line of reasoning which
undermines the whole basis of the Commission's jurisdiction over cases of this sort. Reviewing the legislative
history of Section 2 of the Clayton Act, the court concludes that the section must be construed to prohibit only
discriminations which tend to injure a competitor of the
seller, and does not cover discriminations injurious to
the class of purchasers discriminated against.[37]

The court, however, goes on to deal with the merits of
the case:

What the Mennen Company has done was to allow to "wholesalers" who purchased a fixed quantity of their products a
certain rate of discounts while to the "retailers" who purchased

[37] For reasons previously given, I find some difficulty with the court's
reasoning. As first reported, the bill forbade discriminations "with the
purpose or intent to thereby destroy or wrongfully injure the business
of a competitor, *of either such purchaser or seller."* The phraseology
was obviously unsatisfactory, as the words "such purchaser" had no
ascertainable antecedent. In the conference the section was amended,
in the manner and for the reasons stated by Congressman Webb, who
presented the Conference Report in the House: "But as originally drawn
they were criminal sections, and section 2 made it a crime to discriminate
in price for the purpose of destroying or injuring a competitor. *We
thought that was probably too restricted.* We agreed, instead of retaining the language 'with the purpose or intent thereby to destroy or
wrongfully injure the business of a competitor' and so forth, to insert
this language: 'Where the effect of such discrimination may be to substantially lessen competition or tend to create a monopoly in any line
of commerce.' *We felt that that would tend to give the section more*

the same quantities it denied the discount rates allowed to the "wholesalers." This does not indicate any purpose on the part of the Mennen Company to create or maintain a monopoly. The company is engaged in an entirely private business, and it has a right freely to exercise its own independent discretion as to whether it will sell to "wholesalers" only or whether it will sell to both "wholesalers" and "retailers," and if it decides to sell to both, it has a right to determine whether or not it will sell to the "retailers" on the same terms it sells to the "wholesalers." It may announce in advance the circumstances, that is, the terms, under which it will sell or refuse to sell.[38]

It concludes, moreover, that the cooperative buying agencies are in fact retailers and not wholesalers, since their inherent identity with the retail stores cannot be obscured by the mere device of a corporate fiction.[39]

elasticity and breadth." [My italics.] 51 Cong. Rec., 16273. In view of this statement, which may be considered in interpreting the Act (Duplex Printing Press Co. *v.* Deering et al., 254 U.S. 443, 475), it is difficult to see why a restrictive effect should be given to the change made by the Committee.

[38] 288 Fed. 779-780.

[39] "Whether a buyer is a wholesaler or not does not depend upon the quantity he buys. It is not the character of his buying, but the character of his selling, which marks him as a wholesaler, as this court pointed out in Great Atlantic & Pacific Tea Co. *v.* Cream of Wheat Co., *supra.* A wholesaler does not sell to the ultimate consumer, but to a 'jobber' or to a 'retailer.' The persons who constitute these mutual or co-operative concerns are buying for themselves to sell to ultimate consumers, and not to other 'jobbers' or to other 'retailers.' The nature of the transaction herein involved is not altered by the fact that they make their purchases through the agency of their corporation. For some purposes a corporation is distinct from the members who compose it. But that distinction is a fiction of the law, and the courts disregard the fiction whenever the fiction is urged to an intent and purpose which is not within its reason and policy. And in such a case as this the fiction cannot be invoked. The important fact is that the members of the corporation are all retailers who buy for themselves to sell to the ultimate consumer. The Mennen Company is within its rights in classifying them as retailers." (288 Fed. 782.)

The grounds upon which the court's decision rests are obviously sufficient to put an end to all attempts, on the Commission's part, to attack trade discounts as such, or any policy of classifying cooperative buying agencies as retailers. The decision of the Supreme Court denying *certiorari* does not, it is true, imply an approval of the grounds of the decision or even of the result, but as a matter of principle the court's conclusion seems sound. No reason is given in any decision of the Commission why a trade discount as such is objectionable. I have described its economic basis, and in the absence of controlling considerations of public interest, such a device, found by the trade to fulfill a useful function, should not be disturbed. Whether or not a cooperative buying agency is a wholesaler is a more difficult question, but it does not seem necessary to answer it. A certain leeway must be left for the judgment and policy of the manufacturer. If he believes in good faith that the cooperative agency does not perform the services which he expects from a wholesaler, he should not be compelled by law to give it a wholesaler's compensation.

The facts may, however, point clearly to a different motive. The manufacturer may be entirely satisfied with the services the agency is performing, and entirely willing to allow the regular wholesaler's discount on sales handled by it, but he may be coerced by the concerted economic power of the "legitimate" wholesalers. Such a state of facts presents legal issues of a different character.

TRADE BOYCOTTS

THE scope which the law allows to associative activity in the businesses and professions is one of the most difficult as well as one of the most important of the unsettled questions of modern law. The phenomenal growth of the trade association as a factor in the economic life of the nation, and the services which these associations are rendering in improving business standards, disseminating knowledge, and promoting the use of better business methods, will be appreciated by any reader of the excellent review of Trade Association Activities which the Department of Commerce has recently published.[40] Their economic power also can be readily imagined. It will vary, of course, according to trade traditions and personalities, but where a large proportion of the trade belongs to an association, with aggressive leadership and strong financial resources, and with a firm hold on the loyalty of its members, it is obvious that the association is in a position to command the respect of all persons coming into business relations with the trade. The wholesalers especially, perhaps because of the menacing growth of the large retail establishments (the department stores and chain stores) as well as of the cooperative buying agencies, seem to have been particularly successful in welding their membership into a compact, aggressive, and powerful organization.

Obviously these associations exist primarily to protect trade interests, and the most vital interest of the wholesale trade is to preserve and perpetuate the time-honored method of distribution, from manufacturer to wholesaler, from wholesaler to retailer, from retailer to consumer. The natural enemy of the trade is the department store or chain store which buys direct from the manufacturer at wholesale prices. How far may such an association and its members go in insisting that they be recognized as a necessary link in the chain of distribution? Each member may of course use his own judgment in selecting his own customers and clients. If he does not like the policy of a retailer who buys direct from manu-

[40] *Trade Association Activities*, by L. E. Warford and Richard A. May, Washington, 1923. *See* also Jones, *Trade Association Activities and the Law* (1923).

facturers, he can refrain from dealing with him. If he does not like the policy of a manufacturer who sells direct to a chain store, or who gives a jobbers' discount to a cooperative agency, he can refuse to handle his products. Presumably he can inform the manufacturer or retailer or the public of the reasons for his action. But the Sherman Law, as construed by the Supreme Court, forbids him to agree with the other wholesalers in the trade that all will refrain from patronizing a manufacturer or retailer who has offended against the policy of the wholesale trade by "direct" dealing. Probably it forbids any concerted movement or propaganda, through the medium of an association or similar body, to induce members to follow a common course in such matters. The law is a recognition of the public interest in the unfettered development of new methods of distribution, as well as a revolt against the overweening methods which some of the more powerful associations have seen fit to use.[41]

In a series of cases, the Federal Trade Commission has dealt with attempts of this sort to direct by concerted effort the channels of wholesale and retail distribution, and its orders in these cases have been very generally sustained by the courts.

A complaint was filed in 1917 against the Wholesale Saddlery Association and 150 members throughout the United States, comprising the greater part of the wholesale saddlery trade of the country.[42] The National Harness Manufacturers' Association and its officers and executive committee and twenty affiliated local harness

---

[41] *See* on this subject the leading case of Eastern States Retail Lumber Dealers' Asso. *v.* U.S., 234 U.S. 600 (1914). Also pages 261 to 269 of Jones, *Trade Association Activities and the Law,* and Chap. 6 of Stevens, *Unfair Competition.* But *see* also Ware & Defreville *v.* Motor Trade Asso. (1921), 3 K.B. Div. 40.

[42] F.T.C. *v.* The Wholesale Saddlery Asso. of the U.S. et al., 1 F.T.C.D. 335 (1919).

manufacturers' associations were also joined as respondents. In this line of business, it should be noted, the harness manufacturer is really the retailer. Saddlery accessories are made by large producers and sold to the
wholesaler, who in turn sells them to the local harness
manufacturer, for use in making and repairing harness
or for direct sale to consumers. There had been in recent
years, however, a growing tendency on the part of manufacturers of accessories to sell direct to large consumers
and retail stores. Against this tendency the Wholesale
Saddlery Association appears to have opposed its most
vigorous efforts.[43] Until 1907 it published and circulated
in the trade official lists of "recognized" jobbers, and
thereafter it circulated its own membership list, with the
announced desire that it should be recognized as containing all the legitimate jobbers in the United States.
It officially "censored" a jobbers' list published by a
trade paper. Since 1911 it had excluded from its jobbers'
lists all concerns doing a combined or affiliated wholesale
and retail business, unless they were then members of
the association. From time to time the association had
notified accessory manufacturers that certain specified
concerns were not entitled to recognition as legitimate
jobbers, and "as recently as 1914" had notified its members of the names of accessory manufacturers who sold
direct to the retail trade. It gave favorable publicity to
the names of manufacturers who were in harmony with
the policy of the association. Public resolutions were
adopted condemning direct shipments to retailers. In

[43] The association had declared its policy as follows: "It is the
policy of this association to promote trade and commerce in the saddlery
line in the time-honored and regular channels, namely, through sales
of goods by the manufacturer to the jobber, by the jobber to the retailer,
and by retailer to the consumer, thus maintaining the stability of business and contributing to the prosperity of all in their respective stations." (1 F.T.C.D. 353.) *See* par. 15 of findings, 1 F.T.C.D. 353.

these efforts the National Harness Manufacturers' Association, representing the retail harness makers, actively cooperated. Specifically, it requested and secured the cooperation of the members of the wholesale association in preventing direct sales to mail order houses, general stores, and hardware stores. It established an "associate membership" to which accessory manufacturers were eligible only if their conduct was in harmony with the policy of the association. Salesmen of associate members were given "credentials," and retailers were systematically and persistently urged to withhold patronage from concerns whose salesmen were not equipped with such credentials. Such is a brief summary of the Commission's findings. The order forbade conspiring and combining to induce manufacturers to refuse to recognize non-members as legitimate jobbers; compiling, censoring or distributing lists of legitimate jobbers; reporting or circulating the names of manufacturers not in harmony with the association's policy, and "withdrawing, withholding, threatening to withdraw or withhold, or urging the withdrawal and withholding of patronage" from any such manufacturers, and, in short, to give the substance of seventeen separate paragraphs of the order, from establishing any standard of legitimacy in the jobbing business and using cooperative means of enforcing those standards. The National Harness Manufacturers' Association filed a petition for review (the other respondents apparently acquiescing in the order), but on a review of the findings and testimony, the Circuit Court of Appeals unanimously affirmed the order.[44]

This was a case in which a general trade boycott was sought to be enforced by associative activity. Several cases involve attempted boycotts against particular concerns.

[44] National Harness Manufacturers' Asso. *v.* F.T.C., 268 Fed. 705 (C.C.A. 6th, 1920).

In one case[45] the Wholesale Grocers Association, of El Paso, was charged with endeavoring to organize a boycott against the Standard Grocery Company. This company operated a chain of retail stores and conducted a wholesale department, at first directly and later through a subsidiary incorporated for the purpose. The local wholesalers objected to the "recognition" of this company by the manufacturers, and made vigorous representation to the local agents and brokers of the larger manufacturers of specialties, including verbal threats that they would concertedly discontinue handling the products of any manufacturer who sold to the concern in question. Both the wholesalers and the local brokers were made parties respondent, and they were ordered to cease and desist from combining and conspiring to prevent manufacturers from dealing with the Standard Grocery Company. On petition for review, the order was affirmed by the Circuit Court of Appeals, Fifth Circuit.[46]

In a case in southern California[47] the facts were very similar, except that the concern against which the boycott was directed was a cooperative buying agency for approximately 250 Los Angeles retailers. The extent and methods of the boycott are fully set forth in the findings. The Commission found that the Los Angeles Grocery Company was at first a mere buying exchange, pricing all sales to members at cost. It was then transformed into a regular jobbing house, invoicing at straight list prices and distributing profits to members at the end of the year as dividends. The Food Administration appears to have given it a license as a jobber, and the Commission found that it was doing a regular wholesale business. The

[45] F.T.C. v. Wholesale Grocers Asso. of El Paso et al., 3 F.T.C.D. 109 (1920).

[46] Wholesale Grocers Asso. of El Paso v. F.T.C., 277 Fed. 657 (C.C.A. 5th, 1922).

[47] F.T.C. v. Western Sugar Refinery Co. et al., 2 F.T.C.D. 151 (1919).

Circuit Court of Appeals, considering this question vital, reviewed the testimony and concluded that there was evidence to support the finding. It sustained the order against all petitioners found to have engaged in concerted efforts to prevent the recognition of the concern as a jobber. The order was reversed, however, against two sugar refiners who refused to sell to the concern as a jobber, but whose refusal was found to have been based on their individual judgment as to the classification to be given to the company. "This classification," said the court, "appears from the testimony to have been erroneous, but as long as it was the individual opinion and action of the refiners, it could not be made the basis of a finding of conspiracy or combination between the two refiners, or between them and the jobbers, or between them and the brokers."[48] Circuit Judge Ross, however, dissented from the affirmance of the order, on the ground that the company was in fact a buying exchange and not a wholesaler, and that therefore "the petitioning wholesale dealers, whose legitimate business, mainly if not entirely, depends upon the custom of retailers, were justified in combining to protect such legitimate business."[49]

Two other cases[50] involve similar facts, there being in each case an alleged attempt by wholesalers to organize a boycott of cooperative wholesale agencies.

The reader will have observed in these cases an apparent conflict between the decision in the Second Circuit, in the Mennen case, and the decision in the Los Angeles case in the Ninth Circuit. One court took the view that a buying agency organized by a group of retailers on a

[48] Western Sugar Refinery Co. et al. v. F.T.C., 275 Fed. 725, 741.
[49] Ibid., p. 742.
[50] F.T.C. v. Southern Hardware Jobbers Asso. et al., 4 F.T.C.D. 428 (1922), and F.T.C. v. The Atlanta Wholesale Grocers et al., 4 F.T.C.D. 466 (1922).

mutual basis was a wholesaler, the other that it was not. The cases can be reconciled, however, upon the assumption that a manufacturer may, at least within a reasonable range, use his own judgment in classifying distributing agencies, even if the Commission or the court might take a different view, but that concerted action to enforce an agreed classification is unlawful, regardless of the correctness of the classification. The position of the dissenting judge in the Los Angeles case, that concerted action to enforce an agreed classification is lawful provided the court believes the classification to be correct, does not seem tenable, in view of the authorities. It would result in legalizing an organized boycott by wholesalers against a manufacturer selling direct to retailers, or by retailers against a manufacturer or jobber who sold direct to consumers, although under the authorities such a concerted boycott is clearly illegal.[51]

In these cases the findings of the Commission are on the whole full and informative, and the cases appear on the face of the record to have been fairly and competently handled. The effectiveness of the remedy is of course weakened by the inability of the Commission to award damages, as well as by the length of time which expired, perhaps necessarily, before an effective order could be issued. However, a case of this sort generally involves a trade controversy of great magnitude, in which the public interest may be much at stake, and often the contest would, in the absence of governmental intervention, be a very unequal one. Judging by the cases I have reviewed, the action of the Commission seems to have been both warranted and helpful.

Some other cases involving boycotts are not so satisfactory. A case in Nebraska involved the act of a single wholesaler in protesting to a manufacturer against direct

[51] Eastern States Retail Lumber Dealers Asso. *v.* U.S., 234 U.S. 600, 614; Grenada Lumber Co. *v.* Mississippi, 217 U.S. 433, 440.

sales to the wholesale department of a chain of retail stores.[52] On petition for review, the Circuit Court of Appeals held that such action was not unlawful, in the absence of concerted action, and set aside the order.[53] In another case,[54] three wholesale grocery concerns in Cairo, Illinois, were charged with conspiring with local brokers of certain manufacturers, to prevent the manufacturers from selling direct to a cooperative buying agency. All the overt acts charged were done by the wholesalers individually, but there are general findings that the respondent wholesalers "have agreed and conspired among themselves" to induce manufacturers not to deal with the cooperative agency, and that the respondent brokers, "induced by coercion, persuasion, boycott and threats of boycott," agreed and conspired to recommend to their principal not to deal with the agency. The general allegations of conspiracy are so vague and so much broader than the facts stated in the findings, that one is left in doubt whether the finding of concerted action and agreement was a finding of fact, or merely a legal conclusion based on the fact that the three wholesalers acted in the same way under the circumstances. In an earlier case[55] the complaint charged a combination and conspiracy of two Baltimore jobbers to hamper and obstruct competitors by inducing manufacturers to refuse to recognize "such competitors" as jobbers. The findings ignore the charge of conspiracy, but state that each respondent "has corresponded with a manufacturer of automobile accessories," informing him that unless he ceased allowing the jobbers' discount to certain retailers,

[52] F.T.C. v. Raymond Bros.-Clark Co., 3 F.T.C.D. 295 (1921).

[53] Raymond Bros.-Clark Co. v. F.T.C., 280 Fed. 529 (1922).

[54] F.T.C. v. McKnight-Keaton Grocery Co. et al., 3 F.T.C.D. 87 (1920).

[55] F.T.C. v. Baltimore Hub-Wheel & Mfg. Co. et al., 1 F.T.C.D. 395 (1919).

the respondent in question would cease buying his accessories. Under the decision in the Raymond Bros.-Clark case, the complaint should, upon this finding, have been dismissed. There was also the elaborate proceeding, already referred to in another connection,[56] against a number of retail lumber dealers of the Middle West, charging the promotion of a boycott against the mail order houses. The complaint charged both concerted and individual action designed to induce manufacturers to cease supplying the mail order houses. This was the case in which a stipulation was entered into "that each of the stipulating respondents, and some of them without concert or conspiracy with any one or more of the others, . . ." and so forth, "has done or caused to be done one or more of the acts charged in paragraphs 8 and 10 of the complaint . . ." There are no formal findings, and obviously an order based on such a stipulation, even though consented to, is legally worthless.

PRICE MAINTENANCE

The controversy over trade discounts and also many of the trade boycott cases which I have discussed are but a phase of the constant struggle between those who are interested in maintaining the traditional processes of wholesale and retail distribution, and the innovators, the department and chain stores and cooperative buying agencies. Another aspect of the same struggle, in which also the Federal Trade Commission has intervened actively, is the controversy over price maintenance.

The business basis of the attempt to maintain set prices, both wholesale and retail, is much the same as in the case of trade discounts. A manufacturer produces an article, generally under a trade mark or name, and ad-

[56] F.T.C. v. Botsford Lumber Co. et al., 1 F.T.C.D. 60 (1918). *See supra*, p. 122.

vertises it on a lavish scale in the national market. A minimum of quality is of course a *sine qua non,* but apart from this commercial success will depend first on creating an effective demand among consumers, and second upon persuading the army of wholesale and retail distributors to give satisfactory and aggressive service in moving the article to the consumer. Technically and legally, as I have said, the relation between manufacturer and wholesaler is that of vendor and purchaser, and the manufacturer may have no direct relation whatever with retail trade. Actually, however, his eye is on the ultimate consumer. His advertising and his sales policy are directed toward selling the article to the man who uses it, and all intermediate factors in the process of distribution are merely agencies which he employs for the purpose. Since the manufacturer is directing the sales campaign, he will expect to determine for himself the major questions of retail sales strategy, instead of leaving them to the haphazard decision of several thousand retail stores. He will determine the scope and character of the advertising, and the size and shape of the package, and, since price is one of the principal factors of sales strategy, he will expect to prescribe to his retail distributors the price at which the article shall be offered to the public.

Obviously if he expects the retailer to carry out his sales policy, instead of acting merely as a buyer and seller of personal property, the manufacturer must be prepared to compensate him on a scale that will make the business satisfactory. Since large scale operations must be to some extent standardized, he will arrive at a fixed allowance per package or other unit, which will in his opinion make the business sufficiently attractive to the average retailer to induce him to handle the product, and he will arrange, through wholesalers, to supply the retailer with the product at a price sufficiently below the set retail price to net him, upon resale, the amount allowed. The wholesaler also, performing as he does an essential service, must be assured a fair return, hence the manufacturer allows him a further standard discount, sufficient in amount to assure good service. The price to the consumer and the discounts to retailers and wholesalers are as much elements of the manufacturer's business policy as are the salaries he pays to his own officers, and the price he pays for his materials.

To be effective, however, such a policy must be enforced, and it may be necessary to adopt means to ensure that wholesalers and retailers comply with the manufacturer's instructions. The manufacturer cannot afford to advertise an article widely at a stated price, say, a dollar watch or a five cent cigar, only to find that his retailers are selling it at a different price. Moreover, he feels himself under a certain obligation to protect the wholesaler and distributor who is faithfully carrying out his policy, against the competing dealer who is cutting prices. A contract is the most obvious means of securing the performance of a business understanding, and it may be advisable to have a corps of agents to report on sales methods of the various distributors, and to adopt disciplinary means in flagrant cases. In addition, precautions must be taken to prevent large quantities of the article from getting in the hands of dealers who have not agreed to adhere to the sales policy in question, and who for their private ends may see fit to engage in "predatory" price cutting. In view of the large amounts at stake, it is obvious that the technique of such a system may be brought to a high degree of perfection.

Such is the price maintenance system from the point of view of the manufacturer. The two principal antagonists of the system are the department store and the chain store, and of course their version is a different one. These retail establishments, large in resources and often aggressive in management, quite naturally insist on having a sales policy of their own. They may be unwilling to act merely as agencies engaged in carrying out the sales policies of a manufacturer. As compared with the small retail store, the department or chain store is generally a large advertiser, and it is a part of the advertiser's art to create for his establishment a distinct personality which customers will remember. One may make a specialty of sales at 5 and 10 cents. Another may use as an advertising "feature" a custom of selling 50 cent articles for 48 cents, or one dollar articles at 97 cents. Another may rely on special "sales," cut price campaigns, bargain counters, and similar artifices. Such devices are of course utterly inconsistent with a policy of set prices, or indeed with any system of distribution which regards the retailer as a mere agency in the service of the manufacturer.

It is undoubtedly true to a large extent that chain stores and department stores, owing to rapid turnover and large volume of sales, can handle many products at a lower unit cost than can the smaller retailer, and hence feel entitled to compete for the retail trade by operating on a smaller margin of profit. But the prime motive seems to be the advertising value of the cut price, and from this point of view, of course, the more thoroughly the set price is enforced elsewhere, the greater the effect of a much advertised cut of a few cents. Hence great efforts are directed toward securing, at wholesale or even at "distress" prices, supplies of nationally advertised articles which the "legitimate" dealers are expected to sell only at a set price, and sales of such articles at cut prices are heavily advertised. Correspondingly great are the efforts of the manufacturers and regular dealers to thwart their efforts.

The controversies engendered by this struggle have been much in the courts, and before the Federal Trade Commission Act had become law the Supreme Court had

spoken authoritatively as to the legal rights of the parties.
The leading case[57] involved the sales policy of a manufacturer of proprietary medicines, made according to a
secret though unpatented process. The manufacturer
entered into a series of standard contracts with wholesale and retail dealers, each dealer agreeing not to sell
the medicines at less than the full retail price printed on
the package, or to any dealers not "accredited agents"
of the manufacturer. A large wholesaler declined to enter
into such a contract, but succeeded in obtaining from
some of the regular wholesale and retail "agents," in
violation of their contracts, supplies of the medicine.
These "contraband" supplies he offered for sale at cut
prices. The manufacturer brought a bill for an injunction, but in the Circuit Court, and the Circuit Court of
Appeals on appeal, the relief was denied. On *certiorari*
the decision was affirmed by a majority of the Supreme
Court. The decision rests upon technical grounds. Under
the common law doctrine against restraints upon aliena-
tion of chattels the court held that the manufacturer could
not, except by contract, limit the right of a purchaser or
sub-purchaser to sell the article to any one or at any
price he pleased. A contract limiting his rights in this
respect would only be valid, again under the traditional
common law doctrine, if it was (a) limited to what was
fairly necessary to protect the covenantee, and (b) reasonable with respect to the public and the parties. So far
as the interests of the covenantee (the manufacturer)
were concerned, the court apparently inclined toward the
opinion that they could be disregarded, since "the advantage of established retail prices primarily concerns
the dealers. The enlarged profits which would result from
adherence to the established rates would go to them and
not to the complainant."[58] Even if it be of advantage to

[57] Dr. Miles Medical Co. *v.* Park & Sons Co., 220 U.S. 373 (1911).
[58] *Ibid.*, p. 407.

the manufacturer, however, the court found that the sales plan restricted "the freedom of trade on the part of dealers who own what they sell," and that agreements or combinations "having for their sole purpose the destruction of competition and the fixing of prices, are injurious to the public interest and void." The court concluded that "the complainant having sold its product at prices satisfactory to itself, the public is entitled to whatever advantage may be derived from competition in the subsequent traffic."[59]

In a subsequent case,[60] the article in question was patented, and the package in which it was sold contained a statement that the sale of the package below $1 would be a violation of the license and an infringement of the patent. A drug store obtained a supply from wholesalers, and offered them at cut prices. The manufacturer brought a bill claiming patent infringement, but the Supreme Court held that the privilege conferred by the patent law did not include the right to fix the price at which a purchaser could resell the patented article.

Such was the state of the law when the Federal Trade Commission was established, and as soon as it had got fairly in motion it took up the problem. In the latter part of 1917 complaints were filed against several concerns, among them the manufacturer of "Old Dutch Cleanser," charging them with unfair methods of competition in that they were fixing the prices at which their products should be resold, and refused and threatened to refuse to sell to dealers who failed to adhere to the policy.[61] Subsequently other complaints were filed,[62] and in all no

[59] *Ibid.*, p. 409.

[60] Bauer *v.* O'Donnell, 229 U.S. 1 (1913).

[61] F.T.C. *v.* Chester Kent & Co., Inc., 1 F.T.C.D. 149 (1918); F.T.C. *v.* The Cudahy Packing Co., 1 F.T.C.D. 199 (1918); F.T.C. *v.* Mishawaka Woolen Mfg. Co., 1 F.T.C.D. 506 (1919).

[62] F.T.C. *v.* Clayton F. Summy Co., 1 F.T.C.D. 413 (1919); F.T.C.

less than thirteen cases have been carried through to final order, besides a number of cases in which complaints were dismissed without prejudice.[63] The position taken by the Commission in these cases appears to have been that any attempt by a manufacturer to induce retailers to charge fixed prices in the resale of the manufacturer's products was illegal. The orders not merely prohibited the manufacturer from entering into contracts having price maintenance in view, but from "indicating" resale prices, refusing to sell to dealers who failed to adhere to the prices indicated, and discriminating in price against them or in favor of dealers who maintained prices, or indeed "carrying out a price maintenance policy by any other means." Generally there was a proviso permitting respondent to issue price lists or to print prices on containers, so long as he did not directly or indirectly recommend, require, or by any means whatsoever bring about the resale of the products at such resale prices.

In the meantime a case had come before the Supreme Court involving an indictment under the Sherman Law for enforcing a price maintenance policy.[64] The indictment, as construed by the district court, charged that Colgate & Company had urged and requested wholesalers and retailers to resell only at fixed prices, and had refused to sell to any that failed to comply, but it did not charge any contract or combination. The district court

v. Auto Strop Safety Razor Co., 1 F.T.C.D. 418 (1919); F.T.C. v. The Eli Lilly & Co., 1 F.T.C.D. 442 (1919); F.T.C. v. C. W. Baker & Sons, 1 F.T.C.D. 452 (1919); F.T.C. v. Gregory Furniture Mfg. Co., 1 F.T.C.D. 499 (1919); F.T.C. v. Beech-Nut Packing Co., 1 F.T.C.D. 516 (1919); F.T.C. v. Ruud Mfg. Co., 1 F.T.C.D. 530 (1919); F.T.C. v. Mutual Candy Co., Inc., 2 F.T.C.D. 1 (1919); F.T.C. v. The Aeolian Co., 3 F.T.C.D. 124 (1920), and F.T.C. v. Paul Forbriger & Co., 4 F.T.C.D. 17 (1921).

[63] See post, p. 299.

[64] U.S. v. Colgate & Co., 250 U.S. 300 (1919).

quashed the indictment, and on writ of error the Supreme
Court affirmed the judgment. Mr. Justice McReynolds
said:

The purpose of the Sherman Act is to prohibit monopolies,
contracts and combinations which probably would unduly interfere with the free exercise of their rights by those engaged,
or those who wish to engage, in trade and commerce—in a word,
to preserve the right of freedom to trade. In the absence of any
purpose to create or maintain a monopoly, the act does not restrict the long recognized right of trader or manufacturer
engaged in an entirely private business, freely to exercise his
own independent discretion as to the persons with whom he will
deal. And, of course, he may announce in advance the circumstances under which he will refuse to sell. . . . In Dr. Miles
Medical Co. v. Park & Sons Co., *supra,* the unlawful combination was effected through contracts which undertook to prevent
dealers from freely exercising the right to sell.[65]

On this authority, another district court sustained a
demurrer to an indictment against Schrader's Son, Inc.,
which did charge a series of agreements looking to price
maintenance.[66] The court took the view that the Colgate
case overruled the Dr. Miles Medical Company case, observing that whether or not there was a contract was "a
distinction without a difference." The Supreme Court,
however (two Justices dissenting), reversed the decision,
holding that the Dr. Miles Medical Company case was still
law, and was applicable wherever contracts were involved.

Such was the state of the authorities when the first of
the Federal Trade Commission's price maintenance cases
came before the court. The case was against the Beech-
Nut Packing Company, and involved price maintenance in
the sale of chewing gum and similar products. The find-

---

[65] *See* pp. 307-308.

[66] U.S. v. A. Schrader's Son, Inc., 252 U.S. 85 (1920). *See* also Frey
& Son v. Cudahy Packing Co., 256 U.S. 208 (1921).

ings of the Commission indicate that the company was using every practicable means to enforce fixed resale prices, except that in deference to the law it had no contracts with dealers calling for price maintenance. It maintained a list of "selected" or "desirable" dealers, both wholesale and retail, the test being, aside from credit standing and proficiency as a merchandiser, a willingness to maintain the indicated resale prices and refrain from selling to price cutters. To enforce the Beech-Nut sales policy, the company announced broadcast to jobbers, wholesalers, and retailers that it would refuse to sell to any dealer who failed to carry out the policy. Card records of dealers were kept, and whenever a complaint of price cutting was received, a salesman was sent to investigate, and if the charge was sustained an appropriate entry (such as the letters "DNS," for "do not sell") was made on the card of the dealer affected. Until the dealer gave assurance that he would not offend again he was refused further supplies. As soon as such assurances were received, however, instructions were sent to "clear the record," appropriate notation was made on the dealer's card, and he was reinstated as a "desirable" dealer. As an additional check, the company devised a system of symbols or key numbers, stamped on the cases, to enable it to trace back any package sold at cut prices, and thus to detect the offender.

On this state of facts (much condensed in this review) the Federal Trade Commission ordered respondent to cease and desist "from directly or indirectly recommending, requiring, or by any means bringing about the resale of Beech-Nut products . . . according to any system of prices fixed or established by respondent . . ." More particularly, the order covered refusal to sell to a distributor because of failure to adhere to fixed prices, or because of sales to price cutters; seeking or securing the cooperation of distributors in maintaining or enforcing a system of resale prices; or "carrying out or causing others to carry out a resale price-maintenance policy by any other means."

The company petitioned the Circuit Court of Appeals for review, and the court set aside the order on the authority of the Colgate case, there being no evidence of contracts or agreements.[67] The case went to the Supreme Court on *certiorari,* and there, by a five to four decision, the Circuit Court of Appeals was reversed.[68] "The facts show," said the majority opinion, "that the Beech-Nut system goes far beyond the simple refusal to sell goods to persons who will not sell at stated prices, which in the Colgate case was held to be within the legal right of the producer." The court continued:

The system here disclosed necessarily constitutes a scheme which restrains the natural flow of commerce and the freedom of competition in the channels of interstate trade which it has been the purpose of all the antitrust acts to maintain. In its practical operation it necessarily constrains the trader, if he would have the products of the Beech-Nut Company, to maintain the prices "suggested" by it. If he fails to do so, he is subject to be reported to the company either by special agents, numerous and active in that behalf, or by dealers whose aid is enlisted in maintaining the system and the prices fixed by it. Furthermore, he is enrolled upon a list known as "Undesirable— Price Cutters," to whom goods are not to be sold, and who are only to be reinstated as one whose record is "clear" and to whom sales may be made upon his giving satisfactory assurance that he will not resell the goods of the company except at the prices suggested by it, and will refuse to sell to distributors who do not maintain such prices.

From this course of conduct a court may infer, indeed cannot escape the conclusion, that competition among retail distributors is practically suppressed, for all who would deal in the company's products are constrained to sell at the suggested prices.

[67] Beech-Nut Packing Co. *v.* F.T.C., 264 Fed. 885 (C.C.A. 2d, 1920).
[68] F.T.C. *v.* Beech-Nut Packing Co., 257 U.S. 441 (1922).

Jobbers and wholesale dealers who would supply the trade may not get the goods of the company, if they sell to those who do not observe the prices indicated or who are on the company's list of undesirables, until they are restored to favor by satisfactory assurances of future compliance with the company's schedules of resale prices. Nor is the inference overcome by the conclusion stated in the Commission's findings that the merchandising conduct of the company does not constitute a contract or contracts whereby resale prices are fixed, maintained, or enforced. The specific facts found show suppression of the freedom of competition by methods in which the company secures the cooperation of its distributors and customers, which are quite as effectual as agreements express or implied intended to accomplish the same purpose. By these methods the company, although selling its products at prices satisfactory to it, is enabled to prevent competition in their subsequent disposition by preventing all who do not sell at resale prices fixed by it from obtaining its goods.[69]

The order of the Commission, was, however, directed to be modified in important respects. I quote again from the court's opinion:

The order should have required the company to cease and desist from carrying into effect its so-called Beech-Nut policy by cooperative methods in which the respondent and its distributors, customers, and agents undertake to prevent others from obtaining the company's products at less than the prices designated by it—(1) by the practice of reporting the names of dealers who do not observe such resale prices; (2) by causing dealers to be enrolled upon lists of undesirable purchasers who are not to be supplied with the products of the company unless and until they have given satisfactory assurances of their purpose to maintain such designated prices in the future; (3) by employing salesmen or agents to assist in such plan by reporting dealers who do not observe such resale prices, and giving orders of purchase only to such jobbers and wholesalers as sell at the suggested prices and refusing to give such orders to

[69] *Ibid.*, pp. 454-455.

dealers who sell at less than such prices, or who sell to others who sell at less than such prices; (4) by utilizing numbers and symbols marked upon cases containing their products with a view to ascertaining the names of dealers who sell the company's products at less than the suggested prices, or who sell to others who sell at less than such prices in order to prevent such dealers from obtaining the products of the company; or (5) by utilizing any other equivalent cooperative means of accomplishing the maintenance of prices fixed by the company.[70]

Justices Holmes, McKenna, and Brandeis dissented, on grounds apparently favorable to price maintenance. Mr. Justice McReynolds, who had spoken for the majority in the Colgate and Schrader cases, dissented on the ground that no contracts were involved.

It can hardly be denied that the decision leaves the law, in its practical aspects, in a very unsatisfactory state. A manufacturer may, in accordance with this decision, indicate, on the article or container or otherwise, the price at which he expects the article to be resold. He may, it seems, announce to all distributors his expectation and desire that the price be adhered to. If it comes to his knowledge that a dealer is cutting prices, he may refuse to have further dealings with him, and may advise him or anyone else of the reason. But apparently knowledge that the dealer has cut prices must come to the manufacturer spontaneously. He cannot instruct or request dealers or even his own agents to report the names of price cutters. Apparently also he must trust to his own memory as to the price-cutting proclivities of dealers; certainly he cannot cause their names to be "enrolled upon lists," and it would seem by analogy that entries on card records were likewise forbidden. Of course numbers and symbols to assist in tracing shipments at cut prices are forbidden, as is "any other equivalent cooperative means" of accomplishing the

[70] *Ibid.*, pp. 455-456.

maintenance of resale prices. In other words, a system of price maintenance, enforced by a policy of refusing to sell to price cutters, is permitted, but modern business methods may not be used to make it effective.

While the Beech-Nut case was in the courts, a number of cases then pending before the Federal Trade Commission were in virtual suspension, and after the decision was announced, the Commission ordered the complaints in these cases dismissed, "without prejudice to the commencement of another proceeding by the Commission against this respondent."[71]

The quality of the findings in these price maintenance cases varies greatly, depending doubtless upon the competence of the examiner or attorney who drafted them. In some of them the findings are somewhat scant and unsatisfactory.[72] Such cases, on the other hand, as the

[71] Thirty-eight such complaints were dismissed, some of them dating back more than four years. The text of the order of dismissal was as follows:

"A complaint having been issued herein by the Federal Trade Commission, including the charge of a violation of sec. 5 of the Federal Trade Commission Act declaring unlawful unfair methods of competition, by reason of the respondent . . . having adopted a policy of maintaining resale prices fixed by it, and the respondent having answered; and an order of the Commission in a proceeding brought by it against the Beechnut Co., for the same cause having meanwhile been taken to the United States Supreme Court for final determination, and further proceedings herein having been suspended to await its decision, and the Supreme Court having thereafter decided said Beechnut case and set forth the law therein in an opinion. (January 3, 1922,— 257 U.S. 441.)

"Now, in view of said decision, and the lapse of time since the beginning of this proceeding,

"IT IS HEREBY ORDERED, That the complaint herein be, and it hereby is, dismissed without prejudice to the commencement of another proceeding by the Commission against this respondent."

See footnote, 5 F.T.C.D. 135, for the order and a list of the cases.

[72] See, for instance, F.T.C. v. Chester Kent & Co., Inc., 1 F.T.C.D.

Beech-Nut Packing case, the case against the Mishawaka Woolen Manufacturing Company,[73] and the Old Dutch Cleanser case[74] are among the best in the Commission's reports. They present much valuable information as to distributing costs and methods, and bring out clearly the economic theory of the Commission's case. The substance of it is that operating costs of jobbers and retailers vary greatly, and that a standardized margin of profit tends to keep the inefficient, high-cost dealer in business, while preventing the more efficient dealer from competing for business by operating on a lower margin of profit. As a consequence, the public is deprived of the benefit of competition among dealers, and is compelled to pay prices based upon the costs of the least efficient dealer. The findings are, it is true, entirely formal, and suggest that they were prepared primarily with an eye to the legal result desired, rather than as an impartial and informative description of the practice. The economic arguments against the practice are stated, at least inferentially, but the arguments in its favor are neither referred to nor disposed of. However, as I have pointed out before, the formal character of the Commission's findings does not easily lend itself to impartial and informative exposition, nor is it permitted to inject argumentative matter. As compared with the usual run of decisions, these cases were on the whole exceptionally well handled.

"TIEING CLAUSES" AND CONTRACTS FOR EXCLUSIVE DEALING

IN the group of cases next to be considered, the Federal Trade Commission has been less successful in the courts, and its findings have also been less satisfactory, than

149 (1918); F.T.C. v. Clayton F. Summy Co., 1 F.T.C.D. 413 (1919), and F.T.C. v. Auto Strop Safety Razor Co., 1 F.T.C.D. 418 (1919).

[73] F.T.C. v. Mishawaka Woolen Mfg. Co., 1 F.T.C.D. 506 (1919).

[74] F.T.C. v. The Cudahy Packing Co., 1 F.T.C.D. 199 (1918).

in the price maintenance cases. I refer to the cases involving "tieing clauses" and contracts for exclusive dealing.

Here also the subject has a previous history. In the well-known case of Henry v. A. B. Dick Company,[75] a majority of the Supreme Court had held, over the emphatic dissent of the Chief Justice, that the manufacturer of a patented article could "license" the purchaser to use it, upon condition that he use with it only supplies and accessories, not patented, made by the same manufacturer. A violation of the condition was held to be an infringement of the patent. This case, as well as the proceedings then pending against the United Shoe Machinery Company, involving the same practice, played, it will be recalled, an important part in the political history of Section 3 of the Clayton Act. In the first case of this kind that came before the Supreme Court after the passage of the Clayton Act, the court expressly overruled the Dick case.[76] A clause in a contract for the sale of patented motion picture apparatus, that it should be used only with an unpatented film made by the vendor, was held invalid. The court did not directly rely upon Section 3 of the Clayton Act, although it recognized the section as "a most persuasive expression of the public policy of our country," but expressed clearly its opinion that the Dick case was wrongly decided. However, in the following year a majority held that the tieing clauses of the United Shoe Machinery Company, requiring lessees of patented machinery to use in connection with them only certain unpatented machines of the lessor, did not constitute contracts in restraint of trade subjecting the maker to indictment under the Sherman Law.[77] Here again the Clayton Act was not in issue, the alleged of-

[75] 224 U.S. 1 (1912).

[76] Motion Picture Patents Co. v. Universal Film Mfg. Co. et al., 243 U.S. 502 (1917).

[77] U.S. v. Winslow, 227 U.S. 202.

fense having been committed before the law took effect. The change made by the Clayton Act was recognized, however, in the second United Shoe Machinery case,[78] where the tieing clauses of the company were held illegal.

There are in the published reports of the Commission only three cases dealing with tieing contracts, in the strict sense of the word, that is, contracts by which an article is sold or leased to the ultimate user with a stipulation that it be used only in conjunction with accessories, supplies, or other machinery made by the vendor or lessor. One of the first complaints filed by the Commission was against the A. B. Dick Company, upon substantially the facts involved in the case in the Supreme Court.[79] There is another case against the National Binding Machine Company upon similar facts,[80] and a case against a manufacturer of shooting traps, who leased the traps on condition that they be used only with clay pigeons made by the lessor.[81]

In cases of this character there is a difficulty arising out of the unfortunate phrasing of Section 3 of the Clayton Act. The section applies to the lease or sale of an article on the condition, agreement, or understanding "that the lessee or purchaser thereof shall not use or deal in the goods, wares, merchandise, machinery, supplies, or other commodities of a competitor or competitors of the lessor or seller." A "tieing clause" is merely an agreement not to use machinery or supplies of a competitor *in conjunction with the article sold or leased*. The "license restriction" of the A. B. Dick Company, for instance, would forbid the use of a competitor's stencil paper and ink in the operation of an A. B. Dick mimeograph, but it

[78] United Shoe Machinery Corp. et al. *v.* U.S., 258 U.S. 451 (1922).
[79] F.T.C. *v.* A. B. Dick Co. et al., 1 F.T.C.D. 20 (1917).
[80] F.T.C. *v.* National Binding Machine Co., 1 F.T.C.D. 44 (1917).
[81] F.T.C. *v.* The Chamberlain Cartridge & Target Co., 2 F.T.C.D. 357 (1920).

would not prevent the purchaser from buying also some other make of stencil duplicating machine and using with it any kind of ink or paper he might choose to purchase. In the second United Machinery case this argument seems to have been pressed, but was rejected by the court. The opinion states that "while the clauses enjoined do not contain specific agreements not to use the machinery of a competitor of the lessor, the practical effect of these drastic provisions is to prevent such use." In this case the Shoe Machinery Company was found by the district court to control more than 95 per cent of the business in which it was engaged in the United States, and to manufacture certain patented machines which a shoe manufacturer was compelled to use and could not obtain from any other source. "When it is considered," said the Supreme Court, "that the United Company occupies a dominating position in supplying shoe machinery of the classes involved, these covenants, signed by the lessee and binding upon him, effectually prevent him from acquiring the machinery of a competitor of the lessor, except at the risk of forfeiting the right to use the machines furnished by the United Company, which may be absolutely essential to the prosecution and success of his business."

As thus defined, the issue is closely related to the question whether the condition or agreement is such that its effect may be, in the words of the Clayton Act, to substantially lessen competition or tend to create a monopoly. The question is whether or not a manufacturer, having a legal or practical monopoly of an article, is trying to acquire by contract or stipulation a similar monopoly over another article used in connection with the first.

The findings in the cases before the Federal Trade Commission, however, do not deal as satisfactorily with this difficulty as did the Supreme Court in the Shoe Ma-

chinery case. In the A. B. Dick case,[82] it is found that the
company controls about 85.1 per cent of the commerce in
stencil duplicating machines, and there is a finding that
the restrictive conditions "have compelled, and do compel, purchasers and users of such machines to purchase
stencil duplicating paper, stencil duplicating ink, and
other stencil duplicating supplies exclusively from the
respondents." Why they should have this effect is not
stated, and it is difficult to say whether the "finding"
implies that there was in fact economic compulsion, or
whether it is merely an argumentative interpretation of
Section 3 of the Clayton Act. The findings in the National
Binding Machine case[83] are even less satisfactory. The
text of the "license agreements" is not given, but it is
said that by their terms the "owners and users of tape-
moistening machines other than the National Binding
Machine are permitted to continue their use only upon
condition that they shall purchase their supply of gummed
sealing tape from respondent." It is found that these
restrictions "have compelled and may compel lessees
and users of such binding machine to purchase gummed
sealing tape exclusively from respondent . . . and
. . . have prevented and do prevent competing manufacturers from selling their gummed sealing tape for
use with National Binding Machines leased by respondent." Whether the user of National Binding Machines
may also use a competing binding machine, and use with
it some other brand of sealing tape, and whether, if such
is the case, the Clayton Act has been violated, is not discussed in the findings. It is stated that the company has
about 15,000 machines under lease, but it is not shown
what proportion this is of the total number in use in the
United States. In the clay pigeon case it is clear that the
contract merely prevents the lessor from throwing from

[82] F.T.C. v. A. B. Dick Co. et al., 1 F.T.C.D. 20 (1917).
[83] F.T.C. v. National Binding Machine, 1 F.T.C.D. 44 (1917).

the traps leased by respondent any targets not made by respondent, and no facts are given bearing on the question whether, in the language of the Supreme Court, the "practical effect" is to prevent the lessee from using any other clay pigeons than those made by respondent.

In both the binding machine case and the clay pigeon case the findings show the extent of respondent's sales of the supplies in question. The National Binding Company controlled 38 per cent of the commerce in gummed sealing tape, and the pigeon trap company sold substantially more clay pigeons than did all its competitors. Perhaps it is intended to suggest that the dominating position (if such it was) was due to the tieing clause rather than to the excellence of the product, but no facts are given bearing upon this issue. From the absence of specific findings of fact it may be assumed from these cases that the Commission believes that the sale or lease of an article, with a condition that it be used only in conjunction with another article also made by the vendor or lessor, is of itself illegal—in other words, that a farmer who sells his horse to a neighbor across the state line, with an agreement that the horse be fed only with oats bought from him, has violated the Clayton Act.

That such a legal position is unwarranted is suggested by a case which, while it did not involve a tieing clause in the strict sense, raised a question that is closely analogous. The Carnegie Steel Company manufactures, among other things, steel ties for use in binding bales of cotton, and markets them through the sole agency of Messrs. Warren, Jones & Gratz, as distributors. This firm is also distributor of jute bagging made by the American Manufacturing Company of St. Louis. A complaint was filed against Warren, Jones & Gratz, charging that they refused to sell steel ties unless the purchaser would also buy from them the necessary jute bagging to be used with the ties. The purpose, intent, and effect

to stifle competition was, as usual, alleged, and the practice was said to be a violation of both Section 5 of the
Trade Commission Act and Section 3 of the Clayton Act.
The findings show that the Carnegie Steel Company
makes about 75 per cent of the steel ties made for the
purpose in the United States, and "sufficiently dominates
the cotton tie situation in the United States to enable it
to fix and control the price of such ties throughout the
country." As to jute bagging, 45 per cent of the amount
used annually in the United States is made by the American Manufacturing Company, 20 per cent by a Boston
concern, and the remainder is secondhand bagging or a
substitute called sugar bag cloth. The Commission found
that respondents "had what amounted to a monopoly of
the cotton-tie business of the country," that their dominating and controlling position "made it possible for
them to force would-be purchasers of ties to also buy
from them bagging manufactured by the American Manufacturing Co.," and that "in many instances" they refused to sell ties unless the purchaser would also buy a
corresponding amount of bagging. This was found to
be an unfair method of competition, but it was found that
there was not sufficient proof to sustain the charge that
Section 3 of the Clayton Act had been violated. The latter conclusion was obviously correct, since there was no
condition or agreement as to the use of the article sold,
but merely a refusal to sell one article without the other.

Respondent petitioned the Circuit Court of Appeals
for review, and that court unanimously set aside the
order.[84] The court's version of the practice was as follows:

It is the natural and prevailing custom in the trade to sell
ties and bagging together, just as one witness testified it is to
sell cups and saucers together. Such evidence as there is of a
refusal to sell is a refusal to sell at all to certain persons with

[84] F.T.C. *v.* Gratz et al., 258 Fed. 314 (C.C.A. 2d, 1919).

whom the respondents had previous unsatisfactory relations and a refusal to sell ties without bagging at the opening of the market in 1916 and 1917 when there was fear that owing to scarcity of ties and the prospects of large crops, the marketing of the cotton crop might be endangered by speculators creating a corner in ties. The evidence is that with these exceptions the respondents sold ties without any restrictions to all who wanted to buy and indeed made extraordinary efforts to induce the manufacturers of ties to increase their output so that all legitimate dealers and all cotton raisers should get enough ties and bagging at reasonable rates to market their cotton. It is only these exceptional and individual cases, which established no general practice affecting the public, that can sustain the findings in paragraph 4.[85]

The case went to the Supreme Court, and there the majority took the view, already referred to,[86] that regardless of evidence or findings, the order must be reversed if the complaint does not set forth facts sufficient to show a violation of law. The complaint, the court held, failed to show what amount of the business was controlled by respondents, or that they had acquired or were attempting to acquire a monopoly of either ties or bagging. "All question of monopoly or combination being out of the way, a private merchant, acting with entire good faith, may properly refuse to sell, except in conjunction, such closely associated articles as ties and bagging." The decision setting aside the order was therefore affirmed. The opinion does not show whether the result would have been different if the findings, showing the extent of respondent's control of the cotton tie situation, could have been considered.

Further light is thrown on the lawfulness of "tieing clauses" in a group of cases which involve a practice apparently common in the marketing of gasoline. As is

[85] *Ibid,* p. 317.
[86] *Supra,* p. 90.

well known, gasoline is commonly sold by the refiner, out
of tank wagons, to retailers, who in turn sell it to consumers from pumps, set on storage tanks, and fitted out
with measuring devices. The pump fulfills a threefold
purpose. It is an apparatus for measuring out the gasoline. It is also designed to be an advertisement of the
particular brand of gasoline in question, and is therefore
given, a distinctive color and shape, and bears prominently the name of the company or brand. Finally, it provides the necessary storage for the local supply of gasoline, thus reducing the frequency with which gasoline
must be supplied from the tank wagon, and consequently
decreasing the cost of distribution.

Under the stress of competition, and also, it was
claimed, to induce the retailer to increase his storage
facilities, many of the leading oil refiners adopted the
practice of ''leasing'' tanks and pumps, bearing the
lessor's name or distinctive mark, to retailers at virtually nominal rentals, upon the understanding that the
retailer would use them only to sell the lessor's brand of
gasoline. The agreement did not attempt to prevent the
dealer from selling competing brands through other
pumps, but it would prevent a dealer from selling, say,
''Tydol'' gasoline from a ''Socony'' pump. Where, therefore, the dealer's business only warranted the installa-
tion of a single pump, he was practically compelled to
handle only one brand of gasoline.

The Federal Trade Commission launched a nation-
wide attack on the practice. Trade Practice Submittals
were held in 1920, in Denver and Chicago, at which independent oil interests of the intermountain states and of
the Middle West were represented, and the practice was
condemned in formal ''rules of conduct'' adopted at each
meeting.[87] Complaints were filed against the Standard
Oil Companies of Indiana, New Jersey, Ohio, and New

[87] Trade Practice Submittals, p. 52.

York, against the Atlantic Refining Company, the Sinclair Oil Company, and the Texas Company, and against a long list of lesser competitors. The published reports contain thirty-five separate orders condemning the practice.[88] In many of the cases there are voluminous records, and the proceedings were prolonged and costly. From the point of view of time and expense, probably these cases represent the greatest single effort of the Federal Trade Commission to deal with a trade practice deemed to be injurious.

The result was, however, a complete failure. In four circuits petitions for review were filed,[89] and in each case the orders of the Commission were set aside. *Certiorari* was granted by the Supreme Court in cases in two circuits,[90] and the decisions of the Circuit Courts of Appeal were unanimously affirmed. In all the cases the arguments were substantially the same. There was no agreement not to deal in the gasoline of a competitor, and no purpose of acquiring an unlawful monopoly. In the Second Circuit, Judge Hough put the matter succinctly. "The reasoning of the Commission," he said, "confounds commerce with convenience, besides introducing into

[88] F.T.C. *v.* Standard Oil Co. of Indiana, 2 F.T.C.D. 26 (1919), and Same *v.* Same, 2 F.T.C.D. 46 (1919); F.T.C. *v.* Maloney Oil & Mfg. Co., 2 F.T.C.D. 346 (1920), and *see* footnote 2 F.T.C.D. 357, for list of firms against which the Commission entered similar orders in cases involving substantially the same facts; F.T.C. *v.* Lubric Oil Co., 3 F.T.C.D. 68 (1920), and *see* footnote 3 F.T.C.D. 86, for list of firms against which the Commission entered similar orders in cases involving substantially the same facts; F.T.C. *v.* Bartles Oil Co., 3 F.T.C.D. 77 (1920), and F.T.C. *v.* The Motor Fuel & Lubricating Co., 3 F.T.C.D. 78 (1920).

[89] Sinclair Refining Co. *v.* F.T.C., 276 Fed. 686 (C.C.A. 7th), Standard Oil Co. of N.Y. *v.* F.T.C., and The Texas Co. *v.* Same, 273 Fed. 478 (C.C.A. 2d), Canfield Oil Co. *v.* F.T.C. 274 Fed. 571 (C.C.A. 6th), and Standard Oil Co. of N.J. *v.* F.T.C., 282 Fed. 81 (C.C.A. 3d).

[90] F.T.C. *v.* Sinclair Refining Co., 257 U.S. 631 (C.C.A. 3d and 7th).

trade an element of unfairness and indeed dishonesty. There is no contract, agreement, or understanding by which any retailer is prevented from selling any brand of oil, and he can own or lease as many pumps as he likes or can use. It is unfair and dishonest to give out from a pump bearing one brand another maker's oil, and all that secures any one retailer's trade for any one wholesaler is the amount of business the retailer can gather from the community.''[91]

The outcome as well as the merits of the controversy suggest that the Commission did not exercise the best of judgment in selecting this particular practice as the object of so expensive and far-reaching a campaign. Nor can much be said for the way in which the cases were handled. In the first proceeding instituted, that against the Standard Oil Company of Indiana,[92] the complaint contained a number of loosely worded charges, which were completely ignored in the findings. There was also a charge that respondent allowed a commission to dealers only if they "use or deal in respondent's products exclusively," but the findings merely show a condition that pumps and tanks leased from respondent shall be used only in selling respondent's gasoline. In addition there was a finding that respondent leased equipment at a nominal rental, and that this was an unfair method of competition against other manufacturers of equipment. This practice, however, was not alleged in the complaint. Another complaint against the same company charged numerous unfair practices, including price discrimination, misrepresentation of competitor's products, and other dishonest acts, but these charges again were ignored in the findings, which were confined to the sale and lease of equipment at nominal rates and with the restrictive covenant. It was in these cases that the Com-

[91] 3 F.T.C.D. 626-627.
[92] *Supra,* p. 156.

mission formally "disapproved" parts of the agreed statement stipulated by its counsel, and subsequently amended its findings by eliminating certain portions favorable to respondents, although specifically admitted in the stipulation.[93] In the Canfield Oil Company case, the Commission was reproved by the court for adopting "one general form of findings" for all cases in the group, although in direct conflict with the evidence or even with stipulations in some of the cases.[94] In none of the cases is the economic basis of the practice adequately discussed, nor is there anywhere a comprehensible analysis of the supposed legal theory upon which the orders rest.

While the decisions are not conclusive, the Gratz case and the "pump and tank" cases suggest that where there is no agreement not to use the goods of a competitor, but merely an agreement not to use them in conjunction with a specific article, the law is not violated unless there are special facts which as a practical matter compel the purchaser or lessee to refrain from using the competitor's product at all. In the United Shoe Machinery case, such facts existed, it being found that certain machines made by the company, and covered by patent, were essential in the manufacture of shoes. Whether anything less is sufficient, it is not yet possible to tell.

A tieing clause, in the strict sense, is an agreement or condition designed to affect, directly, the purchases of the ultimate user. A contract for exclusive dealing, although dealt with in the same section of the Clayton Act, has a different economic purpose. From the manufacturer's point of view, it is a means of securing the undivided loyalty of his retail distributor. No manufacturer would permit a traveling sales agent to interest himself, on the side, in a competing product, and as I have said in

[93] See supra, pp. 157, 158.
[94] Canfield Oil Co. v. F.T.C., 274 Fed. 571 (C.C.A. 6th, 1921).

another connection, there is a strong tendency among manufacturers of nationally advertised brands to regard the wholesale and retail distributors as mere merchandising agencies of the manufacturer. The manufacturer feels that when he has at great expense and trouble selected his distributing agencies throughout the country, has taught them how to display and sell his wares, and has advertised his product widely for their benefit, he can reasonably require that they do not enter the service of his competitors. There is, however, another side to the picture. In a large city, where there are retail stores at every corner, there can be no great harm if each such store confines itself to a particular brand. A small town, however, may have only one or two drug stores, or a single drygoods store, or there may be only the old-fashioned "general store," handling everything from gasoline to galoshes. If both the drug stores and the single drygoods store bind themselves by contract to carry only one brand, they are depriving the public of the benefit of a larger choice, while the general store, if it pursued such a policy, would belie its historic function. And if a manufacturer of a widely advertised brand succeeds in tieing up the retailers in all the small towns in the country, he may effectively close to his competitors a substantial part of the normal channels of distribution.

It is not surprising that this conflict of policy has led to much uncertainty in court decisions. For many years, Whitwell *v.* Continental Tobacco Company[95] was the leading case. It involved the legality of the practice of allowing discounts to tobacco dealers who refrained from handling brands of plug and chewing tobacco which competed with the manufacturer's brand. The court found that the practice had no tendency to restrict competition or restrain trade, and dismissed the plaintiff's suit for

[95] 125 Fed. 454 (1903).

triple damages under the Sherman Law. In the Continental Wall Paper case,[96] on the other hand, there was a combination of 95 per cent of the manufacturers of wall paper in the United States, and a concerted policy of entering into exclusive contracts with dealers. The Supreme Court held that contracts immediately connected with this attempt to monopolize the trade were unenforceable. These cases arose, of course, before the enactment of the Clayton Act. More recently, in Standard Fashion Company v. Magrane-Houston Company,[97] the court considered the effect of the Clayton Act upon contracts of a pattern maker, requiring retail drygoods stores to handle its patterns to the exclusion of those of competitors. It was found that of the 52,000 so-called pattern agencies in the United States approximately two-fifths were controlled under exclusive contracts by the Standard Fashion Company. The court unanimously affirmed the decision of the district court and the Circuit Court of Appeals, holding the contracts to be in violation of Section 3 of the Clayton Act, and quoted with approval the following from the opinion of the Circuit Court of Appeals:

The restriction of each merchant to one pattern manufacturer must in hundreds, perhaps in thousands, of small communities amount to giving such single pattern manufacturer a monopoly of the business in such community. Even in the larger cities, to limit to a single pattern maker the pattern business of dealers most resorted to by customers whose purchases tend to give fashions their vogue, may tend to facilitate further combinations; so that the plaintiff, or some other aggressive concern, instead of controlling two-fifths, will shortly have almost, if not quite, all the pattern business.

The Federal Trade Commission has had occasion to deal with exclusive contracts of this character in a num-

[96] Continental Wall Paper Co. v. Voight & Sons Co., 212 U.S. 227 (1909).

[97] 258 U.S. 346 (1922).

ber of cases. A manufacturer of horse-clipping and sheep-
shearing machinery made it a practice, fully acknowledged in its printed announcements, of paying a 7 per
cent premium to such of its jobbers and wholesalers as
refrained from handling any competing makes. The findings show that out of 603 jobbers and wholesalers dealing
in such machinery, 493 handled respondent's products.
It does not appear how many earned the premium. A
violation of Section 3 of the Clayton Act was found, and
respondent was ordered to cease and desist.[98] In a case
against a motion picture booking corporation,[99] the complaint charged that respondent, with the intent, purpose,
and effect of stifling and suppressing competition in the
sale and leasing of moving picture films in interstate
commerce, had leased and sold films on condition that
lessee or purchaser do not exhibit or deal in the films of
competitors. The findings were in substantially the same
words, except that instead of the intent, purpose, and
effect of stifling and suppressing competition, they
charged that the effect of the practice "may be to substantially lessen competition or tend to create a monopoly." The text of the exclusive contract is not given,
nor do any facts appear bearing on the size and extent
of respondent's business or the economic effect of the
practice. The case is therefore quite worthless. More recently there was a case against a manufacturer of oleomargarine,[100] which is equally unsatisfactory. The complaint charges the offense substantially in the language
of the statute, without specification or detail. The findings
add only one fact, namely, that twenty competitors of
respondent use similar contracts, while practically all of
the remaining forty-five enter into informal understandings to the same effect. The only finding bearing on the

[98] F.T.C. *v.* Chicago Flexible Shaft Co., 1 F.T.C.D. 181 (1918).
[99] F.T.C. *v.* Stanley Booking Corp., 1 F.T.C.D. 212 (1918).
[100] F.T.C. *v.* B. S. Pearsall Butter Co., 5 F.T.C.D. 127 (1922).

issue of monopoly is the formal refrain that the effect is
to substantially lessen competition and to tend to create
a monopoly. Respondent petitioned the Circuit Court of
Appeals to review the order, and it was unanimously set
aside.[101] The court mentioned the fact, apparently established by the evidence though not referred to in the findings, that the company controlled only 1 per cent of the
output of oleomargarine, and found no evidence that a
monopoly had been acquired or sought after.

I have left to the last the Curtis Publishing Company
case,[102] the most important of the cases involving "exclusive dealing" cases, because it sums up clearly the
weakness of the Commission's handling of these cases. I
have given elsewhere a full review of the case,[103] and need
not go over the ground again. There were, it will be recalled, two crucial issues in the case: first, whether or not
there was a contract of sale between the Curtis Publishing Company and its retail distributors, and second,
whether or not there was, in the peculiar system of distribution built up by respondent, an economic justification for the exclusive contract. The first issue the
Commission's findings evade, by calling the contracts,
ambiguously, "contracts for sale." The text of the contracts was not given. The contracts were held by both
reviewing courts to be contracts of agency, and not of
sale, thus disposing of any question under the Clayton
Act. Upon the second issue, respondent presented an
elaborate defense and voluminous testimony, and strenu-
ously asserted that the object of the restrictive clause
was merely to protect the company's system of distribution from unfair appropriation by competitors. The
defense was not alluded to in the findings, and it was
necessary for the reviewing court to perform the task,

[101] Pearsall Butter Co. v. F.T.C., 292 Fed. 720 (1923).
[102] F.T.C. v. Curtis Pub. Co., 2 F.T.C.D. 20 (1919).
[103] *Supra,* p. 127.

which the Commission should have performed, of analyzing the evidence and reporting the true facts. It is not surprising that the Supreme Court treated the Commission's findings in this case with scant respect. In the Supreme Court the decision sustaining the reversal of the Commission's order was unanimous, two Justices "doubting" merely certain expressions in the majority opinion as to the reviewing power of the courts.

The net result of the cases under Section 3 of the Clayton Act has therefore been substantially nil.[104] Every order which has been appealed has been annulled by the courts. The Commission itself has made no contribution toward the juristic development of the subject, but seems to have contented itself with the dogmatic assumption that all tieing contracts and all contracts for exclusive dealing are unlawful. What meagre progress there has been toward clarification of the law has been made by the courts and not by the Commission. This is the more regrettable because the subject matter is one that should be peculiarly within the competence of the Federal Trade Commission. Fundamentally, the issue is whether a tieing contract or a contract for exclusive dealing is justified by the business facts, in a particular case, or whether it represents merely an attempt by a powerful manufacturer to use his strategic position as a lever to induce

---

[104] Reference should be made at this point to F.T.C. v. Fruit Growers' Express, 2 F.T.C.D. 369 (1920), involving a charge that respondent, as owner and lessor of refrigerator cars, required its lessees to agree to use its equipment exclusively. The Commission found that "by reason of the contracts hereinbefore mentioned" at least 95 per cent of fruits and vegetables on the lines in question were carried in respondent's cars. The findings are fairly satisfactory in their description of the business. The order was, however, set aside by the Circuit Court of Appeals on petition to review, on the ground that the practice affected common carriers, and was therefore within the jurisdiction of the Interstate Commerce Commission rather than of the Federal Trade Commission. Fruit Growers' Express v. F.T.C., 274 Fed. 205 (1921).

dealers or consumers to boycott his competitors. A more
fertile field for legal and economic study could hardly
be desired. The powers and procedure of the Commission,
conducive as they are to deliberation and thorough research, lend themselves peculiarly well to a problem of
this kind, and the experience which the Commission may
be supposed to have accumulated should render it particularly well fitted to speak with enlightened authority.
Yet it is in these cases that the Commission's findings
appear to be peculiarly barren of the fruits of economic
research and understanding, and to an unusual degree
the products of legalism and dogma.

"VOLUNTARY" RESTRAINTS OF COMPETITION

ALL the cases that have been considered heretofore, both
in this and the preceding chapter, have involved practices
condemned because of their injurious effect upon competitors of the respondent, or because they involved injurious discrimination between customers of the respondent. Where two competitors consolidate, or by agreement
restrict or eliminate competition, no such injurious conduct is involved. The wrong, if any, is to the public, which
relies upon competition as the regulator of the quality
and price of the things it buys. Such conduct is peculiarly
within the province of the Sherman Act, with which, of
course, the Federal Trade Commission has no direct concern. One small part of the field is, however, covered by
two sections of the Clayton Act. Section 7 forbids intercorporate stockholding between competing corporations,
whether directly or through a holding company, where
the effect may be to substantially lessen competition between the corporations involved, or to restrain trade or
tend to create a monopoly. Section 8 forbids interlocking
directorates between companies of which any one has a
capital, surplus, and undivided profits over $1,000,000,

where the companies are competitors, "so that the elimination of competition by agreement between them would
constitute a violation of any of the provisions of any of
the anti-trust laws." I have discussed some general questions involved in the interpretation of these provisions,[105]
and it remains to consider the cases, few in number, which
the Commission has dealt with under the sections in question.

Section 8 is easily disposed of, as no order has been
issued by the Commission dealing with interlocking directorates. Under Section 7 there have been several important cases.

The first was against the American Agricultural
Chemical Company, and charged acquisition of the stock
of The Brown Company.[106] This was the company, it will
be recalled, which the Commission found had been forced,
by a combination of the Philadelphia renderers, to "sell
out" after a prolonged price war.[107] The complaint
charged that the effect of the acquisition "may be" to
substantially lessen competition between the companies.
The findings suggest, however, although they do not
clearly so state, that the two companies were not competitors and no order was issued as to this phase of the
case.

Early in 1919 a complaint was issued against the
Aluminum Company of America, charging that respondent had acquired a large part of the stock of the Aluminum Rolling Mill Company, and that the effect may be
to substantially lessen competition between the two companies, or to restrain commerce, or to tend to create a
monopoly. The findings show that respondent was the
sole producer of pig aluminum in the United States, and

[105] *See supra,* p. 38.
[106] F.T.C. *v.* American Agricultural Chemical Co., 1 F.T.C.D. 226
(1918).
[107] *See supra,* p. 248.

produced about half of the world's output of the metal.
Through subsidiaries, the company manufactured sheet
aluminum, and a large assortment of fabricated and
finished products. Three competitors also manufactured
sheet aluminum, using imported raw materials. Of these
one was absorbed by the Aluminum Company in 1919;
another was unimportant; the third was the Cleveland
Metal Products Company. In 1918 this latter competitor
and the respondent organized a third corporation, known
as The Aluminum Rolling Mills Company, with a capital
of $600,000, of which $400,000 was taken by the Aluminum
Company of America, and $200,000 by the Cleveland com-
petitor. The new corporation took over the Cleveland
Company's sheet aluminum business. In this way the
only competing maker of sheet aluminum (with one in-
considerable exception) came under the control of the
respondent company.[108] The technical difficulty which the
case presents is obvious. The Aluminum Company did
not directly buy the stock of a competitor. It organized
an affiliated company which purchased certain assets of
the competitor, but a purchase of assets is not within the
terms of Section 7 of the Clayton Act. The Commission
found, however, that the acquisition of stock in the new
company "was in effect equivalent to" a direct acquisition of stock of the Cleveland company, and that its effect
was to eliminate "actual existing competition" between
respondent and the Cleveland company. The company
was ordered, within a year, to divest itself of the stock,
and directed not to sell it to any affiliated person or corporation. The case went to the Circuit Court of Appeals,
and upon a careful analysis of the facts, the order was

[108] Most of these facts appear in the formal findings of the Commission, F.T.C. *v.* Aluminum Co. of America, 3 F.T.C.D. 302 (1921),
but the statement in the opinion of the Circuit Court of Appeals is
both more complete and more easily comprehensible. *See* 284 Fed. 401
(1922).

sustained, one judge dissenting. The court found that the new company took over not only physical assets, but a rolling mill business; that it began operating this business before the transaction resulting in the acquisition of its stock by respondent was fully completed; that the Aluminum Company did therefore technically purchase the stock of a corporation engaged in commerce; and that the effect was to create a monopoly. This decision was final, as the Supreme Court denied *certiorari*.[109]

Two other cases involved complaints against Armour & Company[110] and Swift & Company,[111] respectively, in each case based upon the acquisition of stock in local packing plants alleged to have been competitors. A third involved a similar charge against the Western Meat Company, a concern jointly owned by several of the large packers.[112] The facts in each case are stated in great detail and the material is well handled.

The principal difficulty in cases of this character is the one presented in the Aluminum case, and even more strikingly present in the cases against Armour and Swift. It is inherent in the defective draftsmanship of the law. Section 7 does not prohibit corporate consolidations or combinations, unless they are effected by purchase of the competitor's stock, or by purchase of stock of two competitors by a holding company. A consolidation by any other means is not affected. Where stock has been unlawfully acquired, the respondent may be ordered to "cease and desist" from the violation, and to "divest itself of the stock held,"[113] but the Commission is not directly authorized to order respondent to undo the consolidation. In the Armour & Company case, it seems that

[109] 67 U.S. L. Ed., 419 (1923). (Advance sheets.)
[110] F.T.C. *v.* Armour & Co., 4 F.T.C.D. 457 (1922).
[111] F.T.C. *v.* Swift & Co., 5 F.T.C.D. 143, 5 F.T.C.D. 293 (1922).
[112] F.T.C. *v.* Western Meat Co., 5 F.T.C.D. 417 (1923).
[113] Clayton Act., Sec. 11, par. 2.

a few months after stock of the competitor had been acquired, the corporation executed a deed of all its property to Armour & Company.[114] In the Swift case the same procedure was followed.[115] Merely to order the respondents to divest themselves of the stock was therefore useless. The Commission met the situation by a finding that the deed was for a nominal consideration and was a "mere paper transfer," and it ordered respondents to restore the property, by proper conveyance to the corporation whose stock was acquired, and then to divest themselves of the stock. It is an interesting question whether the Commission has the power to make such an order, in view of the limited authority conferred in Section 11 of the Clayton Act. If it has not, its action in a case of this kind must generally be ineffective. At best, it is only dealing, in these cases, with one of a number of methods by which the desired result can be achieved. Since the Clayton Act, consolidations in which the parties are well advised have been effected by some other means than by purchase of stock.

In conclusion, mention should be made of a few cases in which the Commission has endeavored to deal with voluntary agreements between competitors, with respect to prices, or concerted efforts to maintain or enhance prices. Such cases are, of course, frequently met with in the decisions under the Sherman Law. As far as the Federal Trade Commission is concerned, the difficulty lies in finding any intelligible basis for its jurisdiction. Thus, complaints were issued, during the war, against a number of book paper manufacturers, charging "a concerted movement unduly to enhance the prices of book paper."[116] It seems that they had organized a "Bureau of

[114] Par. 10 of findings.

[115] Par. 5 (w) and (y) of findings.

[116] F.T.C. *v.* Bureau of Statistics of The Book Paper Mfrs. et al., 1 F.T.C.D., 38 (1917).

Statistics,'' but the functions of the Bureau can only be guessed at from the vague generalities of the complaint. By stipulation an order was entered that the dissolution of the Bureau was "hereby approved" by the Commission, and that respondents should thereafter cease and desist from joining any such bureau, or engaging in any concerted movement to enhance or maintain prices. No findings were made, nor does the stipulation admit any facts; indeed, in several cases the docket shows that attorneys for respondents made the specific reservation that they did not admit any of the facts charged. There was a similar proceeding against the Association of Flag Manufacturers and certain of its members, charging a concerted movement to enhance the price of American flags.[117] Here again there were no findings, other than a finding that the Association had dissolved, but orders were entered against the members, as in the book paper manufacturers' case. In a case against an association of manufacturers of gold leaf, findings were made, sustaining the charge of a concerted movement to enhance prices.[118] The findings are upon an agreed statement, and are very meagre. Finally there was a proceeding against concerns engaged in printing railway tariffs, charging mutual price fixing agreements.[119] In all these cases a violation of Section 5 of the Federal Trade Commission Act was alleged, but upon what theory a concerted movement to refrain from competing in certain respects is a method of competition at all, is not stated. None of these cases have found their way into the courts, and it does not seem that they are to be taken very seriously.

[117] F.T.C. *v.* Association of Flag Mfrs. of America et al., 1 F.T.C.D. 55 (1918).

[118] F.T.C. *v.* U.S. Gold Leaf Mfrs'. Asso., 1 F.T.C.D. 173 (1918).

[119] F.T.C. *v.* Blakely Printing Co. et al., 1 F.T.C.D. 277 (1918).

MISCELLANEOUS CASES

ONLY brief mention can be made of a few additional cases which properly belong in this chapter.

There are several cases in which the Commission entered orders against concerns which have either misquoted or misrepresented patent claims, or have threatened to sue for patent infringement but have failed to do so. The orders in such cases forbid threats of patent litigation, unless made in good faith, and unless followed up within a reasonable time by infringement suits.[120] One case went farther, and ordered respondent to cease threatening suits unless he "owns or controls a valid subsisting patent" and clearly specifies the nature of the alleged infringement.[121] It seems doubtful whether this attempt to assume jurisdiction over the validity of a patent can be sustained, and indeed the whole subject matter would seem to be more appropriate to the jurisdiction of a court of equity.

There is also a somewhat unsatisfactory group of cases in which respondents are charged with inducing customers to "cancel and rescind" orders and contracts placed with competitors,[122] or with "enticing" away the

---

[120] See F.T.C. v. National Binding Machine Co., 1 F.T.C.D. 44 (1917); F.T.C. v. Chicago Lino-Tabler Co., 1 F.T.C.D. 110 (1919); F.T.C. v. Gartside Iron Rust Soap Co., 1 F.T.C.D. 310 (1919); F.T.C. v. Nulomoline Co., 1 F.T.C.D. 400 (1919); F.T.C. v. Brown Portable Conveying Machinery Co., 2 F.T.C.D. 143 (1919); F.T.C. v. Sunbeam Chemical Co., 3 F.T.C.D. 365 (1921); F.T.C. v. Albany Chemical Co., 3 F.T.C.D. 369 (1921); F.T.C. v. Eskay Harris Feature Film Co., 5 F.T.C.D. 219 (1922).

[121] F.T.C. v. Champion Blower & Forge Co., 3 F.T.C.D. 137 (1920).

[122] F.T.C. v. Stanley Booking Corp., 1 F.T.C.D. 212 (1918); F.T.C. v. Wayne Oil Tank & Pump Co., 1 F.T.C.D. 259 (1918); F.T.C. v. Milwaukee Tank Works, 1 F.T.C.D. 272 (1918); F.T.C. v. Sunlight Creameries, 4 F.T.C.D. 55 (1921).

employees of a competitor.[123] From the findings it is not entirely clear whether the respondents were held to have induced the breach of a valid and subsisting contract, or whether in the opinion of the Commission any persistent policy of winning away customers and employees of competitors is a violation of the act. The question of substantive law is interesting and important, but the findings are too meagre for profitable discussion.[124]

Again, there are some interesting cases in which respondents are charged with tampering with the samples or advertising of their competitors. Thus two retailers of vacuum cleaners were found to have been "especially interested in" a certain brand of vacuum cleaners. They carried competing brands in stock, however, and it was found that in making demonstrations, respondent's salesmen had tampered with the mechanism of the competing makes, so that they would make an unfavorable impression on the prospective customer. The practice was found to be unfair.[125] Another order condemned the practice of bribing employees of customers to adulterate and spoil varnishes and lacquers supplied by a competitor. The facts are so meagrely stated, however, that it is not quite clear what happened.[126] One aspect of the Fleischmann case[127] suggests a more difficult problem. It was found that respondent's representatives had "occasionally" removed samples of yeast left with bakers by competing yeast companies, leaving Fleischmann samples in their place, and that they had "occasionally" purchased or

[123] F.T.C. *v.* Standard Car Equipment Co., 1 F.T.C.D. 144 (1918). *See* this case analyzed *supra,* p. 115.

[124] *See,* in this connection, the trade practice submittal of the butter manufacturers, Trade Practice Submittals, pp. 1, 3, par. I.

[125] F.T.C. *v.* Muenzen Specialty Co., 1 F.T.C.D. 30 (1917); F.T.C. *v.* Vacuum Cleaner Specialty Co., Inc., 3 F.T.C.D. 377 (1921).

[126] F.T.C. *v.* Essex Varnish Co., 1 F.T.C.D. 138 (1918).

[127] F.T.C. *v.* Fleischmann Co., 1 F.T.C.D. 119 (1918).

offered to purchase the competing samples. The practice was forbidden in the order. In another case the Commission found that a distributor of automobile tire rim parts had instructed its salesmen wherever possible to remove from the stores of dealers the display cards of makers of competing parts.[128] This practice was also condemned. In both cases the removal of the competitor's samples or advertising seems to have been effected with the consent of the dealer. A recent case presents yet another aspect of the problem.[129] It seems that the Chamber of Commerce of Missoula, Montana, sharing the hostility of most of its members toward the large mail order houses in New York and Chicago, arranged with a local moving picture house to designate a certain day as "mail order catalogue day." On that day any child presenting and surrendering at the box office a mail order catalogue was admitted free, and in addition special prizes were given for the newest catalogue, and for the oldest and most thumbed catalogue. Several hundred of the offending catalogues were turned in and destroyed. Both the chamber and the moving picture house were ordered to abandon the practice.

Of course the Commission was not organized primarily to restrain competitive guerilla warfare of this kind. The local courts can take cognizance of such practices, and are generally better able to render effective justice than is a commission in Washington. The significant cases in this chapter are those which involve practices in some way related to the trust problem, the problem of monopoly, and restraint of trade. It is to these cases that we turn to ascertain whether the Federal Trade Commission has made any real contributions either to substantive law or to administrative practice.

[128] F.T.C. *v.* Keaton Tire & Rubber Co., 5 F.T.C.D. 335 (1922).

[129] F.T.C. *v.* Chamber of Commerce of Missoula, 5 F.T.C.D. 451 (1923).

A summary of this chapter will show that the contributions have not been very substantial. In the cases involving price cutting and other unfair price tactics there was, it will be recalled, no attempt to grapple with the difficult questions of law and accounting involved, or to analyze the business facts necessary to a decision. The trade boycott cases were as a rule more satisfactory, but the Commission has handled them just as a court would handle them, except that its powers are more restricted, its procedure less flexible, and its remedy less prompt. In the cases involving trade discounts, the Commission's work proved to be ineffective because it was based on a theory of law which the courts found to be erroneous. The price maintenance cases were on the whole more successful, but here the Commission itself has admitted that it was merely following the lead of the Supreme Court. "The Commission itself," says the 1921 Annual Report, "has not undertaken to pass on the general principle, but has considered the matter in concrete cases before it, issued its order and has carried the matter to the Supreme Court of the United States, where such controverted practices must be finally adjudicated." As I have indicated, the result has not been very satisfactory from the practical point of view. In the cases involving tieing clauses and contracts for exclusive dealing, the Commission has a consistent record of failure. Every order which has been appealed has been reversed. As to cases arising under Section 8 of the Clayton Act it is not yet clear that the Commission can issue an effective order, in view of the inadequate powers conferred in the act. In the anomalous cases involving conspiracies and concerted price tactics, no rational basis for the Commission's jurisdiction is suggested in the findings, and it is doubtful whether any exists. Taken as a whole, the record in these cases, up to date, is somewhat discouraging.

CHAPTER VI

CONCLUSION

I SHALL endeavor in this closing chapter to present a few general conclusions gathered in the course of this study, and to suggest some alterations in method and procedure which would, in my opinion, make the Federal Trade Commission more effective as an administrative agency. For I am fully convinced, despite the many matters of detail which can justly be criticised, and despite the meagre results which have been achieved to date, that the fundamental policy embodied in the Federal Trade Commission Act is sound, and that the Commission itself is in a position to render services of great value to the business community and to the country as a whole.

I pointed out in an early chapter that the most difficult task which has confronted the Commission has been to preserve its own judicial impartiality, in the face of the statutory procedure which requires that it be the formal complainant in the very litigation in which it is also the judge.

Primarily, of course, impartiality and fair-mindedness are personal qualities. There are men who can preserve a detached and judicial point of view, however much their relation to the controversy may draw them toward one side or another. There are other men who become bitter partisans at the first opportunity, although every condition of formal impartiality has been carefully observed. In any problem of administration, these personal factors are in reality far more important than the questions of form and procedure dealt with in this study.

Questions of personality, however, are beyond the

scope of this study, and what little I have to say on the subject should not be taken to refer to any particular men or group of men. In the long run, and until current ideals of public service change very radically, it cannot be expected that a government commission, paying modest salaries and exposed to the vicissitudes of political life, can command the services of those super-men whose decisions are always made of the substance of justice and wisdom, and who can scorn the adventitious aids of a correct formal procedure. The science of administration owes its being to the fact that most government affairs are run by men of average capabilities, and that it is necessary to supply such men with a routine and a ready-made technique, and to confine them to a formal procedure which may indeed at times clip the wings of genius, but which will serve to create conditions under which average men are more likely to arrive at just results.

I shall not, therefore, be accused of neglecting substance for form if I urge certain changes in procedure and method which, in my opinion, will tend to improve the quality and, therefore, the influence of the Commission's work. A few such changes I have already suggested. As long as evidence is heard by employees sitting as examiners, rather than by the Commission itself, it seems clear that the findings should be prepared by the examiner himself, and that the irregular practice of allowing the trial attorney to have a hand in their preparation should be prohibited. I have also suggested that the trial examiner be selected from an independent panel, rather than from the division of the Federal Trade Commission which initiated the complaint. These are relatively minor details. The crux of the matter is that the Commission has not been able to overcome the handicap of a procedure which makes it both complainant and judge, and to impress upon its findings that stamp of impartiality and of disinterested justice which alone can give them weight and authority.

It will be helpful to recall, for a moment, why this anomalous procedure was adopted, instead of the time-honored triangle of plaintiff, defendant, and judge. It was in part, as I have said, because it was desired that the Commission should represent the public interest, and should be in a position to take the initiative in behalf of the public, where private parties might prefer to let matters rest. In part, also, it was because the legislators feared that the Commission would be overwhelmed with a host of petty squabbles, and therefore provided that the formal machinery of the Commission could be set in motion only by the Commission itself, where the case seemed to be of sufficient importance. I can conceive of no other valid reasons than the two which I have mentioned. Certainly the procedure was not adopted because it was desired to subject the persons complained of to the jurisdiction of a tribunal which would be predisposed to rule against them.

It seems to me that a slight change in the statutory procedure would do away with the present anomaly, and yet preserve all the objects which the draftsmen of the Trade Commission Act had in mind. The law should be amended to provide that whenever it appears to the Commission that a particular trade practice or method of competition is in violation of Section 5 of the Trade Commission Act, or of the relevant sections of the Clayton Act, and is being employed, in interstate or foreign commerce, to such an extent that the public interest is affected, it should issue, not a complaint, but an interlocutory order or citation, addressed to and served upon the persons employing the practice or method in question. The citation should recite that complaints have come to the Commission that the persons addressed are engaged in practices claimed to be in violation of law, describing them with sufficient particularity, and that the Commission has determined, under its statutory power, to inquire into the matter and determine whether or not the complaints are justified. A day would be set for a hearing, at which not only the persons complained of, but any other interested parties, would be permitted to be heard. Thus it might be that certain manufacturers of imitation silk hosiery were the persons complained of. An association of silk manufacturers might appear as complainant, present evidence that the respondents had employed certain trade names, and urge upon the Commission the legal and business considerations which were believed to render the brands misleading. An association of makers of mercerized cotton might present testimony and arguments to the contrary. The Commission, directly or through examiners, would hear the matter impartially, without interest in either side of the controversy. If the Commission's counsel appeared at the hearing, and presented testimony or argument, it would not be with a view to sustaining or defeating the complaint, but merely to make sure that the facts were fully developed and that impartial expert testimony was available. Such a proceeding would still be completely within the control of the Commission. It could act on complaint or on its own motion. It could refuse to act if the matter did not appear to be of public moment. But it would preserve, in fact as well as in form, the disinterested impartiality so essential in an administrative tribunal.

Such a procedure would have additional advantages quite apart from the one which I have mentioned. A complaint frequently heard among business men and attorneys who have had to do with the Commission, is directed against the injustice of a formal complaint by a governmental tribunal, publicly charging serious offenses against reputable citizens, and based merely upon a provisional and tentative belief that the charges may be true. The complaint is given to the newspapers and naturally attracts much attention. Many months later it may be withdrawn or dismissed, but the injury to the respondent's reputation has already been done. It is unfair to respondents, and it lessens the dignity of the Commission, to require it to form and publish a provisional opinion that a citizen has violated the law.

Another complaint also would be met by the change in procedure which I have suggested. At the present time the Commission's attorneys, at least so far as the formal record is concerned, and generally off the record as well, assume the burden of preparing and presenting the cases which come before the Commission. The attorney in charge naturally desires to make a record, and the Commission is doubtless loth to interfere with his conduct of the proceeding. The case, therefore, runs its appointed course, testimony is taken, motions are entertained and argued, briefs are filed, all without any real control by the responsible members of the Commission. In the meantime the actual controversy may have become moot. The practice may, for instance, have been abandoned, without any intention of resuming it. Nevertheless, the cumbersome machinery of the Commission continues inexorably, and time and money are expended in lengthy trials and arguments, merely because the respondent does not care to admit that he has violated the law, and the Commission's attorney wishes to add another victory to his record. When the final order is issued, it may direct the respondent to cease and desist from using a method or practice which he has abandoned months or even years ago. Attorneys who have practiced before the Commission will recognize the situation which I have described. It exists because the Commission itself, being the judge, does not wish to interfere with the prosecution of the case by its attorneys, and because the real complainants in the controversy, the competitors who are the injured parties, have nothing to say as to the conduct of the case. If the injured competitors were recognized as formal parties, and compelled to assume the burden of presenting evidence in support of their complaint, they would be the first to request a discontinuance of a case in which the controversy had become moot. Of course the Commission should reserve the right, in exceptional cases, to insist that a hearing continue even if the complainants withdraw, for the Commission must ultimately represent the public interest in every such controversy. But such cases would doubtless be rare. The typical case represents a conflict of interest between competitors or groups of competitors, and where the conflict is solved the controversy should be at an end.

If the changes which I have suggested are made, it will, of course, be necessary to adopt certain safeguards, in the interest of respondents as well as in the Commission's interest. Since there would be no formal complaint there must be some limitation as to the practices which may be dealt with in the order. The rule in the Gratz case,[1] that an order, though warranted by the testimony, must be set aside if all the elements of the offense which it forbids are not alleged in the complaint, seems unnecessarily rigid. It is based on the peculiar language of the statute, and if the section is redrafted it would seem to be sufficient to provide that no order may be issued against any party not served with the citation, or with respect to any practice not fairly specified in the citation, with a proviso that the citation may on proper notice be amended to conform to the proof, so long as no substantial injustice is thereby done to respondents. It would doubtless be necessary, also, to give the Commission some discretion as to the parties which may be permitted to intervene and be heard either for or against the charges under consideration, so that the proceeding may be kept

[1] *Supra,* p. 90.

within reasonable bounds. These are matters of detail; I am dealing here only with the main thesis, that the present form of partisan proceeding is unfair and unwise, and that the changes which I have suggested, with such elaboration of detail as may be found desirable, will remedy the most serious defects without sacrificing any of the advantages of the present procedure.

Even without an amendment of the statute, it seems that the Commission could by a change of its rules conform in some degree at least to the procedure which I am suggesting. There is a provision in Section 5 of the present Federal Trade Commission Act, that where a complaint has been issued by the Commission, "any person, partnership or corporation may make application, and upon good cause shown may be allowed by the Commission to intervene and appear in said proceeding by counsel and in person." The text is not very explicit, but there seems to be no reason to doubt that it permits an intervention as party complainant, as well as an intervention as party respondent. In practice, the provision has been largely a dead letter, but I see no reason why the Commission could not put it to effective use. Where a business concern complains informally that a competitor is using unfair methods of competition, or where a trade association objects to practices in a competing trade, the Commission could state that it would, on a provisional showing, issue a formal complaint, on the understanding that the applicant would at once intervene and assume the burden of the litigation. This would, of course, be a makeshift, and would not meet the situation fully. The Commission would still be a formal complainant, and would still be required to prejudge the case before hearing it on the merits. The hearing, however, would take on a more impartial tone and the real parties in interest would at least be formally represented.

The second change which I have to suggest is one

which the Commission could put into effect at once, without additional legislation. I have pointed out in a previous chapter that the one feature which distinguishes the Federal Trade Commission from a mere prosecuting agency, and gives it powers of a judicial character, is its capacity to make findings of fact which must be respected by the courts if supported by testimony. We have seen also how meagre and unconvincing, in many cases, these findings have been, and how little respect has been paid to them by the courts. I have already discussed the matter at length, and will not go over the ground again. It seems to me that the most important single step which the Commission could take toward enhancing the value and the authority of its decisions would be to abandon the formal and legalistic "findings" to which it is now addicted, and to adopt instead narrative and descriptive reports and signed opinions of the kind employed for generations in the courts of England and of the United States.

Such a practice would greatly enhance the quality and justice of the Commission's decisions. Where an examiner must in his report review the evidence presented by the respondent, analyze and dispose of his arguments, give convincing reasons for his decision, and distinguish or reconcile the precedents, he is much more likely to reach a just and well-considered conclusion than if he is permitted merely to state in legal phraseology his ultimate findings of fact and law. Moreover, an opinion which deals impartially with the respondent's case and meets conscientiously the arguments which he has presented is much more likely to dispose of the controversy and satisfy the parties. Nothing is so exasperating to a lawyer as to find that a tribunal has ignored his carefully prepared defense. To do so is to create dissatisfaction and encourage appeals to a higher court.

The educational value of the Commission's reports

would be greatly enhanced if the form were changed in the manner suggested. The Commission deals with a subject matter of vital importance to the business interests involved. Many of the questions which come before it relate to long standing controversies in the trades, and are eagerly debated at conventions and in the trade journals. If the Commission were to issue reports of actual controversies which were really informative and readable, and to give forcefully the reasons which led them to a decision, these reports would, I believe, have an influence far beyond the immediate controversy.

To the attorney called upon to advise a business client such a published opinion would be immensely valuable. There is a general complaint among attorneys, at the present time, that it is impossible to ascertain from the published decisions of the Federal Trade Commission what points were decided and what were the grounds of decision. Every attorney knows the characteristics of a well-considered leading case. It states clearly and fully the relevant facts. It summarizes the contentions of the opposing parties in such a way as to bring out the main issue of law involved. Upon this issue, it reviews the precedents, reconciling conflicts and tracing the law through to the latest utterance of an authoritative tribunal. In the light of these precedents, the precise new issue presented in the case at bar is clearly formulated, and a decision is reached, with a forceful statement of the reasons in support of the decision. Such a case at once takes its place as a precedent, and, if the point is important, may profoundly influence the future course of the law. The very same case, however, involving the same facts and decided the same way, may be utterly without influence if the opinion leaves the issues obscure or the grounds of decision uncertain. The Federal Trade Commission was intended to explore and develop a field of the law in which much pioneer work was needed. It was expected to establish precedents by which business men and attorneys could be guided in the conduct of affairs. I do not see how this important duty can be performed, unless the Commission is ready to publish its decisions in such form that the reader can tell what has been decided and by what reasoning the decision is supported.

I have referred to the tendency in the courts to restrict within the narrowest limits the scope of the clause which declares that the findings of the Commission as to the facts, if supported by testimony, shall be conclusive.[2] Whether or not a method of competition is unfair, and whether or not a practice may substantially lessen competition or tend toward monopoly, are said to be questions of law for the decision of the courts. According to these dicta, all that is left to the Commission is to decide mere questions of physical fact. Indeed, a search of the opinions of Circuit Courts of Appeals and of the Supreme Court does not reveal a single case in which it can be said with assurance that the findings of the Commission have in any way affected the decision of the court. Where the courts have disagreed with the findings they have waived them aside as mere conclusions, or have relied upon other facts revealed by the record, upon which no findings were made. Yet if the Federal Trade Commission is worth maintaining at all, it should have a more important function than merely to record physical facts and occurrences for the benefit of an appellate court. I am not suggesting that the court decisions which have dealt cavalierly with the Commission's findings were not fully justified. But I do feel that where a Commission, created to deal in an expert way with a special field of controversy, has made findings of an expert character which involve elements of practical judgment rather than of law, those findings should be respected by

[2] *Supra,* p. 101.

the courts. Any other point of view seems to me to be inconsistent with the whole theory of administrative rather than of judicial enforcement. The expert judgment of the Interstate Commerce Commission is, as I have said, respected by the courts, and the only reason I can think of for not giving the same treatment to the findings of the Federal Trade Commission is that it is difficult to tell from the great majority of the findings that the Commission has ever exercised an expert judgment, since the reasons for the decision are never given. Despite the dicta of the Supreme Court, I venture the opinion that the matter is not yet foreclosed, and that if it should appear in some future case that the Commission has based its decision on an expert judgment of a practical nature, the court is still in a position to state that it will not substitute its own judgment for the judgment of the Commission. So long as the Commission adheres to its present formal findings of fact, however, there can be little hope of such an outcome.

To the two recommendations which I have made, I should add a third. It seems to me that the Commission is handling too many cases, and that it should exercise a greater discretion in selecting those cases which involve questions of public importance. It does not seem necessary that public funds should be employed to prosecute cases involving controversies between private parties, where a full and adequate remedy can be obtained in a court of law or equity. The same comment applies to other cases to which I have referred, involving trivial or merely technical offenses, in which the public interest is not always easy to discern. There is constant complaint of the crowded condition of the Commission's docket. It takes months to bring a case to a hearing, and additional months to reach a decision. At the end of the fiscal year 1922, there were 231 applications for complaints docketed with the Commission which had been on hand an average of six months and thirteen days,[3] and 123 applications docketed with branches which had been on hand an average of four months and eight days. These were cases in which formal complaints had not yet been issued. At the same time there were pending 257 cases in which formal complaints had been issued.[4] The largest number of formal complaints ever disposed of in a single year was 166, the average being much lower,[5] so that it would apparently take at least a year and a half to work off the cases which had then accumulated, without considering new business. The 1922 Annual Report mentions the accumulation of cases and the complaints of delay, and blames the Commission's "limited force and funds." Yet the Commission has an annual appropriation close to a million dollars, and a personnel, as revealed by its last annual report, of over 300 employees. It would seem that the remedy lay rather in a more careful selection of the cases in which complaints are filed, and a greater readiness to drop proceedings in which the practice has been abandoned voluntarily or the controversy has in some other way become moot.

Of course, if the suggestion at the beginning of this chapter is adopted, and private complainants are compelled in usual cases to stand the burden and expense of prosecuting complaints before the Commission, a great saving can be effected, not only in the time of the Commissioners and of their assistants, but in the expense of running the organization. At a time when such efforts are being made to promote economy in the administration of the Government, it would seem to be worthy of consideration whether the Commission should continue in such

[3] 1922 Annual Report, p. 38.

[4] *Ibid.*, p. 17. The table shows that up to the end of the fiscal year 1922, 899 formal complaints had been served, of which 642 had been disposed of, leaving 257 on hand.

[5] *Ibid.*, p. 17.

cases to bear the cost of litigating business controversies between competitors.

It should not be forgotten that the Federal Trade Commission was organized primarily to deal with the trust problem, the problem of monopoly and restraint of trade. All other matters were incidental, and it is therefore doubly important that time should not be wasted upon petty squabbles and dishonesties. Even in the field of misbranding and of deceptive advertising, valuable though the work has been, the Commission's jurisdiction has been a more or less fortuitous by-product rather than the result of a clear legislative design. Probably if the question of merchandise misbranding had been taken up on its merits, a law similar to the Food and Drugs Act would have been drafted, with its effective combination of administrative and criminal enforcement.

In the history of the relation of government to business, the legislation of 1914 marked, so far as the United States is concerned, a change of attitude in two important respects. I refer to the legislation rather than to the Federal Trade Commission itself, because the change does not yet appear to be fully reflected in the Commission's work.

The legislation recognized, in the first place, that the trust problem was not a single problem but a large number of problems. It had usually been supposed that there was a form of economic wickedness, known as monopoly and restraint of trade, which could be identified by name and denounced in a criminal statute. It was, in the popular mind, like stamping out robbery and arson. In the new legislation, the emphasis was shifted from monopoly and restraint of trade, as such, to the host of trade practices and methods of competition by which the objectionable results had been achieved. As a matter of draftsmanship, the details were not, as I have said, very successfully carried through, but the change in point of view was none the less apparent. This of itself was a great gain. The Standard Oil Company had used methods of competition which had aroused the resentment of competitors. The methods were enumerated and described in the opinion of the Supreme Court. But whether the practices themselves were condemned, or whether the vice lay in the combination of them all, coupled with the size and power of the concern which used them, no reader of the opinion could tell. All that was certain was that the result was an illegal monopoly. In the new legislation, attention was directed toward the competitive methods and practices themselves, and machinery was devised by which these methods and practices could be isolated and studied.

The second departure from the traditional point of view was even more important. Neither the Trade Commission Act nor the Clayton Act was a criminal statute. The machinery set up to administer them was corrective rather than punitive. As I have said, the traditional view had been that monopoly and restraint of trade were species of crimes which needed the attention of the district attorney and the deterrent influence of a jail sentence. A long and discouraging experience with Sherman Law indictments had finally satisfied the country that the problem could not be dealt with in this way. It was only in those flagrant cases in which economic power had been brutally misused, and selfish ends gained by the ruin of innocent men, that juries could be brought to the point of moral indignation at which a conviction was possible. The usual case, however, involved merely a conflict of interests between different economic groups. A large manufacturer might be in conflict with a group of wholesalers. An association of jobbers might be pitted against a mail order house or a department store. A retail association, representing the group interests of its members, might be at odds with a single retail trader, determined to pursue his own policy. Or it might be a case of a whole industry in conflict with a group of consumers. Either side in such a controversy might, it is true, use weapons which would shock the moral sense, and fall within the popular conception of criminal conduct. The controversy itself, however, would not be a conflict between right and wrong, but a conflict between opposing interests.

Such a conflict calls for adjustment rather than for a moral crusade. Everyone knows how useless in a negotiation is the man who sees a profound moral issue in every small business difference. To remain on friendly terms with a man although your economic interests are opposed to his, to recognize that men may have legitimate business conflicts, to concede that your competitor may be an honest man and a gentleman, these are signs of the growing maturity of civilization, just as the trust-busting fervor of the first decade of the century and the crusades of the Middle Ages were signs of immaturity.

Of course, in the field of government this conception of the trust problem calls for a certain degree of abnegation on the part of the men engaged in administering the law. A crusade is more spectacular than a scientific inquiry, and a moral issue has greater political value than a practical adjustment. It is precisely for this reason, however, that the enforcement of the new laws was entrusted to a non-partisan commission, to be composed of men of training and experience whose tenure would not depend upon political considerations. It seems to me that from this point of view the Commission has a great and important opportunity. I conceive it to be, potentially, an expert tribunal, of steady tenure and scrupulous judicial poise, firm in the public interest but impartial as between the private economic groups affected by its action. I do not look upon it as a prosecuting agency, at war with the forces of evil. Where a crusade is necessary, as of course it may be at times, the matter should be left to the political branch of the Government. The Commission's procedure should be such that a trade practice or a method of competition, deemed by some to be injurious and defended by others, could be brought before it for calm and impartial study, the facts and arguments developed in a formal procedure, and an order issued which, if confirmed in the courts, would settle for the benefit of the business world whether or not the practice was consistent with the letter and spirit of the law. With the amendments which I have suggested, the Commission can be relieved of the stigma of partiality now conveyed by the very words of the statute. With a corresponding change in the spirit in which the proceedings are conducted, I see no reason why the Federal Trade Commission should not realize fully the promise of the legislation of 1914.

APPENDIX

ACTS OF CONGRESS FROM WHICH THE COMMISSION DERIVES ITS POWERS.

I.

FEDERAL TRADE COMMISSION ACT.

AN ACT To create a Federal Trade Commission, to define its powers
and duties, and for other purposes.

[Pub. No. 203, 63d Cong. Chap. 311, 38 Stat. at L. 717]

*Be it enacted by the Senate and House of Representatives of the
United States of America in Congress assembled,* That a commission
is hereby created and established, to be known as the Federal Trade
Commission (hereinafter referred to as the commission), which shall
be composed of five commissioners, who shall be appointed by the
President, by and with the advice and consent of the Senate. Not more
than three of the commissioners shall be members of the same political
party. The first commissioners appointed shall continue in office for
terms of three, four, five, six, and seven years, respectively, from the
date of the taking effect of this Act, the term of each to be designated
by the President, but their successors shall be appointed for terms of
seven years, except that any person chosen to fill a vacancy shall be
appointed only for the unexpired term of the commissioner whom he
shall succeed. The commission shall choose a chairman from its own
membership. No commissioner shall engage in any other business, voca-
tion, or employment. Any commissioner may be removed by the President for inefficiency, neglect of duty, or malfeasance in office. A vacancy in the commission shall not impair the right of the remaining
commissioners to exercise all the powers of the commission.

The commission shall have an official seal, which shall be judicially
noticed.

SEC. 2. That each commissioner shall receive a salary of $10,000 a
year, payable in the same manner as the salaries of the judges of the
courts of the United States. The commission shall appoint a secretary,
who shall receive a salary of $5,000 a year, payable in like manner,

and it shall have authority to employ and fix the compensation of such attorneys, special experts, examiners, clerks, and other employees as it may from time to time find necessary for the proper performance of its duties and as may be from time to time appropriated for by Congress.

With the exception of the secretary, a clerk to each commissioner, the attorneys, and such special experts and examiners as the commission may from time to time find necessary for the conduct of its work, all employees of the commission shall be a part of the classified civil service, and shall enter the service under such rules and regulations as may be prescribed by the commission and by the Civil Service Commission.

All of the expenses of the commission, including all necessary expenses for transportation incurred by the commissioners or by their employees under their orders, in making any investigation, or upon official business in any other places than in the city of Washington, shall be allowed and paid on the presentation of itemized vouchers therefor approved by the commission.

Until otherwise provided by law, the commission may rent suitable offices for its use.

The Auditor for the State and Other Departments shall receive and examine all accounts of expenditures of the commission.

SEC. 3. That upon the organization of the commission and election of its chairman, the Bureau of Corporations and the offices of the Commissioner and Deputy Commissioner of Corporations shall cease to exist; and all pending investigations and proceedings of the Bureau of Corporations shall be continued by the commission.

All clerks and employees of the said bureau shall be transferred to and become clerks and employees of the commission at their present grades and salaries. All records, papers, and property of the said bureau shall become records, papers, and property of the commission, and all unexpended funds and appropriations for the use and maintenance of the said bureau, including any allotment already made to it by the Secretary of Commerce from the contingent appropriation for the Department of Commerce for the fiscal year nineteen hundred and fifteen, or from the departmental printing fund for the fiscal year nineteen hundred and fifteen, shall become funds and appropriations available to be expended by the commission in the exercise of the powers, authority, and duties conferred on it by this Act.

The principal office of the commission shall be in the city of Washington, but it may meet and exercise all its powers at any other place. The commission may, by one or more of its members, or by such examiners as it may designate, prosecute any inquiry necessary to its duties in any part of the United States.

SEC. 4. That the words defined in this section shall have the following meaning when found in this Act, to wit:

"Commerce" means commerce among the several States or with foreign nations, or in any Territory of the United States or in the District of Columbia, or between any such Territory and another, or between any such Territory and any State or foreign nation, or between the District of Columbia and any State or Territory or foreign nation.

"Corporation" means any company or association incorporated or unincorporated, which is organized to carry on business for profit and has shares of capital or capital stock, and any company or association, incorporated or unincorporated, without shares of capital or capital stock, except partnerships, which is organized to carry on business for its own profit or that of its members.

"Documentary evidence" means all documents, papers, and correspondence in existence at and after the passage of this Act.

"Acts to regulate commerce" means the Act entitled "An Act to regulate commerce," approved February fourteenth, eighteen hundred and eighty-seven, and all Acts amendatory thereof and supplementary thereto.

"Antitrust acts" means the Act entitled "An Act to protect trade and commerce against unlawful restraints and monopolies," approved July second, eighteen hundred and ninety; also the sections seventy-three to seventy-seven, inclusive, of an Act entitled "An Act to reduce taxation, to provide revenue for the Government, and for other purposes," approved August twenty-seventh, eighteen hundred and ninety-four; and also the Act entitled "An Act to amend sections seventy-three and seventy-six of the Act of August twenty-seventh, eighteen hundred and ninety-four, entitled 'An Act to reduce taxation, to provide revenue for the Government, and for other purposes,'" approved February twelfth, nineteen hundred and thirteen.

SEC. 5. That unfair methods of competition in commerce are hereby declared unlawful.

The commission is hereby empowered and directed to prevent persons, partnerships, or corporations, except banks, and common carriers subject to the Acts to regulate commerce, from using unfair methods of competition in commerce.

Whenever the commission shall have reason to believe that any such person, partnership, or corporation has been or is using any unfair method of competition in commerce, and if it shall appear to the commission that a proceeding by it in respect thereof would be to the interest of the public, it shall issue and serve upon such person, partnership, or corporation a complaint stating its charges in that respect, and containing a notice of a hearing upon a day and at a place therein fixed at least thirty days after the service of said complaint. The person, partnership, or corporation so complained of shall have the right to appear at the place and time so fixed and show cause why an order should not be entered by the commission requiring such person, partnership, or corporation to cease and desist from the violation of the law so charged in said complaint. Any person, partnership, or corporation may make application, and upon good cause shown may be allowed by the commission, to intervene and appear in said proceeding by counsel or in person. The testimony in any such proceeding shall be reduced to writing and filed in the office of the commission. If upon such hearing the commission shall be of the opinion that the method of competition in question is prohibited by this Act, it shall make a report in writing in which it shall state its findings as to the facts, and shall issue and cause to be served on such person, partnership, or corporation an order requiring such person, partnership, or corporation to cease and desist from using such method of competition. Until a transcript of the record in such hearing shall have been filed in a circuit court of appeals of the United States, as hereinafter provided, the commission may at any time, upon such notice and in such manner as it shall deem proper, modify or set aside, in whole or in part, any report or any order made or issued by it under this section.

If such person, partnership, or corporation fails or neglects to obey such order of the commission while the same is in effect, the commission may apply to the circuit court of appeals of the United States, within any circuit where the method of competition in question was used or where such person, partnership, or corporation resides or carries on business, for the enforcement of its order, and shall certify and file with its application a transcript of the entire record in the proceeding, including all the testimony taken and the report and order of the commission. Upon such filing of the application and transcript the court shall cause notice thereof to be served upon such person, partnership, or corporation and thereupon shall have jurisdiction of the proceeding and of the question determined therein, and shall have power to make and enter upon the pleadings, testimony, and proceedings set forth in such transcript a decree affirming, modifying, or setting aside the order of the commission. The findings of the commission as to the facts, if supported by testimony, shall be conclusive. If either party shall apply to the court for leave to adduce additional evidence, and shall show to the satisfaction of the court that such additional evidence is material and that there were reasonable grounds for the failure to adduce such evidence in the proceeding before the commission, the court may order such additional evidence to be taken before the commission and to be adduced upon the hearing in such manner and upon such terms and conditions as to the court may seem proper. The commission may modify its findings as to the facts, or make new findings, by reason of the additional evidence so taken, and it shall file such modified or new findings, which, if supported by testimony, shall be conclusive, and its recommendation, if any, for the modification or setting aside of its original order, with the return of such additional evidence. The judgment and decree of the court shall be final, except that the same shall be subject to review by the Supreme Court upon certiorari as provided in section two hundred and forty of the Judicial Code.

Any party required by such order of the commission to cease and desist from using such method of competition may obtain a review of such order in said circuit court of appeals by filing in the court a written petition praying that the order of the commission be set aside. A copy of such petition shall be forthwith served upon the commission, and thereupon the commission forthwith shall certify and file in the court a transcript of the record as hereinbefore provided. Upon the filing of the transcript the court shall have the same jurisdiction to affirm, set aside, or modify the order of the commission as in the case of an application by the commission for the enforcement of its order, and the findings of the commission as to the facts, if supported by testimony, shall in like manner be conclusive.

The jurisdiction of the circuit court of appeals of the United States to enforce, set aside, or modify orders of the commission shall be exclusive.

Such proceedings in the circuit court of appeals shall be given precedence over other cases pending therein, and shall be in every way expedited. No order of the commission or judgment of the court to enforce the same shall in any wise relieve or absolve any person, partnership, or corporation from any liability under the antitrust Acts.

Complaints, orders, and other processes of the commission under this section may be served by anyone duly authorized by the commission, either (a) by delivering a copy thereof to the person to be served, or to a member of the partnership to be served, or to the president, secretary, or other executive officer or a director of the corporation to be served; or (b) by leaving a copy thereof at the principal office or place of business of such person, partnership, or corporation; or (c) by registering and mailing a copy thereof addressed to such person, partnership, or corporation at his or its principal office or place of business. The verified return by the person so serving said complaint, order, or other process setting forth the manner of said service shall be proof of the same, and the return post-office receipt for said complaint, order, or other process registered and mailed as aforesaid shall be proof of the service of the same.

SEC. 6. That the commission shall also have power—

(a) To gather and compile information concerning, and to investigate from time to time the organization, business, conduct, practices, and management of any corporation engaged in commerce, excepting banks and common carriers subject to the Act to regulate commerce, and its relation to other corporations and to individuals, associations, and partnerships.

(b) To require, by general or special orders, corporations engaged in commerce, excepting banks, and common carriers subject to the Act to regulate commerce, or any class of them, or any of them, respectively, to file with the commission in such form as the commission may prescribe annual or special, or both annual and special, reports or answers in writing to specific questions, furnishing to the commission such information as it may require as to the organization, business, conduct, practices, management, and relation to other corporations, partnerships, and individuals of the respective corporations filing such reports or answers in writing. Such reports and answers shall be made under oath, or otherwise, as the commission may prescribe, and shall be filed with the commission within such reasonable period as the commission may prescribe, unless additional time be granted in any case by the commission.

(c) Whenever a final decree has been entered against any defendant corporation in any suit brought by the United States to prevent and restrain any violation of the antitrust Acts, to make investigation, upon its own initiative, of the manner in which the decree has been or is being carried out, and upon the application of the Attorney General it shall be its duty to make such investigation. It shall transmit to the Attorney General a report embodying its findings and recommendations as a result of any such investigation, and the report shall be made public in the discretion of the commission.

(d) Upon the direction of the President or either House of Congress to investigate and report the facts relating to any alleged violations of the antitrust Acts by any corporation.

(e) Upon the application of the Attorney General to investigate and make recommendations for the readjustment of the business of any corporation alleged to be violating the antitrust Acts in order that the corporation may thereafter maintain its organization, management, and conduct of business in accordance with law.

(f) To make public from time to time such portions of the information obtained by it hereunder, except trade secrets and names of customers, as it shall deem expedient in the public interest; and to make annual and special reports to the Congress and to submit therewith recommendations for additional legislation; and to provide for the publication of its reports and decisions in such form and manner as may be best adapted for public information and use.

(g) From time to time to classify corporations and to make rules and regulations for the purpose of carrying out the provisions of this Act.

(h) To investigate, from time to time, trade conditions in and with foreign countries where associations, combinations, or practices of manufacturers, merchants, or traders, or other conditions, may affect the foreign trade of the United States, and to report to Congress thereon, with such recommendations as it deems advisable.

SEC. 7. That in any suit in equity brought by or under the direction of the Attorney General as provided in the antitrust Acts, the court may, upon the conclusion of the testimony therein, if it shall be then of opinion that the complainant is entitled to relief, refer said suit to the commission, as a master in chancery, to ascertain and report an appropriate form of decree therein. The commission shall proceed upon such notice to the parties and under such rules of procedure as the court may prescribe, and upon the coming in of such report such exceptions may be filed and such proceedings had in relation thereto as upon the report of a master in other equity causes, but the court may adopt or reject such report, in whole or in part, and enter such decree as the nature of the case may in its judgment require.

SEC. 8. That the several departments and bureaus of the Government when directed by the President shall furnish the commission, upon its request, all records, papers, and information in their possession relating to any corporation subject to any of the provisions of this Act, and shall detail from time to time such officials and employees to the commission as he may direct.

SEC. 9. That for the purposes of this Act the commission, or its duly authorized agent or agents, shall at all reasonable times have access to, for the purpose of examination, and the right to copy any documentary evidence of any corporation being investigated or proceeded against; and the commission shall have power to require by subpœna the attendance and testimony of witnesses and the production of all such documentary evidence relating to any matter under investigation. Any member of the commission may sign subpœnas, and members and examiners of the commission may administer oaths and affirmations, examine witnesses, and receive evidence.

Such attendance of witnesses, and the production of such documentary evidence, may be required from any place in the United States, at any designated place of hearing. And in case of disobedience to a subpœna the commission may invoke the aid of any court of the United States in requiring the attendance and testimony of witnesses and the production of documentary evidence.

Any of the district courts of the United States within the jurisdiction of which such inquiry is carried on may, in case of contumacy or refusal to obey a subpœna issued to any corporation or other person, issue an order requiring such corporation or other person to appear before the commission, or to produce documentary evidence if so ordered, or to give evidence touching the matter in question; and any failure to obey such order of the court may be punished by such court as a contempt thereof.

Upon the application of the Attorney General of the United States, at the request of the commission, the district courts of the United States shall have jurisdiction to issue writs of mandamus commanding any person or corporation to comply with the provisions of this Act or any order of the commission made in pursuance thereof.

The commission may order testimony to be taken by deposition in any proceeding or investigation pending under this Act at any stage of such proceeding or investigation. Such depositions may be taken before any person designated by the commission and having power to administer oaths. Such testimony shall be reduced to writing by the person taking the deposition, or under his direction, and shall then be subscribed by the deponent. Any person may be compelled to appear and depose and to produce documentary evidence in the same manner as witnesses may be compelled to appear and testify and produce documentary evidence before the commission as hereinbefore provided.

Witnesses summoned before the commission shall be paid the same fees and mileage that are paid witnesses in the courts of the United States, and witnesses whose depositions are taken and the persons taking the same shall severally be entitled to the same fees as are paid for like services in the courts of the United States.

No person shall be excused from attending and testifying or from producing documentary evidence before the commission or in obedience to the subpœna of the commission on the ground or for the reason that the testimony or evidence, documentary or otherwise, required of him may tend to criminate him or subject him to a penalty or forfeiture. But no natural person shall be prosecuted or subjected to any penalty or forfeiture for or on account of any transaction, matter, or thing concerning which he may testify, or produce evidence, documentary or otherwise, before the commission in obedience to a subpœna issued by it: *Provided,* That no natural person so testifying shall be exempt from prosecution and punishment for perjury committed in so testifying.

SEC. 10. That any person who shall neglect or refuse to attend and testify, or to answer any lawful inquiry, or to produce documentary evidence, if in his power to do so, in obedience to the subpœna or lawful requirement of the commission, shall be guilty of an offense and upon conviction thereof by a court of competent jurisdiction shall be punished by a fine of not less than $1,000 nor more than $5,000, or by imprisonment for not more than one year, or by both such fine and imprisonment.

Any person who shall willfully make, or cause to be made, any false entry or statement of fact in any report required to be made under this Act, or who shall willfully make, or cause to be made, any false entry in any account, record, or memorandum kept by any corporation subject to this Act, or who shall willfully neglect or fail to make, or to cause to be made, full, true, and correct entries in such accounts, records, or memoranda of all facts and transactions appertaining to the business of such corporation, or who shall willfully remove out of the jurisdiction of the United States, or willfully mutilate, alter, or by any other means falsify any documentary evidence of such corporation, or who shall willfully refuse to submit to the commission or to any of its authorized agents, for the purpose of inspection and taking copies, any documentary evidence of such corporation in his possession or within his control, shall be deemed guilty of an offense against the United States, and shall be subject, upon conviction in any court of the United States of competent jurisdiction, to a fine of not less than $1,000 nor more than $5,000, or to imprisonment for a term of not more than three years, or to both such fine and imprisonment.

If any corporation required by this Act to file any annual or special report shall fail so to do within the time fixed by the commission for filing the same, and such failure shall continue for thirty days after notice of such default, the corporation shall forfeit to the United States the sum of $100 for each and every day of the continuance of such failure, which forfeiture shall be payable into the Treasury of the United States, and shall be recoverable in a civil suit in the name of the United States brought in the district where the corporation has its

principal office or in any district in which it shall do business. It shall
be the duty of the various district attorneys, under the direction of the
Attorney General of the United States, to prosecute for the recovery
of forfeitures. The costs and expenses of such prosecution shall be paid
out of the appropriation for the expenses of the courts of the United
States.

Any officer or employee of the commission who shall make public
any information obtained by the commission without its authority, unless directed by a court, shall be deemed guilty of a misdemeanor, and,
upon conviction thereof, shall be punished by a fine not exceeding
$5,000, or by imprisonment not exceeding one year, or by fine and im-
prisonment, in the discretion of the court.

Sec. 11. Nothing contained in this Act shall be construed to prevent
or interfere with the enforcement of the provisions of the antitrust
Acts or the Acts to regulate commerce, nor shall anything contained in
the Act be construed to alter, modify, or repeal the said antitrust Acts
or the Acts to regulate commerce or any part or parts thereof.

Approved, September 26, 1914.

II.

CLAYTON ACT*

AN ACT To supplement existing laws against unlawful restraints and
monopolies, and for other purposes.

(Pub. No. 212, 63d Cong. Chap. 323, 38 Stat. at L. 730)

*Be it enacted by the Senate and House of Representatives of the
United States of America in Congress assembled,* That "antitrust laws,"
as used herein, includes the Act entitled "An Act to protect trade and
commerce against unlawful restraints and monopolies," approved July
second, eighteen hundred and ninety; sections seventy-three to seventy-
seven, inclusive, of an Act entitled "An Act to reduce taxation, to
provide revenue for the Government, and for other purposes," of
August twenty-seventh, eighteen hundred and ninety-four, an Act entitled "An Act to amend sections seventy-three and seventy-six of the
Act of August twenty-seventh, eighteen hundred and ninety-four, en-

* Secs. 4, 5, 6, 9, 10, 12-26 and portions of Section 8 are omitted, as
they do not concern the Federal Trade Commission.

titled 'An Act to reduce taxation, to provide revenue for the Government, and for other purposes,' " approved February twelfth, nineteen hundred and thirteen; and also this Act.

"Commerce," as used herein, means trade or commerce among the several States and with foreign nations, or between the District of Columbia or any Territory of the United States and any State, Territory, or foreign nation, or between any insular possessions or other places under the jurisdiction of the United States, or between any such possession or place and any State or Territory of the United States or the District of Columbia or any foreign nation, or within the District of Columbia or any Territory or any insular possession or other place under the jurisdiction of the United States: *Provided,* That nothing in this act contained shall apply to the Philippine Islands.

The word "person" or "persons" wherever used in this Act shall be deemed to include corporations and associations existing under or authorized by the laws of either the United States, the laws of any of the Territories, the laws of any State, or the laws of any foreign country.

SEC. 2. That it shall be unlawful for any person engaged in commerce, in the course of such commerce, either directly or indirectly to discriminate in price between different purchasers of commodities, which commodities are sold for use, consumption, or resale within the United States or any Territory thereof or the District of Columbia or any insular possession or other place under the jurisdiction of the United States, where the effect of such discrimination may be to substantially lessen competition or tend to create a monopoly in any line of commerce: *Provided,* That nothing herein contained shall prevent discrimination in price between purchasers of commodities on account of differences in the grade, quality, or quantity of the commodity sold, or that makes only due allowance for difference in the cost of selling or transportation, or discrimination in price in the same or different communities made in good faith to meet competition: *And provided further,* That nothing herein contained shall prevent persons engaged in selling goods, wares, or merchandise in commerce from selecting their own customers in bona fide transactions and not in restraint of trade.

SEC. 3. That it shall be unlawful for any person engaged in commerce, in the course of such commerce, to lease or make a sale or contract for sale of goods, wares, merchandise, machinery, supplies or other commodities, whether patented or unpatented, for use, consumption or resale within the United States or any Territory thereof or the District of Columbia or any insular possession or other place under the jurisdiction of the United States, or fix a price charged therefor, or discount from, or rebate upon, such price, on the condition, agreement or understanding that the lessee or purchaser thereof shall not use or deal in the goods, wares, merchandise, machinery, supplies or other commodities of a competitor or competitors of the lessor or seller, where the effect of such lease, sale, or contract for sale or such condition, agreement or understanding may be to substantially lessen competition or tend to create a monopoly in any line of commerce.

SEC. 7. That no corporation engaged in commerce shall acquire, directly or indirectly, the whole or any part of the stock or other share capital of another corporation engaged also in commerce, where the effect of such acquisition may be to substantially lessen competition between the corporation whose stock is so acquired and the corporation making the acquisition, or to restrain such commerce in any section or community, or tend to create a monopoly of any line of commerce.

No corporation shall acquire, directly or indirectly, the whole or any part of the stock or other share capital of two or more corporations engaged in commerce where the effect of such acquisition, or the use of such stock by the voting or granting of proxies or otherwise, may be to substantially lessen competition between such corporations, or any of them, whose stock or other share capital is so acquired, or to restrain such commerce in any section or community, or tend to create a monopoly of any line of commerce.

This section shall not apply to corporations purchasing such stock solely for investment and not using the same by voting or otherwise to bring about, or in attempting to bring about, the substantial lessening of competition. Nor shall anything contained in this section prevent a corporation engaged in commerce from causing the formation of subsidiary corporations for the actual carrying on of their immediate lawful business, or the natural and legitimate branches or extensions thereof, or from owning and holding all or a part of the stock of such subsidiary corporations, when the effect of such formation is not to substantially lessen competition.

Nor shall anything herein contained be construed to prohibit any common carrier subject to the laws to regulate commerce from aiding in the construction of branches or short lines so located as to become feeders to the main line of the company so aiding in such construction or from acquiring or owning all or any part of the stock of such branch lines, nor to prevent any such common carrier from acquiring and owning all or any part of the stock of a branch or short line constructed by an independent company where there is no substantial competition between the company owning the branch line so constructed and the company owning the main line acquiring the property or an interest therein, nor to prevent such common carrier from extending any of its lines through the medium of the acquisition of stock or otherwise of any other such common carrier where there is no substantial competition between the company extending its lines and the company whose stock, property, or an interest therein is so acquired.

Nothing contained in this section shall be held to affect or impair any right heretofore legally acquired: *Provided,* That nothing in this section shall be held or construed to authorize or make lawful anything heretofore prohibited or made illegal by the antitrust laws, nor to exempt any person from the penal provisions thereof or the civil remedies therein provided.

SEC. 8. . . . That from and after two years from the date of the approval of this Act no person at the same time shall be a director in any two or more corporations, any one of which has capital, surplus, and undivided profits aggregating more than $1,000,000, engaged in whole or in part in commerce, other than banks, banking associations, trust companies, and common carriers subject to the Act to regulate commerce, approved February fourth, eighteen hundred and eighty-seven, if such corporations are or shall have been theretofore, by virtue of their business and location of operation, competitors, so that the elimination of competition by agreement between them would constitute a violation of any of the provisions of any of the antitrust laws. The eligibility of a director under the foregoing provision shall be determined by the aggregate amount of the capital, surplus, and undivided profits, exclusive of dividends declared but not paid to stockholders, at the end of the fiscal year of said corporation next preceding the election of directors, and when a director has been elected in accordance with the provisions of this Act it shall be lawful for him to continue as such for one year thereafter.

When any person elected or chosen as a director or officer or selected as an employee of any bank or other corporation subject to the provisions of this Act is eligible at the time of his election or selection to act for such bank or other corporation in such capacity his eligibility to act in such capacity shall not be affected and he shall not become or be deemed amenable to any of the provisions hereof by reason of any change in the affairs of such bank or other corporation from whatsoever cause, whether specifically excepted by any of the provisions hereof or not, until the expiration of one year from the date of his election or employment.

SEC. 11. That authority to enforce compliance with sections two, three, seven, and eight of this Act by the persons respectively subject thereto is hereby vested: In the Interstate Commerce Commission where applicable to common carriers, in the Federal Reserve Board where applicable to banks, banking associations and trust companies, and in the Federal Trade Commission where applicable to all other character of commerce, to be exercised as follows:

Whenever the commission or board vested with jurisdiction thereof shall have reason to believe that any person is violating or has violated any of the provisions of sections two, three, seven, and eight of this Act, it shall issue and serve upon such person a complaint stating its charges in that respect, and containing a notice of a hearing upon a day and at a place therein fixed at least thirty days after the service of said complaint. The person so complained of shall have the right to appear at the place and time so fixed and show cause why an order should not be entered by the commission or board requiring such person to cease and desist from the violation of the law so charged in said complaint. Any person may make application, and upon good cause shown may be allowed by the commission or board, to intervene and appear in said proceeding by counsel or in person. The testimony in any such proceeding shall be reduced to writing and filed in the office of the commission or board. If upon such hearing the commission or board, as the case may be, shall be of the opinion that any of the provisions of said sections have been or are being violated, it shall make a report in writing in which it shall state its findings as to the facts, and shall issue and cause to be served on such person an order requiring such person to cease and desist from such violations, and divest itself of the stock held or rid itself of the directors chosen contrary to the provisions of sections seven and eight of this Act, if any there be, in the manner and within the time fixed by said order. Until a transcript of the record in such hearing shall have been filed in a circuit court of appeals of the United States, as hereinafter provided, the commission or board may at any time, upon such notice and in such manner as it shall deem proper, modify or set aside, in whole or in part, any report or any order made or issued by it under this section.

If such person fails or neglects to obey such order of the commission or board while the same is in effect, the commission or board may apply to the circuit court of appeals of the United States, within any circuit where the violation complained of was or is being committed or where such person resides or carries on business, for the enforcement of its order, and shall certify and file with its application a transcript of the entire record in the proceeding, including all the testimony taken and the report and order of the commission or board. Upon such filing of the application and transcript the court shall cause notice thereof to be served upon such person and thereupon shall have jurisdiction of the proceeding and of the question determined therein, and shall have power to make and enter upon the pleadings, testimony, and proceedings set forth in such transcript a decree affirming, modifying, or setting aside the order of the commission or board. The findings of the commission or board as to the facts, if supported by testimony, shall be conclusive. If either party shall apply to the court for leave to adduce additional evidence, and shall show to the satisfaction of the court that such additional evidence is material and that there were reasonable grounds for the failure to adduce such evidence in the proceeding before the commission or board, the court may order such additional evidence to be taken before the commission or board and to be adduced upon the hearing in such manner and upon such terms and conditions as to the court may seem proper. The commission or board may modify its findings as to the facts, or make new findings, by reason of the additional evidence so taken, and it shall file such modified or new findings, which, if supported by testimony, shall be conclusive, and its recommendation, if any, for the modification or setting aside of its original order, with the return of such additional evidence. The judgment and decree of the court shall be final, except that the same shall be subject to review by the Supreme Court upon certiorari as provided in section two hundred and forty of the Judicial Code.

Any party required by such order of the commission or board to cease and desist from a violation charged may obtain a review of such order in said circuit court of appeals by filing in the court a written petition praying that the order of the commission or board be set aside. A copy of such petition shall be forthwith served upon the commission or board, and thereupon the commission or board forthwith shall certify and file in the court a transcript of the record as hereinbefore provided. Upon the filing of the transcript the court shall have the same jurisdiction to affirm, set aside, or modify the order of the commission or board as in the case of an application by the commission or board for the enforcement of its order, and the findings of the commission or board as to the facts, if supported by testimony, shall in like manner be conclusive.

The jurisdiction of the circuit court of appeals of the United States to enforce, set aside, or modify orders of the commission or board shall be exclusive.

Such proceedings in the circuit court of appeals shall be given precedence over other cases pending therein, and shall be in every way expedited. No order of the commission or board or the judgment of the court to enforce the same shall in any wise relieve or absolve any person from any liability under the antitrust Acts.

Complaints, orders, and other processes of the commission or board under this section may be served by anyone duly authorized by the commission or board, either (a) by delivering a copy thereof to the person to be served, or to a member of the partnership to be served, or to the president, secretary, or other executive officer or a director of the corporation to be served; or (b) by leaving a copy thereof at the principal office or place of business of such person; or (c) registering and mailing a copy thereof addressed to such person at his principal office or place of business. The verified return by the person so serving said complaint, order, or other process setting forth the manner of said service shall be proof of the same, and the return post-office receipt for said complaint, order, or other process registered and mailed as aforesaid shall be proof of the service of the same.

Approved, October 15, 1914.

INDEX OF CASES

INDEX